CONDITIONING AND EMPOWERMENT OF WOMEN
A Multidimensional Approach

CONDITIONING AND EMPOWERMENT OF WOMEN

A Multidimensional Approach

Editors

Asha Mukherjee

Kumkum Bhattacharya

GYAN PUBLISHING HOUSE

NEW DELHI–110 002

CONDITIONING AND EMPOWERMENT OF WOMEN
A Multidimensional Approach
(Women Studies)

Rs. 690

ISBN: 81-212-0827-0

Published in 2003 in India by
Gyan Publishing House
5, Ansari Road, Daryaganj
New Delhi-110 002
E-mail: gyanbook@vsnl.com
Visit our website at: http//www.gyanbooks.com

Lasertypesetting by: Varsha Graphics, Delhi
Printed at: Chawla Offset Press, Delhi

Contents

Preface

Some of us having interest in women issues decided to have a seminar on empowerment of women and this edited volume was envisaged after the seminar was over at Visva Bharati in 1997. We thank Visva Bharati authorities for providing us the financial support to hold the seminar and to give us the opportunity to think together on the subject matter.

The main topic of this work is the empowerment of women obviously; it does not aim at empowering women over men and thereby bringing imbalance as a reaction. Rather, it aims at empowering women in the sense of equal sharing and cooperation as equals. Many Western ideas have been suggested and contrasted with many types of Indian theories but women is a cultural construct and her problems and solutions need to be looked within her cultural environment. The genesis of the present book could be looked at from this context. An analysis of the status of women in India and the alternative modes of their empowerment is presented. The issue of empowerment is viewed from different dimensions. It deals with the theoretical issues relating empowerment as well as issues involved in practice. It contains articles by well-known feminists like Martha Nussbaum, Bandana Purkayastha, Maitreyi Choudhury, Sutapa Bhattacharya, Mrinal Kanti Dasgupta and others. Some papers deal mainly with the theoretical side of the issues while the others are more related with the means and the goal of empowerment in actual life of Indian women such as environment management, Panchayat institution and the over all change in thinking of the people. The volume aims to argue that the issue of empowering women has to be looked upon as a multidimensional issue rather than from one particular dimension.

While going through the papers we have learnt a lot, specially some of the papers helped us in identifying the problems and their conditioning that need special attention. It provided us the opportunity to think afresh about the Indian women. We owe a deep debt and gratitude to our contributors for their constant inspiration patience and reminders. Our contributors have kept up persistent pressures. Originally, we had planned to include only those articles, which were presented in the seminar but unfortunately for some reason or the other the publication of the volume got delayed, and we could not get all the papers. Later, Martha Nussbaum and Bandana Purkayastha visited Visva Bharati and delivered lectures and we decided to approach them and they readily agreed to contribute paper for this book. We are grateful to both of them for responding to our requests warmly and for their contributions.

In spite of our best efforts, we are afraid, some errors and shortcomings are likely to be noticed by a careful reader, for which we deeply apologize.

We feel, we could have included more articles to fill in the gaps within the scope of the book but for some obvious reasons we did not. We are really sorry for this deficiency.

Asha Mukherjee
Kumkum Bhattacharya

List of Contributors

1. **Martha Nussbaum** is Ernst *Frund* Professor of law and Ethics at the University of Chicago with appointment in Law, Philosophy, Divinity and Classics. She is Co-editor of *The Quality of Life* with Amartya Sen, Oxford 1993, *Women, Culture and Development* with Jonathan Glover (Oxford, 1995), *Sex, Preference and Family* with David Estlund (Oxford, 1997) etc. She is also the author of numerous books, including The *Fragility of Goodness* (1986), *Love's Knowledge* (Oxford 1990), *Cultivating Humanity* (1997), *Sex and Social Justice,* (1999) Women and *Human Development—The Capability Approach* (2000).
2. **Mrinal Kanti Dasgupta** is a Professor in Department of Plant Protection, Palli-Siksha Bhavana (Institute of Agriculture, Visva-Bharati, Sriniketan).
3. **Aparajita Chakraborty** is a Professor in Department of Economics and Politics, Visva-Bharati.
4. **Sutapa Bhattacharya,** Reader in Department of Bengali, Visva-Bharati.
5. **Rama Kundu,** Professor, Department of English, Burdwan University, Burdwan. She is the author of *Vision and Design in Hardy's Fiction,* (1993), *Wrestling with God: Studies in English Devotional Poetry* (1996). She has contributed numerous research articles on Women Issues in Bengali and English.
6. **Aruna Mukherjee** is a Reader in Department of Russian Language, Visva-Bharati.
7. **Bandana Purkayastha,** is an Assistant Professor, Sociology, Asian American Studies and Global Program Director, AASI University of Connecticut. Her published books include *Asian Indians in Connecticut* (1999) and several research articles on Domestic Violence, Asian American Women, Activism and Social Change etc.
8. **Dipali G. Danda,** Suptd. Anthropologist (Cultural), Antropological Survey of India, Calcutta.

9. **Kakoli Chakraborty,** Anthropologist (Cultural), Anthropological Survey of India, Calcutta.
10. **Mallanath Mukherjee** is a research scholar in Department of Geography, Visva-Bharati.
11. **Malay Mukhopadhayay** is a Reader in Department of Geography, Visva-Bharati, editor of a biannual Journal on Environment since 1992 and author of books on the impact of rivers on the astride dwellers and has contributed many articles in various journals.
12. **Ishita Naha** is a social worker and she is doing research on the Status of Women in Tribal Communities in West Bengal.
13. **Sutapa Mukhopadhyay,** Lecturer in Department of Geography, Visva-Bharati has contributed many research articles in various National Journals on Land reforms and Land use of the river basin and resource management processes of tribal area development. She is the co-author of *River Geography*.
14. **Maitreyi Choudhuri** is a Professor at Palli Charcha Kendra, Visva-Bharati.
15. **Ayesa Khatun,** Coordinator, Anandadhara, Seed, Howrah.

Introduction

I

The issue of empowering women has been a focal point of discussion at different levels. And obviously one tries to understand what these issues and the differences are in different groups where women become the prime concern of such discussions. The diversities in women's conditions whether they are cultural, social, religious or simply their educational background, play a very important role in the programme of empowerment. Is empowerment of women different from the empowerment of Schedule Caste/Scheduled Tribe and Other Backward Classes? If it is different, in what sense is it different? At least in the Indian context, we have tried many ways to empower the SC/ST and other backward classes by making reservations and by implementing other Government programmes and many NGO's have helped them to be empowered. One important programme was the Barga system in West Bengal the other programme that is specially meant for women is the Panchayati Raj reservation for women very much similar to the reservation for SC/ST. At the same time, when women's groups are treated at par with other different cultural groups specially when human rights of a particular tribe or community are treated at par with women's rights of a particular group, although women form almost half of the population of the world, things become all the more complicated. Bandana Purkayastha's paper (in this volume) argues that if we insist upon this dichotomy then we will clearly strengthen the other hierarchies of society in general and this would consequently hurt the real cause of women in general. The question still remains what is the "real cause of most women"?

Since United Nations Conference on Population and Development (ICPD, 1994) which was held in Cairo, the concept of women's empowerment has drawn attention of the world over and a commitment to empowerment of women is pervasive throughout. There is a necessary relationship between development and women empowerment. What is the nature of this relationship? Is it necessary or it is necessary as well as sufficient ? Can the concept of women's empowerment help us in understanding the development process? Can we on the basis of empirical data determine or measure directly or indirectly women's empowerment? These are the issues which need to be explored. Concept of 'women empowerment' is also not very well defined; its relationship with development process has not been well defined either theoretically or empirically. Empowerment as a process and empowerment as an end product need to be distinguished. But the question remains how to measure the two? Is there any recognizable method?

Empowerment can be defined as the process by which the powerless gain greater control over the circumstances of their own lives; control relating to both resources and ideology. The power relation that has to be transformed includes women's lives at multiple, interlinked levels; the house hold/family, the community, the market, and the state. Empowering women is important in securing their reproductive and sexual rights which are universally valid. Paula England (1986) offers a model where women's empowerment is based on social and economic conditions. Women's empowerment is the actor's self-interest defining as 'anything the women might want' - food, medical care, shelter, income, respectful treatment for herself, a job, property, freedom from violence, sexual pleasure, the family size she desires and so on. Acting in one's self-interest is influenced by the use of power, which in turn has two interacting components: objective power (economic resources, laws and institutional rules and norms held by others) and subjective power (self efficacy and entitlement). Empowerment also means the 'ability to assert oneself', striving for upward mobility or attaining the psychological state of being powerful. But ability to assert oneself or to do things is dependent on cultural norms and institutional arrangements that regulate their lives. The social rules and roles keep women's needs and achievements outside the purview of the public world. The emphasis on women's rights to move around freely, work outside the home, to bodily integrity and freedom from violence, rising from the rules and roles which govern everyday lives of women, right to vote and access to education are all crucial for women's empowerment. Emphasis is laid on equal rights in practical sphere and also on challenging the patriarchal structure.

But the idea of empowerment through gaining equal right has been challenged by radical feminists who feel that separate sets of rights are required for the full empowerment of women (Jones, 1985, Shiva 1988, Gilligan 1982). According to this view equal rights simply allow women the right to compete for masculine achievements. Equal rights do not attend to the rights necessary for attending to activities which are traditionally associated with women's roles. It can only enable women to get the same education, apply for the same jobs and vote but 'family' issues such as childbirth, childcare, support, nurturing and sustenance of less able members of the family are all left outside the purview of 'real'' work and 'real' social needs. Thus, 'women's rights' need to be redefined as 'human rights' which are specifically women's concerns. Are 'women's rights' equal to men or 'women's rights are the rights specifically attending to the needs of women? Can a 'woman' be treated as an individual or is she always as an individual having a cultural entity? Or are women's rights just like any other cultural group right? Answers to these questions would lead us to different directions of women empowerment. Since it is a global issue the debate continues about the meaning and scope of the term such as 'women empowerment'.

The other question which is also important is "what are the special features of being a woman"? In a sense, women are also a bundle of possibilities. She has emotions, motherhood and nurturing nature inbuilt in her personality but she is equally strong, sometimes even stronger than her male counterparts. Strong are her decisions, she is strong in her commitments, determination and above has all has strong resistance power. She makes her way with all odds even before she is born. Birth of a female child itself is enough proof of her being strong. Now, the question is how and why this strong element gets weakened gradually by the social and environmental pressure? Can't we nurture the female child in such a way that she blooms into a fully strong personality? This is what is meant by empowerment of a woman; woman as a free human being exercising her choice in a rational way.

Social roles in social situations are dependent on the culture of the society in question and they are the results of a historical process. At some point they must be taken as universally valid roles. It is often been argued that these so called universally valid roles rest on an ethno-centric illusion. The male and female roles are defined by different cultures differently and they are not determined by any physiological difference in sex as such. Kant insisted on 'Treating humanity as an end and never as means only'. Woman or man being human has to be treated equally. Thus, the concept of 'equality becomes very much significant in this respect. In what sense man and woman are equal? It is in the sense of 'equality with difference'. Equality does not mean 'sameness'. Equality could only be interpreted as having equal opportunity to decide and live according to one's choice but unless one is aware of the options available to herself one would not be able to exercise one's choice. Thus, the need to make them aware of the choices is felt. The choice has to be a free choice. It does not mean that there is no 'cause' of the choice but there are 'reasons' which are rational reasons for the choice. Some choices could be rational and some may not be but it would be sufficient for a woman to be able to decide to choose certain ways of living or action due to her own choice after due deliberations.

Liberation of womanhood to gain her personhood is fundamental to human right. That idea is gaining new height of battle-readiness with each passing day. We need to blend the practical measures with ideas, we need the institutions to translate the promises and ideas to real life and empower women. The progress of the world is integrally linked with the advancement of women; commissions are set up to empower women to fight against women injustices.

In ancient times, woman was treated as movable property and she was reduced to her sex function only. Women were kept away from public life and *purdah* became the symbol of the 'protected', respectable, 'well-to-do' women. The *purdah* system in a broader sense has even today considerable influence on the relationship between the sexes in the middle classes. The norms that regulate the appearance of women in extremely masculine public spheres are after all were derived from the *purdah* complex of the ruling classes. Even today it is considered normal that the 'society' has to protect the chastity of women, since they themselves are incapable of doing it." (Shakuntala Devi, p. 39)

The process of social change and empowerment also relates essentially to value change. The nuclear family system is an unavoidable consequence of urbanization and industrialization. The family ideology of educated Indian middle class is combined with the mechanism of 'Sanskritization and Westernisation' due to the family conception of the dominant Brahamanic ideals as well as in more recent times the impact of TV culture. It is paradoxical that the western educated elite woman tries to liberate herself from the hands of patriarchichal ideal of womanhood but at the same time maintains 'Hindu ideal of womanhood', the *pativrata* ideal of women, completely dependent on the husband as a sign of a higher stage of culture. In this induced process of empowerment there is a kind of internal colonization through which the culture of the dominant group and with it their conceptions of marriage and family are imposed upon non-conforming minorities in the name of 'higher morality'; exactly as before was done in the name of colonial administration. The middle class woman is facing a conflict due to woman's double role in the home and at work. 'Woman' is not defined any more by her biological function.

In the Indian context, the village women think that they are very happy with their life, they do not need anything to be empowered about, it could be lack of awareness of other alternative ways of life or it could be due to ignorance. Many times their thinking faculties are so molded or conditioned that they can hardly think of any alternatives and the moment they would be aware of such choices they may choose to remain in their original positions. After all, it is their considered decision and we must respect it. Thus any kind of empowerment which is imposed from 'above' could not be desirable. The change of status of women in the family and the change of status of women in public life apart from their family functions are desired under empowerment of women. Modern education and modern economic life are compelling Indian women to come out of the narrow sphere of the family and work side by side with men and this is giving rise to completely new problems for women. To understand these we have to know the change, which regulates the status of women in the public sphere.

Normally, it is believed that empowering women often leads to social instability. Is there any necessary connection between the two? Once women become aware of their rights, and start exercising them, it may disturb the equilibrium of the family. If there was any exploitation, the woman no more tolerates it, she may even revolt against it. Thus the role, which was never questioned, is not performed any more, once she realizes that other family members are using her. It may also be the case that she realizes that she is being used but due to deep emotional involvement, she still performs those roles with some deep psychological disturbance. And this may or may not give rise to instability in the family. The end product will have evidence of control over one's life; but the process has three elements: the environment or the setting of women's lives; women's access to potential sources of empowerment and the evidence of empowerment. Women's empowerment has positive gains for the girl child who benefits from better survival of mothers and from improved infant child health. Perhaps it might be relevant to think of different empowering procedures for women of different stages, for example for female children, adolescents and for older women.

Government organisations translate women's empowerment into policies and programmes, creating new models for the future and the available data regarding the status of women, such as education and empowerment provide useful information. But very often they are not sensitive enough to capture the nuances of gender power relations. We need to move beyond the traditional variables of women's status although we agree that status variables are necessary first step leading to more complex task of conceptualising, meaning and analysing women's empowerment. Empowerment just by being financially or economically strong, politically strong (by making Panchayat Pradhan) would not be sufficient. As it is possible that the woman economically, politically empowered is still mentally dependent on other men or her family. This is not to deny the emotional attachment with the other members of her family or society but to emphasize the rational free choice of women as a process of women's empowerment.

Questions such as whether values are real, objective, absolute etc. are still interesting questions but are not considered so fundamental. It is more or less accepted that these dichotomies such as subjective/objective, relative/absolute, naturalist/non-naturalist, deterministic/non-deterministic etc. do not really stand. They are two sides of the same coin. This gives way to the *holistic approach* which has brought us to a new juncture. The juncture where we have to face the question how much objective, how much subjective, how much relative and how much absolute? Not that these questions were not addressed earlier but they have become the most fundamental questions in the present day context. In the past, the restricted vision of traditional approaches in the West worked to a limited extent only because the world was cut into many self-contained units. But with increasing global interdependence this narrow approach is no more accepted. The reach of many issues today—environmental degradation, racial and sexual oppression, the AIDS epidemic, human rights, racial discrimination, euthanasia, gender issues, rights, justice, liberty, entitlement—is global

Social dimension of a woman is interesting starting point for ethical discussion of women's empowerment. Taking on, a particular role such as 'mother', 'teacher' or 'friend', 'employer' or 'employee', 'citizen', 'member of a society' is often thought to involve a change in one's moral status. Social roles create obligations or expand our responsibilities. Social roles may conflict with intuitions, and worse yet, the different roles each person assumes may again offer conflicting guidance about what is right and wrong in particular cases. So, we cannot regard social roles of a woman as unimpeachable sources of ethics. We need to consider intuitions, rules, codes and social roles as each providing input into a process of ethical deliberation. Amartya Sen and Martha Nussbaum have motivated a discussion in this direction. They have suggested models for betterment of the society, especially women, on the basis of economic and political developments. A society which will be right-based, utility based and would take deontic considerations seriously. The practical issues such as rights, justice, liberty, utility, responsibility, care etc. are the key concepts which need to be discussed in detail under this approach.

Women empowerment shares many features with feminism. Feminism takes reflective side of the movement and takes the shape of understanding social reality of gender and tries to get rid of the patriarchic mode of dominated culture. For feminists ending of sexual oppression and injustice is a moral imperative at the level of thought and practice. And women's empowerment relates to this aspect of feminism where the need of empowering the women is felt. At the level of thought, we need to understand ourselves well enough as human beings - as normal females as a reality. In fact, not all feminists agree that there are distinctive feminist virtues, values. Some are even sceptical regarding the traditional positive virtues such as willingness to nurture or an affinity with caring. Still, there are some important focal points of feminism. First, there is a rejection of *a priori* premise of male superiority. There are distinctive women's social experiences, which are worthy of exploration. Social, cultural women issues which were at the periphery have become the prime issues of discussion such as bodily self, social and moral connectedness, care, trust, friendship, nurturing, emotions etc. Thus, there is a need felt of delicate balancing, on the one hand, the social reality of feminity which is a part of our own experience as social being and on the other, we must avoid the so called 'feminine' roles traditionally assigned to us and are sources of oppression.

Women need to be treated as subject as, women are as capable as men of taking decisions, exercising will and controlling desires. The adult women are competent of making life and death decisions about conception, birth, abortion, the care of the dying etc. Yet there is a massive contrast between male and female subjectivity in respect to their empirical conditions under which each is constructed. Male subjectivity enjoys the support of social institutions "which generate a sense of selfhood and personal importance and which do so - in part at least - by positioning women as the excluded 'other'." (M. Griffiths and M. Whitford, 1988, p.122). But, by contrast, men's absence from women's (traditional) grouping tends to be experienced, precisely, as an *absence.*

It might be pointed out that male selfhood is not really the ideal affairs just outlined. Men too, have to bow to contingencies, to choose and act within a complex social context always not of their own making. Why then are we presenting sex specific criticisms? We gladly accept that there is a kind of descriptive inadequacy in dominant models in relation to man and this is one of the points which feminists are insisting on. Traditional moral and political theories have misunderstood not only *women's difference from men*, but also *men's difference from women*. They thought that men too are embodied and vulnerable; emotional and sexual life for them is a source of insecurity; and that they are caught up as women are, in social structures which they do not know how to alter.

In feminism, on the one hand there is a rejection of 'masculine' values as ideal, 'successful' man as role model, and on the other a refusal to be treated as second sex. The formal 'equality' between man and woman is not desired. In fact, the very idea of 'equality' is challenged. The 'difference' between man and woman is no more seen as a problem but a 'different voice' which would form 'different truths' and 'values' are very much desired by the modern feminists. But there is a problem with affirmation of the difference. There always remains a risk that we may be back with the same sort of qualities and roles, which have been assigned by the traditional male conservatives. The other risk is of an idea of a universal 'feminity' which would generate solidarity between women. Gender difference is central to our social experience, but it is only one of many systems of difference around which that experience is organised. Perhaps the most hopeful outcome of these difficult debates would be an appreciation that 'otherness' extends beyond the phenomenon of gender and a more generous conception of the ideal of *unity difference.*

The other very important question is what kind of society is envisaged after women's empowerment, if at all that state is achieved? Or, in other words, what would be the new world-order once the ideal of women's empowerment is achieved? To answer this question many answers have been suggested which include non-contractual relations between parent and the child, future directed efforts that is not an 'investment', having non-possessive emotional experience, reproductive freedom for women and banishing coercion, elusiveness of the sense of self. The target of empowerment is not simply empirical facts that various sort of goods have to be equally distributed between sexes. Rather, the very existence of the social system by which male and female individual are assigned from birth to distinct classes whose identity is determined by their relation to one another - the relation of dominance in case of 'man' and the relation of subordination in case of 'woman'. This hierarchical relation cuts to the depth of our social being. The very existence of 'gender difference' is an object of suspicion and until this remains, women's empowerment would remain incomplete. As we think, these are not only 'women issues' but are universal human issues.

Another important distinction being made is between emotion and reason. Reason has been associated with male endeavour and emotion with female weakness and of course this is not an accidental association. Maleness was aligned with active, determinate, and defining form; femaleness with mere passive, indeterminate, and inferior matter. (Lloyd, G. 1984 p. 104) Feminists repeatedly argue, if the concept of 'human' were built on what we think about 'woman' rather than what we think about 'man', it would be a very different concept. Still another conceptual distinction between public/private as usually formulated has been to privilege the point of view of men in the public domain of state and law, and later in the market place, and to discount the experience of women. Mothering has been conceptualised as a primary biological activity, even when performed by humans. Mothering, as experienced by women, has never been taken seriously as a source of insight and only recently, feminists have begun to. (Ed. Joyce Trebilcot, 1984) Women were seen as emotional rather than rational beings, and thus were not granted full moral personhood. Women's behavior was regarded as 'natural' and driven by instinct and so was irrelevant to morality and moral principles. (It is worth noting that Rousseau, Kant, Hegel all have ignored the reality of women, although they paid homage to their emotional power and aesthetic sensibility.) Annette Baier recently speculated about why it is that moral philosophy has so seriously overlooked the *trust* between human beings that in her view is a utterly central to the issue (pp. 247-48).

In brief, some of the questions and issues which are the subject of our discussion in this book are the following:

1. Are women to be looked as 'the only' marginalised group or as sharing issues in common with other marginalized groups on various accounts?
2. Is gender to be seen as naturally given phenomena or it is to be viewed as conscious/social/traditional compulsions which determine the rules, roles, capabilities and realities?
3. Does historical analysis of the issues facilitate to understand the conditions in more contemporary times?
4. Why the issue of women empowerment is necessarily connected with the issue of family, society rather than those of individuals with problems of individuation?
5. Is/can women empowerment only (be) a matter of policy or it can be inculcated through sequential development changes brought

about by changing the structure of socialisation and by developing the individual capability?

6. Are present policies free from ambiguities? Do their interpretation and implementation circumvent effectiveness of the policies?
7. What are the reward-cost outcomes of empowerment? Do we need to sée a woman beyond the question of reward and cost in the context of social justice which is a fundamental, moral concern as human being?
8. What is the significance of individual stories of breaking out against the traditional/ *paramparic* roles of women and achieving women's empowerment to a certain extent?

Women have distinct identities and are subject to the law, norms and values of society, class, caste, religion, ethnicity, family, kinship, environment and changing polity. It is difficult, nay impossible to devise an undifferentiated Asian model of women or gender relations. So let us focus on the structure within which they exist and which seemingly control them. It is equally important to break out of the question of universality of male dominance and gender asymmetry. There is a realisation that gender relation is constructed differently in different cultures. It is necessary to exclude the hidden ways in which women exercise their agency.

As the very nature of gendered categories suggests that men and women are dichotomous categories, we need to consider gender distinctions to be part of the same continuum. Thus, we are aware that there can be no complete answers on and for one category, e.g. women, unless we consider relational categories as well. It is valid to foreground women but we do not treat this group as a separate and isolated category Foregrounding women is ethically right and of crucial importance, because most 'general' studies generalize from men's experiences only. In this volume by looking from multiple dimensions and analyzing multifaceted issues, we demonstrate how lives of women are affected.

In India the mentally ill, handicapped, socially and economically disadvantaged people share governmental, social and familial apathy and neglect as much as women do, and in most cases the ability to deal with apathy and neglect is in inverse proportion to the level of handicap. This is true for the situations that women too encounter in their lives. Their ability to deal with these situations varies according to a host of factors some of which are social in nature, some political, and a major portion are individual in nature. Since the focus of this volume is issues regarding women in general, we shall confine ourselves in identifying the different dimensions and aspects for a complete understating. We mentioned the other categories so as to put the issues of women in perspective and not to see the issues in isolation but as part of a *gestalt* in which every part supplements another and are connected to form the whole.

There is another important aspect that needs to be highlighted in the understanding of women's issues and that is the aspect of both creation/designing and delivery of service. It is on these aspects that women differ more than marginally from other groups of handicapped or distressed individuals. In the cases of the latter, services are specific, scientifically and experientially tested, and there are standardized means of training personnel and building institutions and providing facilities therein. Even, a price could be fixed or a cost benefit analysis could be worked out. In the case of women it is indeed difficult to develop a comprehensive package of services or depend on existing data banks for scientific and experiential knowledge as well as to train personnel. Equally difficult is to think in terms of institutions and facilities. Why is this so? One possible reason could be the lack of universal ideas about the conditions of women; in a way there are no yardsticks for prediction or anticipating the changing needs of women of various ages and experiences. It is clear that if we look for specific "problems" in the case of women there would be no end and the picture would be too confusing because in most cases, it is the overall situation of woman that could be a cause for her condition. We could look rather, from the standpoint of an individual having to function in "faulty" paradigms that view her" as mere instruments of the ends of others" (Martha Nussbaum, this volume)

In the present volume an attempt is made to explore and elaborate the multidimensional aspects of the concept of women's empowerment. And it is hoped that this would stimulate further researches in this area. We also want to bring home conceptual clarity by focusing on the gaps that exist between the concepts and empirical researches as well as between concepts and policies. Although the authors of these articles share an ideological commitment to Feminism in general and in particular to women's empowerment, they approach and address the issues differently. Further, this book is an attempt to look afresh at the issue of social conditioning and empowerment of women from a holistic point of view as far as possible. The volume includes articles from philosophers, geographers, anthropologists, social workers, statisticians, literature and from the field of plant protection. The canvas is largely the Indian context covering on the one hand, field based cases and on the other, theoretical and historical analysis which are of global concern.

The papers in this volume might not fit together as tightly as one might ideally wish; it may be regarded as just the beginning.

II

The book consists of two parts; the first deals with the issues regarding the social conditioning of women and the second with the interconnected issues regarding women's empowerment. These two focus areas; we presuppose are the parts of the *gestalt* view of the women related questions/ issues.

The volume opens with "Women's Capabilities and Social Justice", a philosophical analysis with a strong applicability that embodies in many ways the central theme of this volume of providing the multidimensional approach to the understanding of the conditioning of the woman and how she could be empowered. It also deals with the adjustment that paradigms have to make in the light of the changes in culture and society that occur in the course of time. This article articulates the need for having clearer ideas about women, in fact provides categorical verbalisations about where and how to start, depending on the *situ.*

The second article "Ecosociology of Man-Woman Relations: Toward Risking A Comprehensive Paradigm", takes a broad politico-historical view of the "institutions" of patriarchy, misogyny, matriarchy and related concepts. The author insists upon the need for correct understanding so as to how and why man is able to dominate over women through the entire course of history, across races, cultures and communities. Without such understanding, a strategy of feminism cannot be set as the correct agenda of social transformation without gender bias. It contains an overview of the demands of culture and how the biological aspect of woman that is often been ignored in modern understanding of main stream feminism creates the situation that pose problem for women. The article contains a critique of Marxian perspective in the light of the works of Simone de Beauvoir.

The article "Women's Question: Three Distinct Viewpoints" argues for the Marxist viewpoint over the liberal democratic and radical feminist point of view. That history is important to understand changing social realities is the main contention of this article and we cannot hope to look for solutions if we ignore this historical approach. The author makes a strong case against "private property rights, development of class exploitation and the rise of the state as an instrument of class exploitation" as being the reason for women's subjugation and oppression.

"Rabindranath and Gender Politics" contains a critique of the poet's ideas regarding gender. Tagore sees women and men in terms of the nature-culture dichotomy playing conventional gender roles defined by "the limits of the emotional configurations that have been composed over many aeons. Self-aware human beings want to transcend these socially-defined gender roles." Reading Tagore's works in the light of women's issues today, it is apparent that he was an individualist in his viewpoint and even though he accepted the socially approved gender roles in moments of crises he extended his unstinted and pointed support for the woman.

In "Revolutions: Parampara: Women" the author has shown how revolutions that managed to change radically the face and the nature of society failed to dent the roots of tradition or parampara of the "voiceless,(the) imperceptible in the saga of male sound and fury, though it is she who has to bear the brunt at times of war/breaking (or making) of nations." The disturbing tendency of a kind of return to the traditional roles for and of women as a means of stabilizing social disturbances and aberrations through political will seems to be taking an upper hand and is fast becoming a 'revolution' in itself !

"Society, Women in Bengal and Brahmo Samaj: Historicity and Present Relevance" brings into focus the indigenous movement for the emancipation of women as advocated by Brahmo Samaj. It was not just an ideology but a practical set of provisions that were to be fulfilled and exercised in order to retain one's membership in the Samaj. In its time the Samaj did spawn elitism of a sort, apparent from the literature of the time as well as the historical record of families who were members. However, the fact remains that it could be revived to provide a gentler nudge towards women's betterment/ uplift in contrast to the often-threatening strident voice of 'western' feminism (Purkayastha, in this volume).

The first article of the second part "Looking Beyond the Individual: Interaction of Structural Factors and Agency in the Empowerment of Women" discusses how "discourse on women/ human rights is increasingly being framed in terms of individuals vs. cultural group rights… insisting on this dichotomy strengthens other social hierarchies and hurts the cause of most women". To think of empowerment as only an individual right blankets the "multiple causes of women's subordination". There is no doubt of the individual effort that is necessary to exercise one's empowered self as agency, yet there remains the need to be provided such arena to bring into play one's agency by more than individual initiative, rather at the state level. There are many forces acting on the woman making the unitary category 'woman' too narrow.

"Gender Issues in the Perspective of Development" and " A Micro-study of Women and Agency in Chattisgarh Region in Madhya Pradesh" are articles from an anthropological point of view, based on field work exploring in little areas cases of women's daily strives and living. The value of such data cannot be overemphasized if at least for breaking some of the stereotypes or even showing the strength of the foundation of stereotypes! The cases reveal that empowerment is the process of change that does not always have to be forced but women gradually acquire agency in some areas of their decision-making capacities. There has been some positive fall out of the persistent (though slow and not always consistent) endeavours of the Government of India and its development programmes targeted towards rural societies. Anthropologists due to their special training see women as the half component of society and as equal participants (even if more biologically than otherwise).

In "Women in Environmental Management", the authors have looked at the natural advantages that women have in encountering environment not because of just their inherent nurturing tendencies but because it is rooted in their roles and work tasks. This has rarely been exploited when it comes to design schemes of environmental management from which the women are kept out. After all "the problem and crisis of environment and day today life are closely related more with the women than men".

Empowerment has been given a concrete face in "Women's Empowerment and Status in Joint Forest Management". Through the travails of a common woman's daily grind, the authors have brought out the sense of empowering that can be brought about through vesting of responsibility. One avenue leads to another, empowerment and recognition of that power opens up other opportunities and women become more active, not only in discharging of duties but also in being imaginative in exploring other means of exercising power/ capacity.

"Empowerment of Women through Panchayati Raj Institution" presents another avenue of empowering women through political will. There are so many arguments for and against the provisions of reservation for women in political machinery that there is a tendency to gloss over the negative aspects by one group or highlight those very aspects by another. This institution is too young to be dismissed only through arguments. It has to be time-tested and strengthened through a few generation of women before it could hope to achieve some sort of balance.

The present study shows that there are miles to go yet.

The last article "I Find My Voice—A Personal Narrative" is a first person account, not only of a person born on the wrong side of gender but on the other side of culture. Being a member of Muslim community and living in a Muslim dominated village, conservatism and rebelling against it were her companions through the growing years. She asks: is she just a person or is she to be defined by her sex and that too limited by her religiosity. These questions do not have easy answers. There is a bright side of Islam regarding women, sometimes more generous than found in Hindu texts, but the practice of Islam is not always that fair towards women and in order to protect women from men, too many, contrary to textual injunctions and provisions, fetters are put around her in the name of maintaining the sanctity of religion. It is an example of empowerment of women, to a certain extent, in the sense of 'self assertion' in real life experience. This gives us some hope, may not be enough that some changes are taking place and in future many more will take place.

At the end, we feel that the articles in this volume will fill the various lacunae; at least, some of them, as very few of the volumes contain a philosophical underpinning that is so important to understand the situation better. The philosophical underpinning provides a fresh perspective of the problem from a positive frame of reference without being bogged down by negative pulls and thrusts. This perspective goes towards building a theoretical framework that is fairly flexible in its parameters in order to accommodate divergent individual cases of women experiencing a wide variety of social conditioning and situations. It helps in pointing the ways that could be used by the women to empower themselves as well use the structures available by which empowerment could be effected.

We have tried to strike a balance between articles dealing with theoretical and practical aspects of the issues based on actual ground realities to supplement the articles that have a philosophical point of view. The multi-dimensional approach towards analysis of social conditioning and women's empowerment seems to be well situated to the understanding of women's complex situation. There are too many extraneous forces as well as compulsions that work from within that make not only the picture complicated but confusing and this is what we set out to do - extricate the strands that make the complex web and put them in perspective of the *gestalt*. We believe that the whole is much too important and concentration on parts would be akin to losing sight of the woods for the trees.

We hope it will help alter in some way the ways of our thinking about women's issues such as injustice, social inequality, neglect etc. in its totality. Let us see women situated in particular social settings and subject to the laws and norms of society as other members and how they by their own agency "resolve" their conditions and if challenged, could be provided arena for exercising their agency in a just and fair manner.

References

Baier Annette ,"Trust and Anti-Trust", *Ethics*, 96 (1986).

England, Paula "Conceptualizing Women's Empowerment in Countries of the North" in *Women's Empowerment and Demographic Processes*. Ed. H.B. Presser and Gita Sen, Oxford University Press, 2002.

England, Paula and Farkas George, *Households, Employment and Gender: A Social Economic and Demographic View,* Hawthorne, NY: Aldine de Gruyter, 1986.

Gilligan, Carol, *In a Different Voice: Psychological Theory and Women's Development*, Cambridge, Mass: Harvard University Press, 1982.

Griffiths M and M. Whitford (ed.) *Feminist Perspectives in Philosophy*, Macmillan, 1988.

Jones, K. and Jonasdittir, A. (ed.). *The Political Interests of Gender*, London: Sage, 1985.

Lloyd, G. *The man of Reason: "Male" and "Female" in Western Philosophy,* University of Minnesota Press, 1984.

Nussbaum, Martha C. *Sex and Social Justice*, Oxford University Press, 1999.

Women and Human Development, The Capability Approach, Cambridge University Press, 2000.

Sen, Amartya "Gender and Cooperative Conflicts" in Irene Tinker (ed) *Persistent Inequlities: Women and World Development,* New York, Oxford University Press, 1990.

Poverty and Famines, An Essay on Entitlement and Deprivation, Oxford Clarendon Press, 1981.

Shiva, V., *Staying Alive: Women, Ecology and Development*, London: Zed Books, 1988.

Shakuntala Devi, *Women's Status and Social Change*, Pointer Publishers, Jaipur, India, 1999.

Nussbaum, Martha, C., *Women and Human Development: The Capabilities Approach*, Cambridge University Press, 2000.

Joyce Trebilcot, (Ed.) *Mothering: Essays in Feminist Theory*, New Jersey: Rowman and Allanheld, 1984.

1

Women's Capabilities and Social Justice

We come from our family's house to live in our husband's house. If we mention our name in this house, they say, "Oh, that is another family." Yet when it comes to working, they say, "What you earn is ours, because you are in this family's house," or "because you are working on this family's land. Let the land be registered in our names, so that we will not always feel like we are in someone else's family."

Santokbehn, agricultural laborer, Ahmedabad

In your joint family, I am known as the second daughter-in-law. All these years I have known myself as no more than that. Today, after fifteen years, as I stand alone by the sea, I know that I have another identity, which is my relationship with the universe and its creator. That gives me the courage to write this letter as myself, not as the second daughter-in-law of your family....

I am not one to die easily. That is what I want to say in this letter.

Rabindranath Tagore, "Letter from a Wife" (1914)

We not only want a piece of the pie, we also want to choose the flavor, and to know how to make it ourselves.

Ela Bhatt, founder, Self-Employed Women's Association (SEWA) (1992)

I. Development and Sex Equality

Women in much of the world lack support for fundamental functions of a human life. They are less well nourished than men, less healthy, more vulnerable to physical violence and sexual abuse. They are much less likely than men to be literate, and still less likely to have professional or technical education. Should they attempt to enter the workplace, they face greater obstacles, including intimidation from family or spouse, sex discrimination in hiring, and sexual harassment in the workplace — all, frequently, without effective legal recourse. Similar obstacles often impede their effective participation in political life. In many nations women are not full equals under the law: they do not have the same property rights as men, the same rights to make a contract, the same rights of association, mobility, and religious liberty.[1] Burdened, often, with the "double day" of taxing employment and full responsibility for housework and child care, they lack opportunities for play and the cultivation of their imaginative and cognitive faculties. All these factors take their toll on emotional wellbeing: women have fewer opportunities than men to live free from fear and to enjoy rewarding types of love—especially when, as often, they are married without choice in childhood and have no recourse from a bad marriage. In all these ways, unequal social and political circumstances give women unequal human capabilities.

One might sum all this up by saying that all too often women are not treated as ends in their own right, persons with a dignity that deserves respect from laws and institutions. Instead, they are treated as mere instruments of the ends of others — reproducers, caregivers, sexual outlets, agents of a family's general prosperity. Sometimes this instrumental value is strongly positive; sometimes it may actually be negative. A girl child's natal family frequently treats her as dispensable, seeing that she will leave anyhow and will not support parents in their old age. Along the way to her inevitable departure she will involve the family in the considerable expense of dowry and wedding festivities. What use would it be, then, to care for her health and education in the same way that one would care for a boy's? What wonder, that the birth of a girl is often an occasion for sorrow rather than for rejoicing? As the old Indian proverb[2] puts it, "A daughter born, To husband or death, She's already gone." [3]

Nor is the marital home likely to be a place of disrespect for such a daughter, although here her instrumental value may become positive. Her in-laws are likely to see her as a mere adjunct of a beloved son, a means to (especially male) grandchildren, an addition to the number of household workers, perhaps as a device to extract money in dowry payments from her parents. Even when she is not abused, she is unlikely to be treated with warmth, nor is her education likely to be fostered. Should her husband prove kind, he can be a buffer between her and the demands of his parents. Should he prove unkind, the woman is likely to have no recourse from abuse in the marital family, and no good exit options. Her natal family will probably refuse to have her back, she probably has no employment-related skills, and the law is not very interested in her predicament. Should the husband die, her situation is likely to become still worse, given the stigma attached to widowhood in many parts of the world. A tool whose purpose is gone: that is what a widow is, and that's rather like being dead.

These are not rare cases of unusual crime, but common realities. According to the Human Development Report 1999 of the United Nations Development Programme, there is no country that treats its women as well as its men, according to a complex measure that includes life expectancy, wealth, and education.[4] Developing countries, however, present especially urgent problems. Gender inequality is strongly correlated with poverty.[5] When poverty combines with gender inequality, the result is acute failure of central human capabilities. In the group of "medium human development" countries taken as a whole, the male adult literacy rate is 83.3 per cent, as against 67.3 per cent for women; in the "low human development countries" the rate is 57.2 per cent for males, 35.8 per cent for females. School enrollment percentages (combining all three levels) are, in the medium development countries, 60 per cent for females, 68 per cent for males; in the low human development countries, 33 per cent for females, 44 per cent for males. In terms of real GDP per capita, in the medium development countries women control $2220 as against $4414 for men; in the low human development countries, $691 for women, $1277 for men. We do not yet have reliable statistics for rape, domestic violence, and sexual harassment, because in many countries little attention is paid to domestic violence and sexual harassment, rape within marriage is not counted as a crime, and even stranger-rape is so rarely punished that many women are deterred from reporting the crime.[6]

If we turn to the very basic area of health and nutrition, there is pervasive evidence of discrimination against females in many nations of the developing world. It is standardly believed that where equal nutrition and health care are present, women live, on average, slightly longer than men: thus, we would expect a sex ratio of something like 102.2 women to 100 men (the actual sex ratio of Sub Saharan Africa[7]). Many countries have a far lower sex ratio: India's, for example, is 92.7 women to 100 men, the lowest sex ratio since the census began early in this century. If we study such ratios and ask the question, "How many more women than are now present in Country C would be there if they had the same sex ratio as Sub-Saharan Africa?" we get a figure that economist Amartya Sen has graphically called the number of "missing women." There are many millions of missing women in the world today.[8] Using this rough index, the number of missing women in Southeast Asia is 2.4 millions, in Latin America 4.4, in North Africa 2.4, in Iran 1.4, in China 44.0, in Bangladesh 3.7, in India 36.7, in Pakistan 5.2, in West Asia 4.3. If we now consider the ratio of the number of missing women to the number of actual women in a country, we get, for Pakistan 12.9 per cent, India 9.5 per cent, Bangladesh 8.7 per cent, China 8.6 per cent, Iran 8.5 per cent, West Asia 7.8 per cent, North Africa 3.9 per cent, Latin America 2.2 per cent, Southeast Asia 1.2 per cent. In India, not only is the mortality differential especially sharp among children (girls dying in far greater numbers than boys), the higher mortality rate of women compared to men applies to all age groups until the late thirties.[9] In some regions, the discrepancy is far greater than the national average: in rural Bihar, for example, an NGO has counted heads and arrived at the astonishing figure of 75 females to 100 males.[10]

One area of life that contributes especially greatly to women's inequality is the area of care. Women are the world's primary, and usually only, caregivers for people in a condition of extreme dependency: young children, the elderly, those whose physical or mental handicaps make them incapable of the relative (and often temporary) independence that characterizes so-called "normal" human lives. Women perform this crucial work, often, without pay and without recognition that it is work. At the same time, the fact that they need to spend long hours caring for the physical needs of others makes it more difficult for them to do what they want to do in other areas of life, including employment, citizenship, play and self-expression.[11]

Women, in short, lack essential support for leading lives that are fully human. This lack of support is frequently caused by their being women. Thus, even when they live in a constitutional democracy such as India, where they are equals in theory, they are second-class citizens in reality.

II. The Capabilities Approach: An Overview

I shall argue that international political and economic thought should be feminist, attentive (among other things) to the special problems women face because of sex in more or less every nation in the world, problems without an understanding of which general issues of poverty and development cannot be well confronted. An approach to international development should be assessed for its ability to recognize these problems and to make recommendations for their solution. I shall propose and defend one such approach, one that seems to me to do better in this area than other prominent alternatives. My version of this approach is philosophical, and I shall try to show why we need philosophical theorizing in order to approach these problems well.[12] It is also based on a cross-cultural normative account of central human capabilities, closely allied to a form of political liberalism; one of my primary tasks will be to defend this type of cross-cultural normative approach as a valuable basis from which to approach the problems of women in the developing world. Finally, I shall also try to show that my version of the capabilities approach, while attractive for many reasons, has special advantages when we are approaching the special problems faced by women: both intellectually and practically, there is a strong link between a concern for gender justice and reasons we might have to turn to the capabilities approach.

The aim of my project as a whole is to provide the philosophical underpinning for an account of basic constitutional principles that should be respected and implemented by the governments of all nations, as a bare minimum of what respect for human dignity requires. I shall argue that the best approach to this idea of a basic social minimum is provided by an approach that focuses on Human Capabilities, that is, what people are actually able to do and to be — in a way informed by an intuitive idea of a life that is worthy of the dignity of the human being. I shall identify a list of Central Human Capabilities, setting them in the context of a type of political liberalism that makes them specifically political goals and presents them in a manner free of any specific metaphysical grounding. In this way, I argue, the capabilities can be the object of an overlapping consensus among people who otherwise have very different comprehensive conceptions of the good.[13] And I shall argue that the capabilities in question should be pursued for each and every person, treating each as an end and none as mere tools of the ends of others: thus I adopt a principle of each person's capability, based on a principle of each person as end. Women have all too often been treated as the supporters of the ends of others, rather than as ends in their own right; thus this principle has particular critical force with regard to women's lives. Finally, my approach uses the idea of a threshold level of each capability, beneath which it is held that truly human functioning is not available to citizens; the social goal should be understood in terms of getting citizens above this capability threshold.

The capabilities approach has another related, and weaker, use. It specifies a space within which comparisons of life quality (how well people are doing) are most revealingly made among nations. Used in this way, as in the Human Development Reports, it is a rival to other standard measures, such as GNP per capita and utility. This role for the conception is significant, since we are not likely to make progress toward a good conception of the social minimum if we do not first get the space of comparison right. And we may use the approach in this weaker way, to compare one nation with another, even when we are unwilling to go further and use the approach as the philosophical basis for fundamental constitutional principles establishing a social minimum or threshhold. On the other hand, the comparative use of capabilities is ultimately not much use without a determinate normative conception that will tell us what to make of what we find in our comparative study. Most conceptions of quality of life measurement in development economics are implicitly harnessed to a normative theory of the proper social goal (wealth maximization, utility maximization, etc.), and this one is explicitly so harnessed. The primary task of my argument will be to move beyond the merely comparative use of capabilities to the construction of a normative political proposal that is a partial theory of justice.

The capabilities approach is fully universal: the capabilities in question are important for each and every citizen, in each and every nation, and each is to be treated as an end. Women in developing nations are important to the project in two ways: as people who suffer pervasively from acute capability failure, and also as people whose situation provides an interesting test of this and other approaches, showing us the problems they solve or fail to solve. Defects in standard GNP and utility based approaches can be well understood by keeping the problems of such women in view; but of course women's problems are urgent in their own right, and it may be hoped that a focus on them will help compensate for earlier neglect of sex equality in development economics and in the international human rights movement.

III. The Need for Cross-Cultural Norms

Should we be looking for a set of cross-cultural norms in the first place, where women's opportunities are concerned? Obviously enough, women are already doing that, in many areas. To take just one example, women laboring in the informal sector, for example, are increasingly organizing on an international level to set goals and priorities.[14] Many other examples are provided by the international human rights movement and international agreements such as CEDAW. But this process is controversial, both intellectually and politically. Where do these normatives categories come from, it will be asked? And how can they be justified as appropriate ones for cultures that have traditionally used different normative categories? Now of course no critical social theory confines itself to the categories of each culture's daily life. If it did, it probably could not perform its special task as critical theory, which involves the systematization and critical scrutiny of intuitions that in daily life are often unexamined. Theory gives people a set of terms with which to criticize abuses that otherwise might lurk nameless in the background. Terms such as "sexual harassment" and "hostile work environment" give us some obvious examples of this point. But even if one defends theory as valuable for practice, it may still be problematic to use concepts that originate in one culture to describe and assess realities in another — and all the more problematic if the culture described has been colonized and oppressed by the describer's culture. Attempts by international feminists today to use a universal language of justice, human rights, or human functioning to assess lives like those of Vasanti and Jayamma is bound to encounter charges of Westernizing and colonizing—even when the universal categories are introduced by feminists who live and work within the nation in question itself. For, it is standardly said, such women are alienated from their culture, and are faddishly aping a Western political agenda. The minute they become critics, it is said, they cease to belong to their own culture and become puppets of the Western elite.[15]

We should begin by asking whose interests are served by the implicit nostalgic image of a happy harmonious culture, and whose resistance and misery are being effaced. Describing her mother's difficult life, Indian feminist philosopher Uma Narayan writes, "One thing I want to say to all who would dismiss my feminist criticisms of my culture, using my 'Westernization' as a lash, is that my mother's pain too has rustled among the pages of all those books I have read that partly constitute my 'Westernization,' and has crept into all the suitcases I have ever packed for my several exiles." This same pain is evident in the united voice of protest that has emerged from international women's meetings such as those in Vienna and Beijing, where a remarkable degree of agreement was found across cultures concerning fundamental rights for women.

Nonetheless, when we advance a set of universal norms in connection with women's equality, we will also face three more sincere and respectable objections, which must be honestly confronted.

First, one hears what I shall call the *argument from culture.* Traditional cultures, the argument goes, contain their own norms of what women's lives should be: frequently norms of female modesty, deference, obedience, and self-sacrifice. Feminists should not assume without argument that those are bad norms, incapable of constructing good and flourishing lives for women. By contrast, the norms proposed by feminists seem to this opponent suspiciously "Western," because they involve an emphasis on choice and opportunity.

My full answer to this argument will emerge from the proposal I shall make, which certainly does not preclude any woman's choice to lead a traditional life, so long as she does so with certain economic and political opportunities firmly in place. But we should begin by emphasizing that the notion of tradition used in the argument is far too simple. Cultures are scenes of debate and contestation. They contain dominant voices, and they also contain the voices of women, which have not always been heard. It would be implausible to suggest that the many groups working to improve the employment conditions of women in the informal sector, for example, are brainwashing women into striving for economic opportunities: clearly, they provide means to ends women already want, and a context of female solidarity within which to pursue those ends. Where they do alter existing preferences, they typically do so by giving women a richer sense of both their possibilities and their equal worth, in a way that looks more like a self-realization (as Tagore's heroine vividly states) than like brainwashing. Indeed, what may possibly be "Western" is the arrogant supposition that choice and economic agency are solely Western values!

Another general point should be stressed: Cultures are dynamic, and change is a very basic element in all of them. Contrasts between West and non-West often depict Western cultures as dynamic, critical, modernizing, while Eastern cultures are identified with their oldest elements, as if these do not change or encounter contestation. Looking at the relationship between her grandmother's way of life and her own, Narayan comments, "I find it impossible to describe 'our traditional way of life' without seeing change as a constitutive element, affecting transformations that become 'invisible' in their taken-for-grantedness."[16] Criticism too is profoundly indigenous to virtually all cultures,[17] but to none more so than to the culture of India, that extremely argumentative nation.[18] To cite just one famous and typical example, Bengali religious thinker Rammohun Roy, imagining the horrors of death, singles out as especially terrible the fact that "everyone will contest your views, and you will not be able to reply."[19] This too is Indian culture.

In short, because cultures are scenes of debate, appealing to culture give us questions rather than answers. It certainly doesn't show that cross-cultural norms are a bad answer to those questions.

Let us now consider the argument that I shall call the argument from the good of diversity. This argument reminds us that our world is rich in part because we don't all agree on a single set of practices and norms. We think the world's different languages have worth and beauty, and that it's a bad thing, diminishing the expressive resources of human life generally, if any language should cease to exist. So too, cultural norms have their own distinctive beauty; the world risks becoming impoverished as it becomes more homogeneous.

Here we should distinguish two claims the objector might be making. She might be claiming that diversity is good as such; or she might simply be saying that there are problems with the values of economic efficiency and consumerism that are increasingly dominating our interlocking world. This second claim, of course, doesn't yet say anything against cross-cultural norms, it just suggests that their content should be critical of some dominant economic norms. So the real challenge to our enterprise lies in the first claim. To meet it we must ask how far cultural diversity really is like linguistic diversity. The trouble with the analogy is that languages don't harm people, and cultural practices frequently do. We could think that threatened languages such as Cornish and Breton should be preserved, without thinking the same about domestic violence: it is not worth preserving simply because it is there and very old. In the end, then, the objection doesn't undermine the search for cross-cultural norms, it requires it: for what it invites us to ask is, whether the cultural values in question are among the ones worth preserving, and this entails at least a very general cross-cultural framework of assessment, one that will tell us when we are better off letting a practice die out.

Finally, we have the *argument from paternalism.* This argument says that when we use a set of cross-cultural norms as benchmarks for the world's varied societies, we show too little respect for people's freedom as agents (and, in a related way, their role as democratic citizens). People are the best judges of what is good for them, and if we say that their own choices are not good for them we treat them like children. This is an important point, and one that any viable cross-cultural proposal should bear firmly in mind. But it hardly seems incompatible with the endorsement of cross-cultural norms. Indeed, it appears to endorse explicitly at least some cross-cultural norms, such as the political liberties and other opportunities for choice. Thinking about paternalism gives us a strong reason to respect the variety of ways citizens actually choose to lead their lives in a pluralistic society, and therefore to seek a set of cross-cultural norms that protect freedom and choice of the most significant sorts. But this means that we will naturally value religious toleration, associative freedom, and the other major liberties. These liberties are themselves cross-cultural norms, and they are not compatible with views that many real people and societies hold.

We can make a further claim: many existing value systems are themselves highly paternalistic, particularly towards women. They treat them as unequal under the law, as lacking full civil capacity, as not having the property rights, associative liberties, and employment rights of males.

If we encounter a system like this, it is in one sense paternalistic to say, sorry, that is unacceptable under the universal norms of equality and liberty that we would like to defend. In that way, any bill of rights is "paternalistic" vis a vis families, or groups, or practices, or even pieces of legislation, that treat people with insufficient or unequal respect. The Indian Constitution, for example, is in that sense paternalistic when it tells people that it is from now on illegal to use caste or sex as grounds of discrimination. But that is hardly a good argument against fundamental constitutional rights or, more generally, against opposing the attempts of some people to tyrannize over others. We dislike paternalism, insofar as we do, because there is something else that we like, namely liberty of choice in fundamental matters. It is fully consistent to reject some forms of paternalism while supporting those that underwrite these basic values.

Nor does the protection of choice require only a formal defense of basic liberties. The various liberties of choice have material preconditions, in whose absence there is merely a simulacrum of choice. Many women who have in a sense the "choice" to go to school simply cannot do so: the economic circumstances of their lives makes this impossible. Women who "can" have economic independence, in the sense that no law prevents them, may be prevented simply by lacking assets, or access to credit. In short, liberty is not just a matter of having rights on paper, it requires being in a material position to exercise those rights. And this requires resources. The state that is going to guarantee people rights effectively is going to have to recognize norms beyond the small menu of basic rights: it will have to take a stand about the redistribution of wealth and income, about employment, land rights, health, education. If we think that these norms are important cross-culturally, we will need to take an international position on pushing toward these goals. That requires yet more universalism and in a sense paternalism; but we could hardly say that the many women who live in abusive or repressive marriages, with no assets and no opportunity to seek employment outside the home, are especially free to do as they wish.

The argument from paternalism indicates, then, that we should prefer a cross-cultural normative account that focuses on empowerment and opportunity, leaving people plenty of space to determine their course in life once those opportunities are secured to them. It does not give us any good reason to reject the whole idea of cross-cultural norms, and some strong reasons why we should seek such norms, including in our account not only the basic liberties, but also forms of economic empowerment that are crucial in making the liberties truly available to people. And the argument suggests one thing more: that the account we search for should seek empowerment and opportunity for each and every person, respecting each as an end, rather than simply as the agent or supporter of ends of others. Women are too often treated as members of an organic unit such as the family or the community is supposed to be, and their interests subordinated to the larger goals of that unit, which means, typically, those of its male members. However, the impressive economic growth of a region means nothing to women whose husbands deprived them of control over household income. We need to consider not just the aggregate, whether in a region or in a family; we need to consider the distribution of resources and opportunities to each person, thinking of each as worthy of regard in her own right.

IV. Traditional Economic Approaches to Development: The Need for Human Norms

Another way of seeing why cross-cultural norms are badly needed in the international policy arena is to consider what the alternative has typically been. Prior to the shift in thinking that is associated with the work of Amartya Sen[20] and with the Human Development Reports of the UNDP,[21] the most prevalent approach to measuring quality of life in a nation used to be simply to ask about GNP per capita. This approach tries to weasel out of making any cross-cultural claims about what has value — although, notice, it does assume the universal value of opulence. What it omits, however, is much more significant. We are not even told about the distribution of wealth and income, and countries with similar aggregate figures can exhibit great distributional variations. (Thus, South Africa always did very well among developing nations, despite its enormous inequalities and violations of basic justice.) Circus girl Sissy Jupe, in Dickens's novel *Hard Times,* already saw the problem with this absence of normative concern for distribution. She says that her economics lesson didn't tell her "who has got the money and whether any of it is mine".[22] So too with women around the world: the fact that one nation or region is in general more prosperous than another is only a part of the story: it doesn't tell us what government has done for women in various social classes, or how they are doing. To know that, we'd need to look at their lives. But then we need to specify, beyond distribution of wealth and income itself, what parts of lives we ought to look at — such as life expectancy, infant mortality, educational opportunities, health care, employment opportunities, land rights, political liberties. Seeing what is absent from the GNP account nudges us sharply in the direction of mapping out these and other basic goods in a universal way, so that we can use the list of basic goods to compare quality of life across societies.

A further problem with all resource-based approaches, even those that are sensitive to distribution, is that individuals vary in their ability to convert resources into functionings. (This is the problem that has been stressed for some time by Amartya Sen in his writings about the capabilities approach.) Some of these differences are straightforwardly physical. Nutritional needs vary with age, occupation, and sex. A pregnant or lactating woman needs more nutrients than a non-pregnant woman. A child needs more protein than an adult. A person whose limbs work well needs few resources to be mobile, whereas a person with paralyzed limbs needs many more resources to achieve the same level of mobility. Many such variations can escape our notice if we live in a prosperous nation that can afford to bring all individuals to a high level of physical attainment; in the developing world we must be highly alert to these variations in need. Again, some of the pertinent variations are social, connected with traditional hierarchies. If we wish to bring all citizens of a nation to the same level of educational attainment, we will need to devote more resources to those who encounter obstacles from traditional hierarchy or prejudice: thus women's literacy will prove more expensive than men's literacy in many parts of the world. If we operate only with an index of resources, we will frequently reinforce inequalities that are highly relevant to wellbeing. As my examples suggest, women's lives are especially likely to raise these problems: therefore, any approach that is to deal adequately with women's issues must be able to deal well with these variations.

If we turn from resource-based approaches to preference-based approaches, we encounter another set of difficulties.[23] Such approaches have one salient advantage over the GNP approach: they look at people, and assess the role of resources as they figure in improving actual people's lives. But users of such approaches typically assume without argument that the way to assess the role of resources in people's lives is simply to ask them about the satisfaction of their current preferences. The problem with this idea is that preferences are not exogenous, given independently of economic and social conditions. They are at least in part constructed by those conditions. Women often have no preference for economic independence before they learn about avenues through which women like them might pursue this goal; nor do they think of themselves as citizens with rights that were being ignored, before they learn of their rights and are encouraged to believe in their equal worth. All of these ideas, and the preferences based on them, frequently take shape for women in programs of education sponsored by women's organisations of various types. Men's preferences, too, are socially shaped and often misshaped. Men frequently have a strong preference that their wives should do all the child care and all the housework — often in addition to working an eight-hour day. Such preferences, too, are not fixed in the nature of things: they are constructed by social traditions of privilege and subordination. Thus, a preference-based approach typically will reinforce inequalities: especially those inequalities that are entrenched enough to have crept into people's very desires. Once again, although this is a fully general problem, it has special pertinence to women's lives. Women have especially often been deprived of education and information, which are necessary, if by no means sufficient, to make preferences a reliable indicator of what public policy should pursue. They have also often been socialized to believe that a lower living standard is what is right and fitting for them, and that some great human goods (for example education, political participation) are not for them at all. They may be underconsiderable social pressure to say they are satisfied without such things: and yet we should not hastily conclude that public policy should not work to extend these functions to women. In short, looking at women's lives helps us see the inadequacy of traditional approaches; and the urgency of women's problems gives us a very strong motivation to prefer a non-traditional approach.

V. Human Dignity and Human Capabilities

I shall now argue that a reasonable answer to all these concerns — capable of giving good guidance to government establishing basic constitutional principles and to international agencies assessing the quality of life—is given by a version of the capabilities approach—an approach to quality of life assessment pioneered within economics by Amartya Sen, and by now highly influential through the *Human Development Reports* of the UNDP. My own version of this approach is in several ways different from Sen's[24]; I shall simply lay out my view as I would currently defend it.

The central question asked by the capabilities approach is not, "How satisfied is this woman?" or even "How much in the way of resources is she able to command?" It is, instead, "What is she actually able to do and to be?" Taking a stand for political purposes on a working list of functions that would appear to be of central importance in human life, users of this approach ask, is the person capable of this, or not? They ask not only about the person's satisfaction with what she does, but about what she does, and what she is in a position to do (what her opportunities and liberties are). They ask not just about the resources that are present, but about how those do or do not go to work, enabling the woman to function.

To introduce the intuitive idea behind the approach, it is useful to start from this passage of Marx's 1844 *Economic and Philosophical Manuscripts,* written at a time when he was reading Aristotle and was profoundly influenced by Aristotelian ideas of human capability and functioning:

It is obvious that the human eye gratifies itself in a way different from the crude, non-human eye; the human ear different from the crude ear, etc....The sense caught up in crude practical need has only a restricted sense. For the starving man, it is not the human form of food that exists, but only its abstract being as food; it could just as well be there in its crudest form, and it would be impossible to say wherein this feeding activity differs from that of animals.

Marx here singles out certain human functions — eating and the use of the senses, which seem to have a particular centrality in any life one might live. He then claims that there is something that it is to be able to perform these activities in a fully human way — by which he means a way infused by reasoning and sociability. But human beings don't automatically have the opportunity to perform their human functions in a fully human way. Some conditions in which people live — conditions of starvation, or of educational deprivation, bring it about that a being who is human has to live in an animal way. Of course what he is saying is that these conditions are unacceptable, and should be changed.

Similarly, the intuitive idea behind my version of the capabilities approach is twofold: first, that there are certain functions that are particularly central in human life, in the sense that their presence or absence is typically understood to be a mark of the presence or absence of human life. Second, and this is what Marx found in Aristotle, that there is something that it is to do these functions in a truly human way, not a merely animal way. We judge, frequently enough, that a life has been so impoverished that it is not worthy of the dignity of the human being, that it is a life in which one goes on living, but more or less like an animal, not being able to develop and exercise one's human powers. In Marx's example, a starving person just grabs at the food in order to survive, and the many social and rational ingredients of human feeding can't make their appearance. Similarly, the senses of a human being can operate at a merely animal level — if they are not cultivated by appropriate education, by leisure for play and self-expression, by valuable associations with others; and we should add to the list some items that Marx probably would not endorse, such as expressive and associational liberty, and the freedom of worship. The core idea seems to be that of the human being as a dignified free being who shapes his or her own life, rather than being passively shaped or pushed around by the world in the manner of a flock or herd animal.

At one extreme, we may judge that the absence of capability for a central function is so acute that the person isn't really a human being at all, or any longer — as in the case of certain very severe forms of mental disability, or senile dementia. But I am less interested in that boundary (important though it is for medical ethics) than in a higher one, the level at which a person's capability is "truly human," that is, worthy of a human being. The idea thus contains a notion of human worth or dignity.

Notice that the approach makes each person a bearer of value, and an end. Marx, like his bourgeois forebears, holds that it is profoundly wrong to subordinate the ends of some individuals to those of others. That is at the core of what exploitation is, to treat a person as a mere object for the use of others. What this approach is after is a society in which individuals are treated as each worthy of regard, and in which each has been put in a position to live really humanly.

I think we can produce an account of these necessary elements of truly human functioning that commands a broad cross-cultural consensus, a list that can be endorsed for political purposes by people who otherwise have very different views of what a complete good life for a human being would be. The list is supposed to provide a focus for quality of life assessment and for political planning, and it aims to select capabilities that are of central importance, whatever else the person pursues. They therefore have a special claim to be supported for political purposes in a pluralistic society.[25]

The list represents the result of years of cross-cultural discussion,[26] and comparisons between earlier and later versions will show that the input of other voices has shaped its content in many ways. It remains open-ended and humble; it can always be contested and remade. Nor does it deny that the items on the list are to some extent differently constructed by different societies. Indeed part of the idea of the list is that its members can be more concretely specified in accordance with local beliefs and circumstances. Here is the current version:

Central Human Functional Capabilities

1. ***Life.*** Being able to live to the end of a human life of normal length; not dying prematurely, or before one's life is so reduced as to be not worth living.

2. ***Bodily Health.*** Being able to have good health, including reproductive health;[27] to be adequately nourished; to have adequate shelter.
3. ***Bodily Integrity.*** Being able to move freely from place to place; to be secure against violent assault, including sexual assault and domestic violence; having opportunities for sexual satisfaction and for choice in matters of reproduction.
4. ***Senses, Imagination, and Thought.*** Being able to use the senses, to imagine, think, and reason — and to do these things in a "truly human" way, a way informed and cultivated by an adequate education, including, but by no means limited to, literacy and basic mathematical and scientific training. Being able to use imagination and thought in connection with experiencing and producing works and events of one's own choice, religious, literary, musical, and so forth. Being able to use one's mind in ways protected by guarantees of freedom of expression with respect to both political and artistic speech, and freedom of religious exercise. Being able to have pleasurable experiences, and to avoid non-necessary pain.
5. ***Emotions.*** Being able to have attachments to things and people outside ourselves; to love those who love and care for us, to grieve at their absence; in general, to love, to grieve, to experience longing, gratitude, and justified anger. Not having one's emotional development blighted by fear and anxiety. (Supporting this capability means supporting forms of human association that can be shown to be crucial in their development.)
6. ***Practical Reason.*** Being able to form a conception of the good and to engage in critical reflection about the planning of one's life. (This entails protection for the liberty of conscience.)
7. ***Affiliation.***

   (A) Being able to live with and toward others, to recognize and show concern for other human beings, to engage in various forms of social interaction; to be able to imagine the situation of another and to have compassion for that situation; to have the capability for both justice and friendship. (Protecting this capability means protecting institutions that constitute and nourish such forms of affiliation, and also protecting the freedom of assembly and political speech.)

   (B) Having the social bases of self-respect and non-humiliation; being able to be treated as a dignified being whose worth is equal to that of others. This entails protections against discrimination on the basis of race, sex, sexual orientation, religion, caste, ethnicity, or national origin.

8. ***Other Species.*** Being able to live with concern for and in relation to animals, plants, and the world of nature.
9. ***Play.*** Being able to laugh, to play, to enjoy recreational activities.
10. ***Control over one's Environment.***

    (A) Political. Being able to participate effectively in political choices that govern one's life; having the right of political participation, protections of free speech and association.

    (B) Material. Being able to hold property (both land and movable goods); having the right to seek employment on an equal basis with others; having the freedom from unwarranted search and seizure. In work, being able to work as a human being, exercising practical reason and entering into meaningful relationships of mutual recognition with other workers.

The list is, emphatically, a list of separate components. We cannot satisfy the need for one of them by giving people a larger amount of another one. All are of central importance and all are distinct in quality. The irreducible plurality of the list limits the trade-offs that it will be reasonable to make, and thus limits the applicability of quantitative cost-benefit analysis. At the same time, the items on the list are related to one another in many complex ways. One of the most effective ways of promoting women's control over their environment, and their effective right of political participation, is to promote women's literacy. Women who can seek employment outside the home have more resources in protecting their bodily integrity from assaults within it. Such facts give us still more reason not to promote one capability at the expense of the others.

Among the capabilities, two, practical reason and affiliation, stand out as of special importance, since they both organise and suffuse all the others, making their pursuit truly human. To use one's senses in a way not infused by the characteristically human use of thought and planning is to use them in an incompletely human manner. Tagore's heroine, summarizing her decision to leave her husband, says, "I found myself beautiful as a free human mind." This idea of herself infuses all her other functions. At the same time, to reason for oneself without at all considering the circumstances and needs of others is, again, to behave in an incompletely human way.

The basic intuition from which the capability approach begins, in the political arena, is that human abilities exert a moral claim that they should be developed. Human beings are creatures such that, provided with the right educational and material support, they can become fully capable of these human functions. That is, they are creatures with certain lower-level capabilities (which I call "basic capabilities"[28]) to perform the functions in question. When these capabilities are deprived of the nourishment that would transform them into the high-level capabilities that figure on my list, they are fruitless, cut off, in some way but a shadow of themselves. If a turtle were given a life that afforded a merely animal level of functioning, we would have no indignation, no sense of waste and tragedy. When a human being is given a life that blights powers of human action and expression, that does give us a sense of waste and tragedy—the tragedy expressed, for example, in Tagore's heroine's statement to her husband, when she says, "I am not one to die easily." In her view, a life without dignity and choice, a life in which she can be no more than an appendage, was a type of death of her humanity.

Notice that the approach makes each person a bearer of value, and an end. Marx, like his bourgeois forebears, holds that it is profoundly wrong to subordinate the ends of some individuals to those of others. That is at the core of what exploitation is, to treat a person as a mere object for the use of others. Thus, it will be just as repugnant to this Aristotelian/Marxian approach as to a bourgeois philosophy to foster a good for society considered as an organic whole, where this does not involve the fostering of the good of persons taken one by one. Thus, it will be insufficient to promote the good of "the community" or "the family," where that leaves intact gross asymmetries of capability among community or family members. Women are especially likely to be the losers when the good of a group is promoted as such, without asking about hierarchies of power and opportunity internal to the group. The capabilities approach insists on pressing that question. What the approach is after is a society in which persons are treated as each worthy of regard, and in which each has been put in a position to live really humanly. (That is where the idea of a threshold comes in: we say that beneath a certain level of capability, in each area, a person has not been enabled to live in a truly human way.) We may call this the principle of each person as end, which can be further articulated as a principle of each person's capability: the capabilities sought are sought for each and every person, not, in the first instance, for groups or families or states or other corporate bodies. Such bodies may be extremely important in promoting human capabilities, and in this way they may deservedly gain our support: but it is because of what they do for people that they are so worthy, and the ultimate political goal is always the promotion of the capabilities of each person.[29]

We begin, then, with a sense of the worth and dignity of basic human powers, thinking of them as claims to a chance for functioning, claims that give rise to correlated social and political duties. And in fact there are three different types of capabilities that play a role in the analysis. First, there are basic capabilities: the innate equipment of individuals that is the necessary basis for developing the more advanced capability, and a ground of moral concern. Second, there are internal capabilities: that is, states of the person herself that are, so far as the person herself is concerned, sufficient conditions for the exercise of the requisite functions. A woman who has not suffered genital mutilation has the internal capability for sexual pleasure; most adult human beings everywhere have the internal capability for religious freedom and the freedom of speech. Finally, there are combined capabilities, which may be defined as internal capabilities combined with suitable external conditions for the exercise of the function. A woman who is not mutilated but who has been widowed as a child and is forbidden to make another marriage has the internal but not the combined capability for sexual expression (and, in most such cases, for employment, and political participation).[30] Citizens of repressive non-democratic regimes have the internal but not the combined capability to exercise thought and speech in accordance with their conscience. The list, then, is a list of combined capabilities. To realize one of the items on the list entails not only promoting appropriate development of people's internal powers, but also preparing the environment so that it is favorable for the exercise of practical reason and the other major functions.

VI. Functioning and Capability

I have spoken both of functioning and of capability. How are they related? Getting clear about this is crucial in defining the relation of the "capabilities approach" to our concerns about paternalism and pluralism. For if we were to take functioning itself as the goal of public policy, a liberal pluralist would rightly judge that we were precluding many choices that citizens may make in accordance with their own conceptions of the good. A deeply religious person may prefer not to be well-nourished, but to engage in strenuous fasting. Whether for religious or for other reasons, a person may prefer a celibate life to one containing sexual expression. A person may prefer to work with an intense dedication that precludes recreation and play. Am I declaring, by my very use of the list, that these are not fully human or flourishing lives? And am I instructing government to nudge or push people into functioning of the requisite sort, no matter what they prefer?

It is important that the answer to this question is no. Capability, not functioning, is the appropriate political goal. This is so because of the very great importance the approach attaches to practical reason, as a good that both suffuses all the other functions, making them fully human, and also figures, itself, as a central function on the list. The person with plenty of food may always choose to fast, but there is a great difference between fasting and starving, and it is this difference that we wish to capture. Again, the person who has normal opportunities for sexual satisfaction can always choose a life of celibacy, and the approach says nothing against this. What it does speak against (for example) is the practice of female genital mutilation, which deprives individuals of the opportunity to choose sexual functioning (and indeed, the opportunity to choose celibacy as well).[31] A person who has opportunities for play can always choose a workaholic life; again, there is a great difference between that chosen life and a life constrained by insufficient maximum hour protections and/or the "double day" that makes women unable to play in many parts of the world.

Once again, we must stress that the objective is to be understood in terms of combined capabilities. To secure a capability to a person it is not sufficient to produce good internal states of readiness to act. It is necessary, as well, to prepare the material and institutional environment so that people are actually able to function. Women burdened by the "double day" may be internally incapable of play — if, for example, they have been kept indoors and zealously guarded since infancy, married at age six, and forbidden to engage in the kind of imaginative exploration of the environment that male children standardly enjoy. Young girls in poor areas of rural Rajasthan, India, for example, have great difficulty learning to play in an educational program run by local activists — because their capacity for play has not been nourished early in childhood. On the other hand, there are also many women in the world who are perfectly capable of play in the internal sense, but who are unable to play because of the crushing demands of the "double day." Such a woman does not have the combined capability for play in the sense intended by the list.

Capability is thus a demanding notion. In its focus on the environment of choice, it is highly attentive to the goal of functioning, and instructs governments to keep it always in view. On the other hand, it does not push people into functioning: once the stage is fully set, the choice is theirs.

VII. Capabilities and Care

All human beings begin their lives as helpless children; if they live long enough, they are likely to end their lives in helplessness, whether physical or also mental. During the prime of life, most human beings encounter periods of extreme dependency; and some human beings remain dependent on the daily bodily care of others throughout their lives. Of course putting it this way suggests, absurdly, that "normal" human beings do not depend on others for bodily care and survival; but political thought should recognize that some phases of life, and some lives, generate more profound dependency than others.

The capabilities approach, more Aristotelian than Kantian, sees human beings from the first as animal beings whose lives are characterized by profound neediness as well as by dignity. It addresses the issue of care in many ways: under "life" it is stressed that people should be enabled to complete a "normal" human lifespan; under "health" and "bodily integrity" the needs of different phases of life are implicitly recognized; "sense," "emotions," and "affiliation" also target needs that vary with the stage of life. "Affiliation" is of particular importance, since it mentions the need for both compassion and self-respect, and it also mentions non-discrimination. What we see, then, is that care must be provided in such a way that the capability for self-respect of the receiver is not injured, and also in such a way that the care-giver is not exploited and discriminated against on account of performing that role. In other words, a good society must arrange to provide care for those in a condition of extreme dependency, without exploiting women as they have traditionally been exploited, and thus depriving them of other important capabilities. This huge problem will rightly shape the way states think about all the other capabilities.[32]

The capabilities approach has a great advantage in this area over traditional liberal approaches that use the idea of a social contract. Such approaches typically generate basic political principles from a hypothetical contract situation in which all participants are independent adults. John Rawls, for example, uses the phrase "fully cooperating members of society over a complete life."[33] But of course no human being is that. And the fiction distorts the choice of principles in a central way, effacing the issue of extreme dependency and care from the agenda of the contracting parties, when they choose the principles that shape society's basic structure. And yet such a fundamental issue cannot well be postponed for later consideration, since it profoundly shapes the way social institutions will be designed.[34] The capabilities approach, using a different concept of the human being, one that builds in need and dependency into the first phases of political thinking, is better suited to good deliberation on this urgent set of issues.

VIII. Capabilities and Human Rights

Earlier versions of the list appeared to diverge from approaches common in the human rights movement by not giving as large a place to the traditional political rights and liberties — although the need to incorporate them was stressed from the start. This version of the list corrects that defect of emphasis.[35] The political liberties have a central importance in making well-being human. A society that aims at well-being while overriding these has delivered to its members an incompletely human level of satisfaction. As Amartya Sen has recently written, "Political rights are important not only for the fulfillment of needs, they are crucial also for the formulation of needs. And this idea relates, in the end, to the respect that we owe each other as fellow human beings."[36] There are many reasons to think that political liberties have an instrumental role in preventing material disaster (in particular famine[37]), and in promoting economic well-being. But their role is not merely instrumental: they are valuable in their own right.

Thus capabilities as I conceive them have a very close relationship to human rights, as understood in contemporary international discussions. In effect they cover the terrain covered by both the so-called "first-generation rights" (political and civil liberties) and the so-called second-generation rights (economic and social rights). And they play a similar role, providing the philosophical underpinning for basic constitutional principles. Because the language of rights is well-established, the defender of capabilities needs to show what is added by this new language.[38]

The idea of human rights is by no means a crystal clear idea. Rights have been understood in many different ways, and difficult theoretical questions are frequently obscured by the use of rights language, which can give the illusion of agreement where there is deep philosophical disagreement. People differ about what the basis of a rights claim is: rationality, sentience, and mere life have all had their defenders. They differ, too, about whether rights are prepolitical or artifacts of laws and institutions. (Kant held the latter view, although the dominant human rights tradition has held the former.) They differ about whether rights belong only to individual persons, or also to groups. They differ about whether rights are to be regarded as side-constraints on goal-promoting action, or rather as one part of the social goal that is being promoted. They differ, again, about the relationship between rights and duties: if A has a right to S, then does this mean that there is always someone who has a duty to provide S, and how shall we decide who that someone is? They differ, finally, about what rights are to be understood as rights to. Are human rights primarily rights to be treated in certain ways? Rights to a certain level of achieved well-being? Rights to resources with which one may pursue one's life plan? Rights to certain opportunities and capacities with which one may make choices about one's life plan?

The account of central capabilities has the advantage, it seems to me, of taking clear positions on these disputed issues, while stating clearly what the motivating concerns are and what the goal is. Bernard Williams put this point eloquently, commenting on Sen's 1987 Tanner Lectures:

> I am not very happy myself with taking rights as the starting point. The notion of a basic human right seems to me obscure enough, and I would rather come at it from the perspective of basic human capabilities. I would prefer capabilities to do the work, and if we are going to have a language or rhetoric of rights, to have it delivered from them, rather than the other way round.[39]

As Williams says, however, the relationship between the two concepts needs further scrutiny, given the dominance of rights language in the international development world.

In some areas, I would argue that the best way of thinking about what rights are is to see them as *combined capabilities*. The right to political participation, the right to religious free exercise, the right of free speech — these and others are all best thought of as capacities to function. In other words, to secure a right to a citizen in these areas is to put them in a position of combined capability to function in that area. (Of course there is another sense of "right" that is more like my "basic capabilities": people have a right to religious freedom just in virtue of being human, even if the state they live in has not guaranteed them this freedom.) By defining rights in terms of combined capabilities, we make it clear that a people in country C do not really have the right to political participation just because this language exists on paper: they really have this right only if there are effective measures to make people truly capable of political exercise. Women in many nations have a nominal right of political participation without having this right in the sense of capability: for example, they may be threatened with violence should they leave the home. In short, thinking in terms of capability gives us a benchmark as we think about what it is really to secure a right to someone.

There is another set of rights, largely those in the area of property and economic advantage, which seem analytically different in their relationship to capabilities. Take, for example, the right to shelter and housing. These are rights that can be analyzed in a number of distinct ways: in terms of resources, or utility (satisfaction), or capabilities. (Once again, we must distinguish between the claim that "A has a right to shelter"—which frequently refers to A's moral claim in virtue of being human, with what I call basic capabilities)—from the statement that "Country C gives its citizens the right to shelter." It is the second sentence whose analysis I am discussing here.) Here again, however, it seems valuable to understand these rights in terms of capabilities. If we think of the right to shelter as a right to a certain amount of resources, then we get into the very problem I discussed in section iii: giving resources to people does not always bring differently situated people up to the same level of capability to function. The utility-based analysis also encounters a problem: traditionally deprived people may be satisfied with a very low living standard, believing that this is all they have any hope of getting. A capabilities analysis, by contrast, looks at how people are actually enabled to live. Analyzing economic and material rights in terms of capabilities thus enables us to set forth clearly a rationale we have for spending unequal amounts of money on the disadvantaged, or creating special programmes to assist their transition to full capability.

The language of capabilities has one further advantage over the language of rights: it is not strongly linked to one particular cultural and historical tradition, as the language of rights is believed to be. This belief is not very accurate: although the term "rights" is associated with the European Enlightenment, its component ideas have deep roots in many traditions.[40] Where India is concerned, for example, even apart from the recent validation of rights language in Indian legal and constitutional traditions, the salient component ideas have deep roots in far earlier areas of Indian thought — in ideas of religious toleration developed since the edicts of Ashoka in the third century BC, in the thought about Hindu/ Muslim relations in the Moghul Empire, and, of course, in many progressive and humanist thinkers of the nineteenth and twentieth centuries, who certainly cannot be described as simply Westernizers, with no respect for their own traditions.[41] Tagore portrays the conception of freedom used by the young wife in his story as having ancient Indian origins, in the quest of Rajput queen Meerabai for joyful self-expression. The idea of herself as "a free human mind" is represented as one that she derives, not from any external infusion, but from a combination of experience and history.

So "rights" are not exclusively Western, in the sense that matters most; they can be endorsed from a variety of perspectives. Nonetheless, the language of capabilities enables us to bypass this troublesome debate. When we speak simply of what people are actually able to do and to be, we do not even give the appearance of privileging a Western idea. Ideas of activity and ability are everywhere, and there is no culture in which people do not ask themselves what they are able to do, what opportunities they have for functioning.

If we have the language of capabilities, do we also need the language of rights? The language of rights still plays, I believe, four important roles in public discourse, despite its unsatisfactory features. First, when used in the first way, as in the sentence "A has a right to have the basic political liberties secured to her by her government", this sentence reminds us that people have justified and urgent claims to certain types of urgent treatment, no matter what the world around them has done about that. I have suggested that this role of rights language lies very close to what I have called "basic capabilities," in the sense that the justification for saying that people have such natural rights usually proceeds by pointing to some capability-like feature of persons (rationality, language) that they actually have on at least a rudimentary level. And I actually think that without such a justification the appeal to rights is quite mysterious. On the other hand, there is no doubt that one might recognize the basic capabilities of people and yet still deny that this entails that they have rights in the sense of justified claims to certain types of treatment. We know that this inference has not been made through a great deal of the world's history. So appealing to rights communicates more than does the bare appeal to basic capabilities, which does no work all by itself, without any further ethical argument of the sort I have supplied. Rights language indicates that we do have such an argument and that we draw strong normative conclusions from the fact of the basic capabilities.

Second, even at the second level, when we are talking about rights guaranteed by the state, the language of rights places great emphasis on the importance and the basic role of these spheres of ability. To say,

"Here's a list of things that people ought to be able to do and to be" has only a vague normative resonance. To say, "Here is a list of fundamental rights," is more rhetorically direct. It tells people right away that we are dealing with an especially urgent set of functions, backed up by a sense of the justified claim that all humans have to such things, in virtue of being human.

Third, rights language has value because of the emphasis it places on people's choice and autonomy. The language of capabilities, as I have said, was designed to leave room for choice, and to communicate the idea that there is a big difference between pushing people into functioning in ways you consider valuable and leaving the choice up to them. But there are approaches using an Aristotelian language of functioning and capability that do not emphasise liberty in the way that my approach does: Marxist Aristotelianism and some forms of Catholic Thomist Aristotelianism are illiberal in this sense. If we have the language of rights in play as well, I think it helps us to lay extra emphasis on the important fact that the appropriate political goal is the ability of people to choose to function in certain ways, not simply their actual functionings.

Finally, in the areas where we disagree about the proper analysis of rights talk—where the claims of utility, resources, and capabilities are still being worked out—the language of rights preserves a sense of the terrain of agreement, while we continue to deliberate about the proper type of analysis at the more specific level.

VIII. Capabilities as Goals for Women's Development

I have argued that legitimate concerns for diversity, pluralism and personal freedom are not incompatible with the recognition of cross-cultural norms, and indeed that cross-cultural norms are actually required if we are to protect diversity, pluralism, and freedom, treating each human being as an agent and an end. The best way to hold all these concerns together, I have argued, is to formulate the norms as a set of capabilities for fully human functioning, emphasising the fact that capabilities protect, and do not close off, spheres of human freedom.

Used to evaluate the lives of women who are struggling for equality in many different countries, developing and developed, the capabilities framework does not, I believe, look like an alien importation: it squares pretty well with demands women are already making in many global and national political contexts. It might therefore seem superfluous to put these items on a list: why not just let women decide what they will demand in each case? To answer that question, we should point out that the international development debate is already using a normative language.

Where the capabilities approach has not caught on—as it has in the *Human Development Reports*—a much less adequate theoretical language still prevails, whether it is the language of preference-satisfaction or the language of economic growth. We need the capabilities approach as a humanly rich alternative to these inadequate theories of human development.

Of course the capabilities approach supplies norms for human development in general, not just for women's development. Women's issues, however, are not only worthy of focus because of their remarkable urgency. They also help us see more clearly the inadequacy of various other approaches to development more generally, and the reasons for preferring the capabilities approach. Preference-based approaches do not enable us to criticize preferences that have been shaped by a legacy of injustice and hierarchy: men's preferences for dominance and for being taken care of, women's preferences for a low level of attainment when that is the only life they know and think possible. The capabilities approach, by contrast, looks at what women are actually able to do and to be, undeterred by the fact that oppressed and uneducated women may say, or even think, that some of these capabilities are not for them. Resource-based approaches, similarly, have a bias in the direction of protecting the status quo, in that they do not take account of the special needs for aid that some groups may have on account of their subordinate status: we have to spend more on them to bring them up to the same level of capability. This fact the capabilities approach sees clearly, and it directs us to make a basic threshold level of capability the goal for all citizens.[42] Human rights approaches are close allies of the capabilities approach, because they take a stand on certain fundamental entitlements of citizens, and they hold that these may be demanded as a matter of basic justice. In relation to these approaches, however, the capabilities approach is both more definite, specifying clearly what it means to secure a "right" to someone, and more comprehensive, spelling out explicitly certain rights that are of special importance to women, but which have not until recently been included in international human rights documents.

The capabilities approach may seem to have one disadvantage, in comparison to these other approaches: it seems difficult to measure human capabilities. If this difficult arises already, when we think about such obvious issues as health and mobility, it most surely arises in a perplexing form for my own list, which has added so many apparently intangible items, such as development of the imagination, and the conditions of emotional health. We know, however, that anything worth measuring, in human quality of life, is difficult to measure. Resource-based approaches simply substitute something easy to measure for what really ought to be measured, a heap of stuff for the richness of human functioning. Preference-based approaches do even worse, because they not only do not measure what ought to be measured, they also get into quagmires of their own, concerning how to aggregate preferences—and whether there is any way of doing that task that does not run afoul of the difficulties shown in the social choice literature. The capabilities approach as so far developed in the *Human Development Reports* is admittedly not perfect: years of schooling, everyone would admit, are an imperfect proxy for education. We may expect that any proxies we find as we include more capabilities in the study will be highly imperfect also—especially if it is data supplied by the nations that we need to rely on. On the other hand, we are at least working in the right place and looking at the right thing; and over time, as data-gathering responds to our concerns, we may expect increasingly adequate information, and better ways of aggregating that information. As has already happened with human rights approaches, we need to rely on the ingenuity of those who suffer from deprivation: they will help us find ways to describe, and even to quantify, their predicament.

Women all over the world have lacked support for central human functions, and that lack of support is to some extent caused by their being women. But women, like men—and unlike rocks and trees and even horses and dogs—have the potential to become capable of these human functions, given sufficient nutrition, education, and other support. That is why their unequal failure in capability is a problem of justice. It is up to all human beings to solve this problem. I claim that the capabilities approach, and a list of the central capabilities, give us good guidance as we pursue this difficult task.

References

1. Ernst Freund Distinguished Service Professor of Law and Ethics, Department of Philosophy, Law School, and Divinity School, The University of Chicago. The present article is closely related to the arguments of my book *Women and Human Development: The Capabilities Approach* (Cambridge and New York: Cambridge University Press, 2000), Introduction and chapter 1; those who would like more extensive versions of my arguments (and more empirical material, focusing on India) can find them there. For earlier articulations of my views on capabilities see "Nature, Function, and Capability: Aristotle on Political Distribution," *Oxford Studies in Ancient Philosophy*

Supplementary Volume I: 1988, 145-84, hereafter NFC; "Aristotelian Social Democracy," in *Liberalism and the Good*, ed. R.B. Douglass *et al.* (New York: Routledge, 1990), 203-52, hereafter ASD; "Non-Relative Virtues: An Aristotelian Approach," in *The Quality of Life*, ed. M. Nussbaum and A. Sen (Oxford: Clarendon Press, 1993), hereafter NRV, volume hereafter QL; "Aristotle on Human Nature and the Foundations of Ethics," in *World, Mind and Ethics: Essays on the Ethical Philosophy of Bernard Williams*, ed. J. E. J. Altham and Ross Harrison (Cambridge: Cambridge University Press, 1995), 86-131, hereafter HN; "Human Functioning and Social Justice: In Defense of Aristotelian Essentialism," *Political Theory* 20 (1992), 202-46, hereafter HF; "Human Capabilities, Female Human Beings," in *Women, Culture, and Development*, ed. M. Nussbaum and J. Glover (Oxford: Clarendon Press, 1995), 61-104, paper hereafter HC, volume hereafter WCD; "The Good as Discipline, the Good as Freedom," in *Ethics of Consumption: The Good Life, Justice, and Global Stewardship*, ed. David A. Crocker and Toby Linden (Lanham, MD: Rowman and Littlefield, 1997), 312-411, hereafter GDGF; "Women and Cultural Universals," chapter 1 in Nussbaum, *Sex and Social Justice* (New York: Oxford University Press, 1999), 29-54, hereafter WC; and "Capabilities and Human Rights," *Fordham Law Review 66* (1997), 273-300, hereafter CHR.

2. For examples of these inequalities, see chapter 3 of *Women and Human Development*, and my "Religion and Women's Human Rights," in Paul Weithman, ed., *Religion and Contemporary Liberalism* (Notre Dame: University of Notre Dame Press, 1997), 93-137, also in Nussbaum, *Sex and Social Justice* (New York: Oxford University Press, 1999).
3. Throughout this paper, as in my book, I focus particularly on India, because I believe it is more helpful to study one situation in some detail than to pull in examples from all over the place without their context. But the problems described are ubiquitous.
4. For an excellent discussion of these attitudes, see Jasodhara Bagchi, *Loved and Unloved: The Girl-Child in the Indian Family* (Calcutta: Stree, 1997).
5. *Human Development Report 1999,* United Nations Development Programme (Oxford and New York: Oxford University Press, 1999).
6. Among the four countries ranking lowest in the Gender-adjusted Development Index (GDI) (Niger, Ethiopia, Burkina Faso, and Burundi—no ranking being given for Sierra Leone because of insufficient data), three are among the bottom four on the the Human Poverty Index (HPI), a complex measure including low life expectancy, deprivation in education, malnutrition, and lack of access to safe water and health services (the bottom four being Sierra Leone, Niger, Ethiopia, and Burkina Faso—Burundi is fifteen places higher) (see pp. 140-41, 146-8); among the four developing countries ranking highest in the HPI (Barbados, Trinidad and Tobago, Uruguay, and Costa Rica), all have

high rankings on the GDI (Barbados 27, Uruguay 36, Costa Rica 42, Trinidad and Tobago 44).

7. On India, see the special report on rape in *India Abroad,* July 10, 1998. According to the latest statistics, one woman is raped every 54 minutes in India, and rape cases have increased 32 per cent between 1990 and 1997. Even if some of this increase is due to more reporting, it is unlikely that it all is, because there are many deterrents to reporting. A woman's sexual history and social class is sure to be used against her in court, medical evidence is rarely taken promptly, police typically delay in processing complaints, and therefore convictions are extremely difficult to secure. Penile penetration is still a necessary element of rape in Indian law, and thus cases involving forced oral sex, for example, cannot be prosecuted as rape. Rape cases are also expensive to prosecute, and there is currently no free legal aid for rape victims. In a sample of 105 cases of rape that actually went to court (in a study conducted by Sakshi, a Delhi-based NGO) only 17 resulted in convictions.

8. Sub-Saharan Africa was chosen as the "baseline" because it might be thought inappropriate to compare developed with developing countries. Europe and North America have an even higher ratio of women to men: about 105/100. Sub-Saharan Africa's relatively high female/male ratio, compared to other parts of the developing world, is very likely explained by the central role women play in productive economic activity, which gives women a claim to food in time of scarcity. For a classic study of this issue, see Esther Boserup, *Women's Role in Economic Development* (New York: St. Martin's Press, 1970), second edition Aldershot: Gower Publishing, 1986). For a set of valuable responses to Boserup's work, see *Persistent Inequalities,* ed. Irene Tinker (New York: Oxford University Press, 1990).

9. The statistics in this paragraph are taken from Jean Drèze and Amartya Sen, *Hunger and Public Action* (Oxford: Clarendon Press, 1989) and Drèze and Sen, *India: Economic Development and Social Opportunity* (Delhi: Oxford University Press, 1995), chapter 7. Sen's estimated total number of missing women is one hundred million; the *India* chapter discusses alternative estimates.

10. See Drèze and Sen, *Hunger*, p. 52.

11. Personal communication, Viji Srinivasan, Adithi, Patna, Bihar.

12. See Eva Kittay, *Love's Labor: Essays on Women, Equality, and Dependency* (New York: Routledge, 1999); Nancy Folbre, "Care and the Global Economy," background paper for *Human Development Report* 1999; Mona Harrington, *Care and Equality: Inventing a New Family Politics* (New York: Knopf, 1999); Joan Williams, *Unbending Gender: Why Family and Work Conflict and What to Do About It* (New York: Oxford University Press, 1999).

13. On this see my "Public Philosophy and International Feminism," *Ethics* 108 (1998), 770-804; "Why Practice Needs Ethical Theory:

Particularism, Principle, and Bad Behavior," forthcoming in *The Path of the Law in the Twentieth Century,* ed. S. Burton, Cambridge University Press; and "Still Worthy of Praise: A Response to Richard A. Posner, "The Problematics of Moral and Legal Theory," *Harvard Law Review* 111 (1998), 1776-95.

14. The terms "political liberalism," "overlapping consensus," and "comprehensive conception" are used as by John Rawls in *Political Liberalism* (expanded paper edition, New York: Columbia University Press, 1996), hereafter PL.

15. See *Women in Informal Employment: Globalising and Organising,* publication of a public seminar, April 1999, in Ottowa, Canada; the steering committee of WIEGO includes Ela Bhatt of SEWA, and Martha Chen, who has been a leading participant in discussions of the "capabilities approach" at the World Institute for Development Economics Research, in the "quality of life" project directed by me and Amartya Sen: see her "A Matter of Survival: Women's Right to Work in India and Bangladesh," in WCD, and *A Quiet Revolution: Women in Transition in Rural Bangladesh* (Cambridge, MA: Schenkman, 1983).

16. See the excellent discussion of these attacks in the essay "Contesting Cultures" in Uma Narayan, *Dislocating Cultures: Identities, Traditions, and Third World Feminism* (New York: Routledge, 1997).

17. Narayan, p. 26.

18. For one fascinating example of this point, together with a general critique of communitarian fantasies of cultural peace and homogeneity, see Fred Kniss, *Disquiet in the Land: Cultural Conflict in American Mennonite Communities* (New Brunswick: Rutgers University Press, 1997).

19. For a general discussion, with many references, see M. Nussbaum and Amartya Sen, "Internal Criticism and Indian Rationalist Traditions," in *Relativism: Interpretation and Confrontation,* ed. Michael Krausz (Notre Dame: University of Notre Dame Press, 1989), 299-325.

20. Cited by Amartya Sen, in speech at the conference on The Challenge of Modern Democracy, The University of Chicago, April 1998.

21. The initial statement is in Sen, "Equality of What?" in S. McMurrin, ed., *Tanner Lectures on Human Values* 1 (Cambridge: Cambridge University Press, 1980), reprinted in Sen, *Choice, Welfare, and Measurement* (Oxford and Cambridge, MA: Basil Blackwell and MIT Press, 1982), hereafter CWM; see also various essays in *Resources, Values, and Development* (Oxford and Cambridge, MA: Basil Blackwell and MIT Press, 1984), hereafter RVD; *Commodities and Capabilities* (Amsterdam: North-Holland, 1985); *Well-Being, Agency, and Freedom: The Dewey Lectures 1984, The Journal of Philosophy* 82 (1985); "Capability and Well-Being," in QL, 30-53; "Gender Inequality and Theories of Justice," in J. Glover and M. Nussbaum, eds., *Women, Culture, and Development* (hereafter WCD) (Oxford: Clarendon Press,

1995), 153-98; *Inequality Reexamined* (Oxford and Cambridge, MA: Clarendon Press and Harvard University Press, 1992). See also J. Drèze and A. Sen, *Hunger and Public Action* (Oxford: Clarendon Press, 1989), and *India: Economic Development and Social Opportunity* (Delhi: Oxford University Press, 1995).

22. *Human Development Reports: 1993, 1994, 1995, 1996* (New York: United Nations Development Programme). For related approaches in economics, see Partha Dasgupta, *An Inquiry Into Well-Being and Destitution* (Oxford: Clarendon Press, 1993)' Bina Agarwal, *A Field of One's Own: Gender and Land Rights in South Asia* (Cambridge: Cambridge University Press, 1994); Sabina Alkire, *Operationalising Amartya Sen's Capability Approach to Human Development: A Framework for Identifying Valuable Capabilities,* D. Phil. Dissertation, Oxford University, 1999; S. Anand and C. Harris, "Choosing a Welfare Indicator," *American Economic Association Papers and Proceedings* 84 (199), 226-49; Frances Stewart, "Basic Needs, Capabilities, and Human Development," in *In Pursuit of the Quality of Life,* ed. Avner Offer (Oxford: Oxford University Press, 1996); Prasanta Pattanaik, "Cultural Indicators of Well-Being: Some Conceptual Issues," in UNESCO, *World Culture Report; Culture, Creativity, and Markets* (Paris, UNESCO Publishing, 1980, 333-39; Meghnad Desai, "Poverty and Capability: Towards an Empirically Implementable Measure," *Suntory-Toyota International Center Discussion Paper* no. 27, London School of Economics Development Economics Research Programme, 1990; Achin Chakraborty, *The Concept and Measurement of the Standard of Living,* Ph.D. Thesis, University of California at Riverside, 1996. For discussion of the approach, see K. Aman, ed., *Ethical Principles for Development: Needs, Capabilities or Rights* (Montclair, N. J.: Montclair State University Press, 1991); *Choice, Welfare, and Development: A Festschrift in Honour of Amartya K. Sen,* ed. K. Basu, P. Pattanaik and K. Suzumura (Oxford: Clarendon Press, 1995).

23. See the discussion of this example in M. Nussbaum and A. Sen, "Introduction," *The Quality of Life,* ed. M. Nussbaum and A. Sen (Oxford: Clarendon Press, 1993).

24. Chapter 2 of *Women and Human Development* gives an extensive account of economic preference-based approaches, arguing that they are defective without reliance on a substantive list of goals such as that provided by the capabilities approach. Again, this is a theme that has repeatedly been stressed by Sen in his writings on the topic: see above n. 13.

25. See chapter 1 of *Women and Human Development* for an account of these differences.

26. Obviously, I am thinking of the political more broadly than do many theorists in the Western liberal tradition, for whom the nation state

remains the basic unit. I am envisaging not only domestic deliberations but also cross-cultural quality of life assessments and other forms of international deliberation and planning.

27. For some examples of the academic part of these discussions, see the papers by Roop Rekha Verma, Martha A. Chen, Nkiru Nzegwu, Margarita Valdes, and Xiaorong Li in *Women, Culture and Development.*
28. The 1994 International Conference on Population and Development (ICPD) adopted a definition of reproductive health that fits well with the intuitive idea of truly human functioning that guides this list: "Reproductive health is a state of complete physical, mental and coail well-being and not merely the absence of disease or infirmity, in all matters relating to the reproductive system and its processes. Reproductive health therefore implies that people are able to have a satisfying and safe sex life and that they have the capability to reproduce and the freedom to decide if, when, and how often to do so." The definition goes on say that it also implies information and access to family planning methods of their choice. A brief summary of the ICPD's recommendations, adopted by the Panel on Reproductive Health of the Committee on Population established by the National Research Council specifies three requirements of reproductive health: "1. Every sex act should be free of coercion and infection. 2. Every pregnancy should be intended. 3. Every birth should be health." See Amy O. Tsui, Judith N. Wasserheit, and John G. Haaga, eds., *Reproductive Health in Developing Countries* (Washington: National Academy Press, 1997), p. 14.
29. See the fuller discussion in *Women and Human Development,* chapter 1.
30. Chapters 3 and 4 of *Women and Human Development* confront the difficult issues raised by religion and the family for this approach.
31. See Martha A. Chen, *Perpetual Mourning: Widowhood in Rural India* (Delhi and Philadelphia: Oxford University Press and University of Pennsylvania Press, forthcoming 1999; and "A Matter of Survival: Women's Right to Employment in India and Bangladesh," in WCD, 37-57.
32. See my *Sex and Social Justice* (New York: Oxford University Press, 1999), chs. 3 and 4.
33. See the varied proposals in the works cited above n. 12, and also my "The Future of Feminist Liberalism," a Presidential Address to the Central Division of the American Philosophical Association, April 22, 2000, and to be published in *Proceedings and Addresses of the American Philosophical Association.*
34. Rawls, *Political Liberalism* (above), a frequent phrase. For detailed discussion of Rawls's views on this question, see my "Rawls and Feminism," forthcoming in *The Cambridge Companion to Rawls,* ed. Samuel Freeman; and also "The Future of Feminist Liberalism."

35. See the excellent argument in Kittay (above n. 12).
36. Not all political approaches that use an Aristotelian idea of functioning and capability are freedom-focused in this way; thus Aristotle was an inspiration for Marx, and also for many Catholic conservative thinkers. Among historical approaches using Aristotle, my approach lies closest to that of the British social-democratic thinkers T. H. Green in the latter half of the nineteenth century (pioneer of compulsory education in Britain) and Ernest Barker in the first half of the twentieth.
37. Sen, "Freedoms and Needs," *The New Republic* January 10/17, 1994, 31-38, at 38. Compare Rawls, PL, 187-8, which connects freedom and need in a related way.
38. Sen, *Poverty and Famines: An Essay on Entitlement and Deprivation* (Oxford: Clarendon Press, 1981).
39. The material of this section is further developed in CHR.
40. Bernard Williams, *"The Standard of Living:* Interests and Capabilities," in The Standard of Living, ed. G. Hawthorne (Cambridge: Cambridge University Press, 1987), 100.
41. On both India and China, see Sen,"Human Rights and Asian Values," *The New Republic* July 14/21, 1997, 33-41; and also Charles Taylor, "Conditions of an Unforced Consensus on Human Rights," in *The East Asian Challenge for Human Rights,* ed. Joanne R. Bauer and Daniel A. Bell (Cambridge: Cambridge University Press, 1999).
42. See Sen, "Human Rights and Asian Values." On Tagore, see Sen, *New York Review of Books,* June 1997; K. Bardhan, "Introduction" to *Of Women, Outcastes.* For the language of rights in the Indian independence struggls, see Nehru, *Autobiography,* 612.
43. That is my account of the political goal: one might, of course, retain the capabilities approach while defining the goal differently—in terms, for example, of complete capability equality. I recommend the threshold only as a *partial theory of justice,* not a complete theory. If all citizens are over the threshold, my account does not yet take a stand on what distributive principle should govern at that point.

2

Ecosociology of Man-Woman Relation: Toward Risking A Comprehensive Paradigm

Marinal Kanti Dasgupta

Abstract

Instead of an exclusively positivist-reductionist pursuit, New Sociology is increasingly looking forward to scientific realism and holism as its principal philosophy and methodology. New ecology is a synthetic study of organisms in an ecosystem in their interactions among themselves and with the environment. Ecosociology integrates New Ecology into New Sociology, which strives to place human both as a biological and sociocultural entity. Human is gifted with the highest levels of intellectual ability, conscience and ethics. This is the only species capable of understanding the depth and expanse of the knowable cosmos but troubled by and torn between the biological determinism fashioned by the evolutionary past and cultural ethics created by the species itself. Ecosociology accommodates temporal and spatial flexibilities, and is cautiously applied to human psychology, ethology, sociocultural evolution of human. This article addressed itself to the classical and modern theories of patriarchy (which is broadened here to masculinism) and misogyny. The current controversies between sociobiology and social Darwinism (being principally a biological argument) on the one hand and cultural evolutionism (being principally a cultural argument) on the other, towards seeking a synthesis between the two are also also discussed. A correct understanding is needed as to how and why man is able to dominate over woman through the entire course of history, across races, cultures and communities, social and economic strata, levels of literacy, urbanisation, material culture and technology, forms of government, etc. Without which a strategy of feminism cannot be set as the current agenda of transformation without gender bias.

A critique of liberal-democratic radical-feminist viewpoints together with a reconstruction of classical Marxist standpoint has been made. This explodes the myth of matriarchy, which has never been a fact in the social-cultural history of man. Lack of evidences apart, polyandry, which ought to have been a necessary accompaniment of matriarchy, has never been operative except for a transient period of unfavourable sex ratio. But the so-called primitive matriarchy has led to the social traditions of matrilinearity, matrilocality and coparcenary property rights, and cultural paterns of mother cult, motherhood myth and even motherhood mysticism of today. The strongest element in favour of the biological argument arises from this historical fact. Biological differences between sexes are the facts of nature, operative between most individuals of the species. The biological determinism is 'fundamental' in the sense that at all stages in the history of class struggle, before the classes appeared and perhaps if and whenever the classes whenever the classes wither away the man-woman contradictions will remain at the biological chore of the gender structure. However, notwithstanding the sexual differences, the boldest truth in the cultural argument is that it is the man who has built up the patriarchal socio-cultural ethics and laws, mores and traditions, art and literature, ideology and practice, behaviour and attitude, beliefs and values—all human constructs—on this biological edifice. As a result, patriarchy has developed as a structure with a material basc, which includes the unequal and oppressive division of productive roles between he sexes. This extended concept of patriarchy traverses the classical notion and reaches out to masculinism as opposed to feminism. The nature and role of sex in further shaping the sexual and cultural evolution in human remains at the nucleus of the gender relations and family system, social and economic structure, polity and state, even idelogy and philosophy. Therefore, given the sexual differences, the best of man-woman relations on equality of sociocultural status and without mutual hatred shall and can only rest on the best of ethics. Since the sociocultural differences are human constructs their deconstruction—be they in economic, legal, social and political rights.

I. Introduction

The archaeology of knowledge and the epistemological advancements so far made is largely reductive, which has undeniably paid significant dividends. But the lesson from this persistently positivist-reductionist pursuit has also developed the antithesis to look for scientific realism and holism for macro-conceptualisation for a unified field. Even as sociology has often been reduced to psychology, and psychology to neurology, the concept of evolutionary-biological and ecosociological continuity of man as a biological entity has gone amiss, until restored in New Ecology. New ecology places the human both as a biological and socio-cultural entity gifted with the highest levels of intellectual ability, conscience and ethics, capable of understanding the depth and expanse of the knowable cosmos across space and time. Human history is spread through a tiny locus in a continuum of energy flow not readily traceable to the original forms or specks of life (not to speak of its abiogenetic past), as genetic diversity has progressed through evolution. Energy flows in the continuum of and consciousness in the complementary convergence of an infinite flow of energy without a beginning or an end. A species or an individual is merely a transient materialisation—a 'momentary configuration' (*sensu* Heisenberg) or 'moments in the network, knobs in the web of life' (*sensu* Callicott, in Callicott and Ames 1989). Such are the rationale for a comprehensive philosophy. The contemporary society needs seeking complementary convergence pervading all branches of human knowledge and endeavour, perception and thinking, frustrations and aspirations, not merely as an unavoidable and logical legacy of the past but projecting for the humans what and how they should strive to be.

Seeking for a unified field is precisely not opposed to the subaltern belief in the lack of universality of a proposition over time, space and context. On the other hand, subalternism is clearly complementary to the determinism of historical materialism at the core of a universal concept, as of Marx, while being most comprehensive as well as situational across times and places. A science is elevated from a figment of a creative scientist to a real one as it becomes able to stand verifications in unrelated areas, what Darwin called 'consilience of inductions'. Deconstructing a hypothesis, long held to be universal, is a post-modernist argument. A natural or social phenomenon is hardly universal in causation or impact, because the factors are too many and the relations between them are too complex. Yet an analytic hypothesis is always convenient to work with. The dialectical approaches of thesis-antithesis-synthesis, or theory-practice-theory, or shifting a paradigm, or deconstructing-and-reconstructing do not seem to be philosophically very distant.

En passant, the Marxian determinism is merely sequential and consequential (and thereby causal) as it happened and shall happen through the course of history of social evolution. At the same time, admittedly, as there could be alternatives in the past, there is scope for evolutionary alternatives and revolutionary upheavals. Which do occur or shall have to be effected in order to direct the course of history or make it faster but never to revert the process. Marx took upon himself to trace out the historical process with the objectives, strategy and tactics. Lenin (1908) wrote, 'We do not regard Marx's theory as something completed and inviolable. On the contrary, we are convinced that it has only laid the founding stone of the science which socialists must develop in all directions if they wish to keep pace with life' (Materialism and Empirio-Criticism).

Ecology is the study of the ecosystem. An ecosystem exists wherever a system of conspecific or polyspecific community exists. Like philosophy, logic, mathematics or statistics, ecology has no domain of its own. An ecologist delves into others' territory for mutual benefit. Ecosociology is proposed to synthesise ecology and sociology in general and ecology into sociology in particular. Ecosociology encompasses and integrates biogeography, cultural ecology, cognitive neuroscience, evolutionary psychology, sociobiology (as a broad concept, not in the restrictive Neo-Darwinian sense) and cultural sociology of societal interactions involving humans as a species and peoples across time and space in the study of human society with an ecological perspective. A species has the characteristics that it has because these characteristics result from its adaptation to a niche in an ecosystem. For humans, a conscious cultural evolution is not only possible but also it has taken place through the ascent of humans since their appearance.

An ecosociological theory of man-woman relation is sought to be unified and comprehensive enough to accommodate temporal and spatial flexibilities. Such a theory is imperative to set the goal, strategy and tactics for women's movement. All past attempts in this regard have been contingent concepts guiding the contemporary theorists and activists of the past only inadequately and non-comprehensively, often smudging their path instead of providing guidance. This is not at all to belittle the historical role the concepts have played and the glorious achievements such movements - reformist or rebellious - have made in the past.

Ecosociology is to be cautiously and critically applied to human psychology, ethology and sociobiology. However, it shall not mean that they are untenable approaches to the understanding of man in societal context. The simple argument is that more and more genetic evidences are accumulating on the genetic basis of biotic or abiotic human diseases, instincts and behaviours including sexuality and homosexuality as well as on the genetic evolution. Numbers of human genes have been located unaltered in the 'lower organisms'. There is no evidence to suggest that the altered genes tend to competitively exclude the unaltered genes.

A brief review of the past and the present theories and movements becomes imperative for the contextual need for the proposition of a comprehensive conceptualisation of the man - woman relations in its barest outline.

II. A Critique of Classical Theories of Patriarchy and Misogyny

We view classical historical materialism to be reductionist. However, when it is broadened with the ecological and evolutionary-biological perspectives the methodology of historical materialism as a means and tool of the study of human society works well.

In this article, both patriarchy and misogyny have been used in the broadest possible connotations. But the authors referred to may have used them in varied extents of purport which I shall have occasions to point out. Generally, they have not been used interchangeably but more biological, material and social import has been given to the former, and more cultural, psychological and attitudinal import to the latter.

Mahadevan (1989) contains attempts to graphically present the man-woman relation in respect of population policies in the traditional societies in Asia. Such analyses are relevant and important in the understanding of the social conditions that makes the psyche, ethos and culture of such societies. Marx for the first time emphasised the importance of the study of everyday life' as complementary to or being more revealing than the empirical studies. So much so that Lefebrre (1992) remarked, 'Marxism as a whole, is a critical knowledge of everyday life'. In arriving at a generalised theory of man-woman relation references to real life studies have found equal importance. Which are often very different from the type obtained in the European societies of the New World, which overtly influence the classical conceptualisations in this field. Even a modern individual of these traditional societies — man or woman — tends to be increasingly superimposed by and juxtaposed with the modern mainstream Euro-American thought process while cosily nursing and nurturing the contradictions of his or her own culture.

2.1. Liberal-Democratic and Radical-Feminist Viewpoints

In liberal-democratic feminism, the concept of individualism arose objectively for a sudden need for plantation and industrial labour from within and across geopolitical boundaries from among the rural folks, slaves, serfs and women. This was also accentuated by a subjective realisation for enlightenment of man and woman as a fall-out of the renaissance and the Victorian value system. Some of the women's rights and privileges for the bourgeois women were achieved percolating very insignificantly downstream. The liberal feminists, however, never bothered to hypothesise the genesis of women's subjugation in this period of colonialism and pre-capitalism, and consequently the concept of 'patriarchy' was mechanistically applied.

The radical feminists were the first to trace the reasons for women's subjugation to patriarchy which to them meant "from the rule of the father to the rule of the man", to "exploitation of wives' labour by.... husbands based on the institution of marriage which was essentially a labour contract between the husband and the wife", to "a universal mode of power relationship" and domination. Patriarchal oppression, they argued, was primary and fundamental, and pre-dated class oppression (Barston 1969). A major and Marxist variant of this school also held that the root of patriarchy is to be sought in the biologically determined division of labour between man and woman in the process of 'reproduction of species'. That 'biological determination seems to be inadequate in the theoretical understanding of the family and human reproduction in relation to the subordination of woman' (Chakraborty, this volume) is a criticism of the radical-feminist argument from the classical Marxist position, which is anthropocentric too.

Suffice it to say at this point, the classical Marxist position is a rigid theorisation on this issue that even ignores Engels' views and Lenin's position not excluding the seminal views of Marx. Marx considered Fourier as the 'complete feminist' and he quotes him: '...the degree of female emancipation forms the 'natural measure' of the general emancipation achieved by any society (Economic and Philosophic Manuscripts, 1844). Marx perhaps treated domestic labour and family labour in family production as labour incognito who can create use values but can create neither wealth, nor culture (Marx, K. 1975, Moscow edition., Critique of the German Gotha Programme). Marx (*loc.cit.*) wanted the abolition of contradiction between mental and manual labour but did not elaborate that most of women's domestic labour is manual and how sexual division of labour may be confronted. Marx's labour theory of value exposed the contradictions between the owners and the wage labourers, i.e. between capital and labour but the patriarchal bias in Marx excluded private labour of women in the household by restricting labour to wage labour (Hartman 1986, Custers 1998) (emphasis added).

Engels' perception was cogent for his time but has been little reflected in the formal classical Marxist literature and propaganda documents even when co-authored by Marx and Engels. The overbearing reason, as for ignoring many other things in their understanding as of young Marx or as is evident in his later letters and notes, was the more important contingent task of changing history rather than to write it more comprehensively. Notwithstanding the prominent role of economic classes this remains a fact that the role of sexual oppression has been nearly totally ignored in framing the theory of historical materialism and in setting the strategy of the liberation of the proletariat. Engels, in The Origin of Family, Private Property and State (OFPPS, 1884), observes, 'The determining factor in history is, in the last resort, the production and reproduction of immediate life.' Marx and Engels (1845-46) (The German Ideology) also emphasised 'the production of immediate life'. But neither were these developed nor were they brought to bear upon their theory of historical materialism and social revolution (Sargent 1986).

Marxists put family in the superstructure not as an economic unit. But the socialist-feminists give priority status to family being primary and fundamental over the class. The production itself signifies the unity of opposites between social and private production—the basic law of dialectics (Kuhn 1978). The overbearing role of industry and the revolutionary role of industrial labour in shaping the future led Marx to ignore all other forms of labour, may be in greater distress and subjugation. Like which he ignored the revolutionary role of the agricultural labour for several objective and subjective conditions he himself explained.

2.2. Marxist Viewpoints Reconstructed

2.2.1 Matriarchy, Matrilineality, Matrilocality. Until recently, it was believed that matriarchy appeared in the history of the social human in an economic condition of social production and consumption for a transient period of primitive communism. Primitive communism is to be understood as a form of community livelihood more in desperation than by volition and in all respects — hunger, insecurity, uncertainty, sex, etc. It is to be particularly noted that such a society was gravely constrained by the lack of any surplus food or material wealth of any consideration to take private possession of crisis in livelihood of a worst order encouraged both competitions within and between tribes, and collectivism in food gathering, hunting, and fishing, perfected more in big game hunting. Through the cultural history of the human, the two opposite ecological forces, viz. competitive exclusion and cooperation (Dasgupta 1995, 1999a) have to be recognised as the fundamental sociological background at every phase in the transformation of the 'cultural ecologies' (*sensu* Thompson). According to Engels, the biologically determined special and specific role of women in 'the process of reproduction of the species' gave women the special power of dominance over the community. It gave rise to matriarchy so long as the means of production, forms of consumption, division of labour, exchange and distribution were collective, and social division of labour had not appeared on the basis of sex. Leibowitz (1986) traced the development of first human societies to the origin of sexual division of labour. An informal division of tasks slowly gets institutionalised and became oppressive to women (Leydcesdorff 1977, Lewenhak 1980, Milkman 1985, Omvedt 1983, Ilina Sen 1988).

Until recently, it was also believed that even when small families were formed, women performed horticulture and agriculture with small grains and root crops which they themselves may have invented, as well as cooking, weaving, etc. and the family served as an economic unit with women as the true matriarchs. Studies in most isolated of the aboriginal peoples with 'ancient cultures' do not always corroborate this view.

Modern evidences suggest that true matriarchy in the sense of rule by a matriarch (absolute woman power and the matrilineal descent of authority) may not have occurred anywhere at any point of time. Even among the Nairs (=Nayars) who have matrilineal and matrilocal property and habitat, actual power and authority is vested with the mother's brother or mother's mother's brother. The right of coparcenary property traditionally inherited by the daughters still continues in some of the castes even across religions in parts of South India but the husband or his family, in fact, enjoys the property. Matrilinearity for parentage and coparcenary property rights to married daughters in varied extent is still prevailing in some societies, such as those derived from the cultural stock of the pre-Aryan peoples in India (Nayar 1989). More commonly, matrilocality is prevalent even in some such societies, which have otherwise adopted patriarchal values, customs and laws, as in the modern pre-Aryan-Aryan Sangam cultures in South India. Evidences of mother cult are too strongly evident in the Harappan cultures. The tradition has integrated itself into the Hindu (a nomenclature with religious imputation had not been referred to until the Gupta period) religion and tradition as a true synthesis of cultures, not without bouts of attrition still simmering within.

In Bengal, till the 7th to 9th century AD, the Aryan culture had not yet interacted with the pre-existing pre-Aryan cultures. Evidences from *Charya pada* to other contemporary literature indicate no Brahminical influence and is secular, closer to nature and has much empathy to the common human and women in particular. Later, with the influence of *Smriti* through Brahminical interaction, hierarchy in society and subjugation of women were gradually and firmly established. Not all peoples pass through cultural transition at equal pace nor any given society accepts all the characteristics of a later form of cultural transition. For instance, there is an indigenous people in West Bengal which still maintains the practice of megalithic burial. Similar is also the process of biological evolution, which makes little sense as of some early orthodox Darwinians to label an organism 'lower' or 'higher' than another.

Until clans or large families fragmented into big families community reproduction still remained a social activity as anything else, paternity was not discernible and group mating prevailed. Even the role of males in reproduction may not have had yet been fully realised in some societies in antiquity. The evidence of such an understanding may be obtained in the practice of the phallus cult being continued even now. The Hindu mythology is blissfully ignorant of the ideal time of sex, and that it ought to correspond with the time of ovulation, which itself they were unaware of. But the system of community livelihood must have shown the signs of cracking even before the beginning of private property. The need for security of children the women bore must have forced them, out of motherly instinct, to depend on men in general and some stronger, braver and more intelligent and kindly men in particular. Bilateral sexual relations, not without competition among men and personal choice by women, may have been the progenitor of polygyny and at least for a transient period, polyandry. With the establishment of private property, paired marriage appeared to be prompted more by the possessive instincts of men (being stronger than women's) than anything else, which soon resulted in firmly establishing polygyny giving way to open and bipolar polygamy, which might have been exceptional. This is also the beginning of patriarchy. Modern students of cognitive evolution, psychological evolution, evolution of sexual behaviour, and sociobiologists in particular, have brought in new findings and theorisations, which are both interesting and controversial (Richards 1987, Ruse 1985, Ruse and Wilson 1985, Trivers 1985).

Community production and social system gave way to private property — chiefly as a failure of the previous socio-economic system. This was also integratively and synergistically emboldened by muscular power, intellectual prowess and instinctive (chiefly possessive) strength of certain men over the rest of men and women in the community and across communities in interaction. It gave rise to both serfs (including slaves and bonded labours, i.e. with or without productive value and economic independence) and women subjugated to community overlords (all males without exception!) in course of time (Bardhan 1993, .Le Doeuff 1991, Miller 1989).

2.2.2 Mother cult, Motherhood myth, Motherhood mysticism. Indian mythological evidences of *Pramila Rajya* of the pre-Aryan cultures (in the *Ramayana*) till about their interactions with the Aryans may be a figment or, more dubiously, a pre-historic artefact or vestige of an exceptional and by then antiquated system. I believe so because such a strong matriarchy in full glory is not compatible with the patriarchy which has since been strongly established in both the Aryans and the pre-Aryans, being personified in *Rama* and *Ravana*, as depicted in *Ramayana* itself.

Unless the natural, i.e., biological determinist differences are assumed to have favoured men to subjugate women is accepted, I believe, there is no alternative and valid explanation as to why women could not have dominated over men since even before the rise of patriarchy or, maybe, ever in the past. The biological make-up of a man or a woman also includes their instinctive, physiological including hormonal nature, and even the psyche at the root. The cultural force of subjugation of women *could be* strong because it is founded on biological differences.

Once patriarchy appeared the subsequent social and economic forces became strong enough to lessen the biological differences. This went on to the extent that at all micro- and macro-levels the biological differences continued to favour men until value changes for liberal and democratic ideals led humans to think and act differently from what humans had done ever in the past. Therefore, only this assumption can explain the subsequent cultural developments which acted in favour of men who, by virtue of biological differences, instilled in themselves and women a highly biased cultural value system and could increasingly manipulate everything over time. Nonetheless, it does in no way argue that this biological determinism ought to have prevailed or should continue to prevail particularly in view of cultural and intellectual evolution of humans who otherwise strive 'to conquer nature' in almost every other area of human 'civilisation' (Betzig *et al.* 1988, Reed 1979).

While biological determinism cuts across all divisions and pre-dates class formation and thereby class oppression *per se;* the strongest and most overbearing of all social forces came to be class struggle in most times, places and contexts. This is also the Marxist-Leninist position which certainly may have been overemphasised in the course of history of women's movement in Germany and many places later, wherever, the leadership has been provided by the communists overwhelmed by classical Marxism. This is also the reason why many orthodox Marxists argue that feminism has no place in Marxism, or at least they do not go hand in hand. It does not imply that class conflict is on the extinct state, merely a different form has appeared and further new forms may appear. Nor does it imply that the role of class struggle is gone and only new antiestablishment forces are to be sought among the feminists, human rights movement activists, green movement activists, etc.

The biological determinism is 'fundamental' in the sense that at all stages in the history of class struggle, perhaps before that and when classes will wither away, if at all they do, the man-woman contradictions will remain. Though not only biologically, biological differences shall remain to be the most difficult to overcome through cultural and value changes. Surely, it is too naive to expect that a collective choice will take place in favour of cloning from women for survival of the species! Thus, there appears to be no alternative but biology to continue influencing the culture and the superstructure. Indeed, here is the more plausible alternative. It is the survival instinct and the unique intellectual equipment of human to continuously improve the quality of life over time and space, which, I hope, shall slowly lead to the collective ethical choice striving to remove the hindrances imposed by the natural differences between man and woman.

Let us take the case of recent changes in sharing of domestic chores between men and women. Male participation in domestic chores increased in the post-World War II phase in the West — perhaps the best of the achievements —arising as contradictions from within. A study in the Netherlands shows that women's work is invisible and stretches over 14 hours per day (Lycklama and Nijehelt 1987, Science News report). Further, the British husbands used to do 20 per cent of domestic chores in the 60's and do 30 per cent in the nineties and they would take another 30 years to share the drudgery equally. The British married women suffer from the Allerednic effect, whereby the professionally prospective women sacrifice their ambition for the sake of providing support to their husbands. It has been suggested that the work culture in the third millennium should provide enough time for both partners not only to share equally the domestic chores but also to provide enough rest and leisure for both (Gershuny 1998, Science News report). No stretch of imagination may lead one to believe that such things will happen to all men and women in all parts of the world in any foreseeable future. It is, however, needless to emphasise that the feminist movement will fight to this direction only. In spite of that before women's cultural subjugation is eliminated its complexion will change many a time with little change in its 'fundamental biological' character. Meanwhile, the feminist movements in different parts of the world will have to eliminate endless forms of factual social and cultural differences—be they in laws, rights, privileges and many others between man and woman. The cultural and behavioural changes have to be rooted into biology—the genetic and the evolutionary process—to have continuing effects. On the other hand, increased male share did not affect the semi-feudal and semi-capitalist systems, particularly at their lowest rungs. The state and society remained a set of symbiotic material and ideological instruments of subtle and not-so-subtle women's subjugation.

As in traditional societies, even housewives' productive labour in homes, in agriculture and animal husbandry, such as seed and grain storage and preservation, needlework, tailoring or weaving, or in cottage industries such as plastics, binding, and making carpet, toy, *durry, papad,* spices, etc. are also ignored. Societal attitude to women's productive labour is a significant point to note. According to 1991 Census, only 12 per cent women joined in productive labour, compared to 30 per cent men in India. In Calcutta, this participation is about 7 per cent, in spite of literacy rate being at 72 per cent among women. Women tend to leave jobs after marriage, have greater participation in agricultural jobs that are there in the rural areas than in the metropolitan areas, and even solitary male workers are there in cities leaving their families in villages. Both in 1991 and 2001 Censuses, definitions of women's productive labour have been gradually extended.

The best of care a woman receives and the best of authority she commands in the family and the society is during the antenatal and postnatal periods. Which may not be good enough. However, there are evidences to the contrary. Even during marriage as an institution in its rituals and forms across cultures and times it is the bride that holds the sway over the groom being in the limelight and glamour. Of course, there is substance in the argument that even this is a male construct, built upon the precincts of cultural matriarchy. There are indeed marriage rituals across cultures that indicate the overlordship of men over women, religiously and meticulously observed by women and enjoyed by men, because they have been culturally attuned by the conspicuous and not-so-conspicuous fangs of male domination of cultural and ideological variety.

Motherhood has been bloated out of all proportions with an ulterior and sinister attitude and motive. It seems to be a heinous design of men to underplay the human actions of women to dominate or even suppress natural womanly functions. It seeks to ignore the reproductive biological role of women and economic consequences of their domestic servitude. It is also imperative and pertinent to ask why or how could or did such a motive or design arise in men alone but not in women? All said, it is the motherhood of woman that remains as the most significant determinant in man-woman relation. It is a well-nourished myth or a mystic belief that cannot easily be blown off and shall remain for a period of history — short or long whatsoever — depending on the strength of feminism as an integral constituent of mainstream movement involving both men and women across classes, nations, communities, etc. I also do find that the matriarchal values are stronger in the traditional societies than in the industrialised societies as reflected in inhibition around sex in the former, as evident in art, literature, human behaviour and attitudes. But this is also changing with increased industrialisation and westernisation as the ideotype for human cultural ecology during the current Pacific Shift (*sensu* Thompson, in Callicott and Ames 1986) of which globalisation is the most recent syndrome.

Primitive matriarchy, defined as the form of no special status to man *vis-à-vis* woman, thus appeared in the history of the social human in an economic condition of social production and consumption for a transient period of primitive communism. This so-called matriarchy as a social institution has lost all its economic strength with the rise of patriarchy much before state machinery had developed. Matriarchy thus remains in its role of cultural value system as a subtle force in mainstream cultures throughout the world, and is gathering momentum in the form of feminism as a challenge to state power. It is slowly but increasingly gaining ground, at least conjunctively if not integratively, in the movements for people's democracy, human rights and intergenerational rights for environment as in the green movements, principally and conspicuously as in the last quarter of the current century. The need for integration of all democratic movements is strongly felt by the human and woman rights and green movement activists particularly in the poor and developing countries (Ms. Asma Jehangir of Pakistan, interview with The Statesman, 27 Feb., 1999). There are indeed some success stories in this regard.

Women's social role models are derived from stories, legends, songs and folklore, and are cultured in contemporary writings, dance, drama, film, television and other mass media. They mould a girl child from much before she attains her womanhood. In India (and perhaps in all traditional societies), we have two type models or paradigms. The epic heroine type—the sacrificing, chaste loyal wife, from *Sita* to *Behula*—exhibits strength derived from self-effacement, self-abnegation and subjugation as the mother or from the spouse god or hero and only in emboldening and glorifying them. Western feminists (such as Andrea Dworkin 1974, 1987) tried to derive sexless woman identities from their fairy tales as *Snow White, Sleeping Beauty, Cinderella*—models of 'passivity, beauty, innocence and victimisation'. Similarly, some Indian feminists (such as Madhu Kishwar 1986) have re-studied them in deriving indigenous cultural traditions for adding strength to women's movements. Their role as 'exemplary models' will be self-defeating; they may merely be 'revelatory' (Sandra Robinson 1985). On the contrary, Hindu mythology also offers another female paradigm—the all-powerful mother goddess, the *Shakti, Kali* or *Durga* types. Between these two poles lies the tribal folklore and historical female paradigm, the *Virangana* models. They are represented by *Razia Sultana* of Delhi, *Kurma Devi* of Chitor, *Rani Durgavati* of the Gond tribe of Madhya Pradesh, *Chand Bibi* of Aurangabad, *Tarabai* of Thoda of Rajasthan, *Ahalyabai Holkar* of Maharashtra, *Rani Lakshmibai* of Jhansi to the heroines of the Independence Movement, such as *Pritilata* and *Kalpana* of Chattogram and *Matangini* of Medinipur. *Nautankis* and films also make warrior heroines—from *Hunterwali* to *Bandit Queen*. Parallels are to be found in *Godmother* and *Elizabeth*. This model is not polarised as good/bad, chaste/unchaste, self-denying/all-destroying, nor related to a male. She is virtuous, strong powerful, prudent, and moves beyond patriarchal archetypes. She constitutes a transcendent, alternative and challenging womanhood (Kathryn Hansen 1988). The only snag lies in stressing Beauvoirian independence—excelling in masculine role.

2.2.3 Patriarchy. Benston (1986) defined patriarchy as 'a structure with a material base which includes the unequal and oppressive division of productive roles between the sexes'. It is expressed in ideology, culture and practice in all forms and directions. At the stage of agriculture new contradictions arose in the form of new means of livelihood as well as the male's personal possession of his productive tools—marked by his skill, invention, innovation and ingeniousness—the first private property. If and when he would leave the family, he would leave it with his tools and, maybe, with his women too (so we may guess). The form of new means of livelihood as well as the males' personal possession of productive tools—the first private properties—negated the collective rights and collective consumption and enjoyment within the community social system. Wealth particularly increased at this stage with males' initiative and enterprise. The private property alongwith rights, authority and privileges were passed on to the male offspring without ever establishing the rights of their female counterparts. Reproductive and domestic-productive contribution of women to social wealth is being appreciated of late, and is yet to get formalised into the economic system. On the other hand, the woman would cope with her pathetic existence in spite of her contributions through biological and domestic-productive roles including inventing agriculture (at least of some root crops, gardening and even some small grains depending on the geography of the continent), animal rearing and food preservation. Her backbreaking and never-ending labour as well as ingeniousness continued to be ignored by society. It became enamoured with the external and more obvious material achievements of man in land clearing and cultivation, hunting and taming of wild animals, fishing in far-coastal seas, and earning of material wealth in the form of meat for nourishment, labour for manual work and women for sexual indulgence and satiation through battles with other tribes. Each of brainy and skilful men's activities centred round inventing and using various tools, such as plough, spear, bow-and-arrow, fishing tools, canoe or kayak, etc. The women themselves alongwith the weaker men were overwhelmed with their heroism. They invented entertainment rituals. The process of subjugation was easy to follow—of women and other men like the serfs, slaves or bonded labours (Betzig et al. 1988, Boyd and Richerson 1985).

The nature and role of sex in further shaping human sexual evolution has been elaborated by many authors since Darwin and Wallace, and is still pursued by many. The need of security for women themselves and the children they bore led them to adore and coax their heroes with uninterrupted sex in preference to other men keeping them away from the attraction of other women. The prolonged childhood of human is an enigma, unique among all organisms. It serves to carry forward and complete the differentiation and development process initiated in the embryonic phase to the later antenatal postembryonic phase to the postnatal phase, maybe because the human ontogenesis is too complicated to be completed before birth. It certainly necessitates a stronger motherly instinct of women. But that it may lead to adapting to uninterrupted sex regardless of conception, unseasonality of ovulation from adolescence to menopause, failure to perceive ovulation, concealed as it is, which some primates can, unique system of menopause in woman as an adaptation to security of the babies already born are some of the explanations offered. An interesting theory is beginning to establish itself as a possible evolutionary process for adaptation in human, but implies too many assumptions and probabilities difficult to verify at the point of time. The significance lies not in how bold and verifiable it is but that it is well founded in biology.

With the family system created through private control, possession of private tools and domestic animals, newer forms of productive activities and exchange further consolidated the family system itself, bringing about complete reversal of women's position in the community as it was under 'matriarchy', established the male lineage and succession. The concept of incest within clans had been established quite early, marked with tribal totems. The reasons for which might have been more for competition for survival between clans than anything else. But the social customs of incest took varied forms alongwith archetypal matriarchy and patriarchy. Variations granted, the customs of incest continue and tend to be patriarchal.

All activities which needed personal initiative, enterprise and acumen and which could not be performed indoors without social participation became male activities. Men's only functional or biological role is transient. Providing food, shelter and security to women became more cultural than biological, increasingly so with development of technology. Women were left with private duties within the confines of the household and the backyard, routine works of drudgery. A woman was only to be relegated to no better state than that of a beast of burden for the day that never ends and bedmate for the night if the husband so chooses. More so, the women as of the vanquished, the serfs and those of the lower social status as in the hierarchical caste structure of Hindu society had to live in an even more wretched state in all respects. Summarily, men assumed social roles and women were assigned private duties, and this determined the culture. Women's social role became more and more insignificant with that of men's being increasingly larger and more complicated and interesting, creative, intellectual, earning economic significance with well-defined social pursuits. The system consolidated itself later with the rise and establishment of state power. Males acquired immense power in society and by dint of which their authority became unquestionable and grew spirally by leaps and bounds with every step of social consolidation until the antithesis grew from within. Productive role of women came to be secondary.

Monogamous family became the essential institutional framework in society. Monogamy became the law for women. Polygamy and concubine and became males' privilege. Women never gained their right or control over sexuality, maternity, pregnancy, divorce, alimony, bondage to husband's family with or without patrilocality, guardianship over children, protectorate guardianship under father, brother, husband or son depending on the stage and strength of institutionalisation of religion vis-*à-vis* industrialisation as a cultural force. They were fought for only since the women's movements started and are being 'granted by the males' in trickles depending on the strength of movements in different countries and at different times. But the women have been liberally fed with cultural values of virtue, virginity, celibacy, prohibition of polyandry, and were coaxed to accepting thousands of customs that only act as means of subjugation — direct or indirect, naked or subtle. Women became subjugated to male options, desires, happiness, enjoyment and bestiality. It is indeed a world of the male, by the male and for the male. A woman remained a biotic system to procreate the heirs and protectors or labourers for the new generation of males.

Thus patriarchy arose as a new sexual division of labour of socially productive activities which slowly but increasingly and definitely polarised the society until the rise of capitalism when it received its first jerks from within the system itself. Matriarchy as a social institution lost all its economic strength and viability with the rise of patriarchy much before state machinery had developed, except retaining some values from matriarchy to the motherhood mysticism depending on the stage of the culture.

Patriarchy is to be viewed as a definite social form with the rise of private property as the relations of production and consumption with the growth of domestication of plants and animals, i.e. plant and animal agriculture and stationary culture rather than fishing, hunting-food gathering and nomadic existence. Clans must have broken into large families as manageable units even with the late nomadic tribal cultures. The development of private property and patriarchy also signifies the beginning of class society. Oppression on the basis of sex and class was first consequential, then concomitant and in either situation, dialectically interlinked.

Development of patriarchy is closely interwoven in the process of development of private property rights, development of class exploitation and ultimately in the development of state. It has proved to be the hitherto most effective instrument of class exploitation dialectically integrated with its development and growth with various manifestations and flourishing in superstructure, euphemistically called the progress of human civilisation.

Men and women have been polarised and antagonised into social and individual opposites — the pair of biologically, physically, socially, culturally and emotionally empowered males and subjected destitute females as separate identities.

Once the sexual division of labour became established patriarchy was consolidated as the private family system of possession (production) and consumption (distribution) as opposed to the social and communal system. Consequently and even concomitantly, the small family household system became the order with stricter and stricter monogamy on the female side and with liberty and laxity outside the family on the male side. Male authority was firmly established even as the female rights, status and privileges, if there were any left till then, found their degradation and disintegration with time and increasingly so with growing flourish of the pre-capitalist economic systems.

Any form of social division, patriarchy included, is interwoven with the class system that arose as the product of historical development. That patriarchy arose prior to class system and remained as the major social division until class system became the predominant feature is due to its natural origin. It flourished and was strengthened by cultural manipulation.

Erosion of patriarchy occurred for the first time with industrial revolution and the rise of capitalism as an economic, social and political system, but not as an unmixed blessing. Feminism as an unavoidable component of cultural evolution can bring about further erosion.

Surplus production capacity of human labour with newer tools as an improvement in the means of production provided the material condition for the division of society into masters and slaves at one stage in the history and as capitalist and proletariat in the other. At every stage a new condition had been created for furthering and strengthening the domination of women. Also, every advancement in the progress of history in the means and relations of production dialectically implies further consolidation of male authority.

It was the woman who gained little newer relative advantages compared to the past but suffered no less from newer relative disadvantages compared to the contemporary man. For instance, with the advent of industrial capitalism the equation began changing in favour of women for the first time since the olden days of 'matriarchy' in the form of avenues of wage labour on an unprecedented scale. The predominant reason was economic; i.e. the sudden need for additional and reserve labour and procreation of labour for future. This has been met biologically as well as socially, i.e. by raising women's status. Again, as for the newer relative disadvantages the most conspicuous was the degradation of the value about woman. Commercialisation of women's body for male enjoyment as a public commodity across social and economic hierarchies in that order only, was noted for the first time in history with the rise of capitalism and continues unabated still. The need for additional labour could not be met without taking recourse to an identical solution in the feudal past. The need for additional labour must have been marginally small in the past compared to the need of the early industrial society and more so, still later.

In times of war even in the Epic Age in India the hero Arjuna felt concerned with the loss of men (of his male kith and kin ready for the battle on both sides of the divider) and the consequent fall in the social norms of celibacy. Krishna cunningly assuaged this with pragmatism and the hero was goaded into battle. Compare the event with what happened after the Second World War in Europe. The women were to undertake the task of men that remained the domain of men till then, with enough encouragement from the men in the name of women's emancipation. But as soon as the war ended and the soldiers returned from the fronts the women were asked to go back to the kitchen. It is the objective reality, attitude and ethics that can make the difference in problem solving. In the former USSR, however, Lenin took a different stand in favour of women much to the chagrin of some of his colleagues and sought to solve the problem with a vigorous increase in industrial endeavour.

With every stage of increase in technology, i.e. the betterment of the means of production resulting in surplus production capacity of human labour, a need arose for more labour. A new material condition became available for devising new means for the domination of women. The women's reproductive capacity had to be used for both the retention of male inheritance to property and power, and production of more labour for the generation of more surplus.

Together with their men, women of the vanquished community turned into slaves, only to produce more slaves. Values of fidelity, celibacy and virginity for women in the family and the society went parallel to the unbridled promiscuity for men of the master's class but less so down the hierarchy for men alone. The culture passed on to the labourers and the slaves. Women's subjugation generally became the custom and the law being unquestionable across societies and times. But the society views this as moral turpitude with severe punishment prescribed in the religious laws but always more stringent against women than against men. Over all, women's subjugation and monogamous family was fully consistent with the slave mode of production and became the ideological social framework within which the slave mode of production could function and develop. Patriarchy provided the essential ideological and material instrument for the perpetuation and strengthening of class domination. Even in the post-Vedic India of the Epic Age, where the typical feudal system did not operate, women, cattle, grain and gold changed hands in the way of the victor's booty, gifts or priestly dues for the services rendered.

2.2.4 State and patriarchy. Class contradictions gave rise to the function of the state as an instrument for maintaining class authority and class rule of the exploiter upon the exploited. The rise of the state for the first time in human history signalled the overwhelming role of economic power as the motive force of societal development, and thereby the economic classes became the essential infrastructure to maintain and uphold the class relations of production. A strong polemic with orthodox Marxism continues if the family should also be dealt as a part of the infrastructure. With class relations, everything else, sooner or later, was relegated to economic determination. This is what was revealed to Marx and he formulated his social philosophy on this basic proposition. For example, institutionalised religion, one of the strongest of value elements in society, fought tooth and nail with the state system throughout Europe over a considerable period of time in history. The end of the protracted war is not within sight even now. In West Europe, West Asia and South Asia including India, if not as persistently as in the past in medieval Europe or ancient and medieval Asia (State vs. religious institution, Brahman vs. Kshatriya contradiction and conflict, as in the early Vedic-Upanishadic phase, cf. Yagnyabalka anecdotes, rise of Buddhism and Jainism), the religious fundamentalism has raised its head sometimes in league with political power. But religious fundamentalism had to and shall have to come in conflict with and concede to state power, sooner or later.

With the rise of state power, the entire superstructure — ethics, values, customs, norms, statecraft, etc. arose and were transformed to serve the state machinery and power which is the embodiment of patriarchy and class relations, interwoven and symbiotically related for mutual strengthening. Class exploitation concomitant with patriarchy, private property rights, patrilinearity and the male-dominated socio-economic-political system are all interrelated.

Alongwith class system, monogamy and patriarchy provided the essential complementary institution for the functioning of the state system. The state, on its part, strengthens class exploitation through laws and statecraft. Without any conflict with the state, institutionalised religion plays its role through customs, beliefs and practice, strengthens patriarchy through monogamy as a mutually synergistic and reinforcing system.

Thus, both women's total subjugation and unquestioned male authority is drawn within the purview of the state and is established by civil and criminal, property and personal laws. New ethos in the forms of values, ideas, concepts, religious and ceremonial rituals, customs, mores, habits, dictums and everything that constitutes the psyche emerges. Women are condemned to homes, households and courtyards and nowhere beyond. Social practice—enforced physically, legally and morally—ensures absolute male control over women's existence — her body, mind, psyche, culture, emotion, sensuality and sensibility. Value of women to men therefore centres on her feminine functions providing sex, bearing and rearing, and housekeeping. They themselves are conditioned to a secondary and insignificant status.

The rebels arise from within the system and exceptional humanists and activists raise their voice and effect some desirable changes in societies from time to time.

2.2.5 Capitalism. With the advent of industrialisation and the concomitant rise of capitalism as the new political system new contradictions arose. On the one hand, the sudden need for additional and cheap labour was to be met by women best kept as the reserve force, without freeing them from their domesticity but lessening their reproductive burden by restricting the frequency of pregnancies. It is the capitalist system in its revolutionary role that first showed that the feudal shackles could be broken. Women however remained chained to the social production and family system without recognition or remuneration although relief was provided through child-rearing and kitchen technologies but more from crèches, nannies and maids (drawn from the most deprived in the social rung, they are the women again to suffer most!). Here women subjugate women. The in-law conflict is a case in point too.

The state is also being extraneously challenged from modern radical humanist-socialist movements. There is, indeed, strength in the argument that the classical form of class struggle is losing ground because both industrial and agricultural proletariat has lost its classical attributes as also its striking power. They have been divested of the ability to crush the industry to a grinding halt and in yielding under threat. The so-called urban and rural proletariat has a stake in the wellbeing of the industry and agriculture at the level of mere subsistence, and thereby of the status quo. The revolutionary proletariat seems to be non-existent in the developed world and in the organised sector even in developing countries. As I see, the white-collar has earned stronger teeth than the have-nots across nations, economies, industries, more so in the state than in the private sector. But the state power along with the economy of the state sector itself is also losing its cutting edge.

Culturally, male participation in domestic chores began to increase in the post-World War II phase in the West—perhaps the best of achievements. Biologically, natural and cultural differences were economically, culturally and technologically mitigated at least in part. A partial replacement of feudal values was needed and indeed conceded to by renaissance and Victorian humanism, which was also strengthened by the women's rights movements—all arising as contradictions from within. The semi-feudal and semi-capitalist systems remained largely unaffected except when the waves of the western feminist movements and values of renaissance thrashed at the eastern shores but caused little ripples in the lowest rungs of the society because their immediate community had no felt need for the elitist luxury. The state and society remained and behaved as a set of symbiotic material and ideological instruments of subtle and not-so-subtle women's subjugation. The feudal value considered the women's body as the private hold of the gentry at the highest echelons of the society. It was for the first time commercialised in the capitalist society—being made a commodity for public entertainment through public brothels, bars, night clubs, films, advertisements, fashion shows, beauty contests and many other masochist malecrafts in course of time and the process continues till date. An egalitarianism of sorts!

Capitalism led to nuclear families, de-collectivisation, alienation and isolation of all descriptions. Marriage remains a contract highly tilted in favour of man. Conflicts arise about legalised and surreptitious prostitution, illegitimacy, young and single motherhood, crude monetary calculations in man-woman relation, as in every other sphere of life, divorce, alimony, guardianship right of children, guardianship right of husband over wife, forced hormonal changes in the malfunction of the natural regulation of the women's reproductive biology, etc. These are all old and new problems that affect women much more than they do men. Interference with natural biology has an important dimension in most of the new ailments of the modern society, again affecting women more than men. Development of economic wealth has changed the face of the world but neither the heart nor the brain. The inequalities between man and woman have narrowed down only at the individual level. Capitalism needs women, more than ever before in the production system as much as it needs men, and has emancipated women and men both not by intent but by objective compulsions (Barston 1969). For example, an important development is the development of gender-neutral technology, which has been more in the pursuance of commercial interest than anything else has.

Heaven descends in a home when the partners make their relations saner and more ethical, and have mutual respect, understanding and recognition of genuine natural differences and agree on their own accord and understanding to disregard those sociostructural and ideological differences culturally imposed upon them.

Feminist movements in the semi-feudal and semi-capitalist poor and developing societies do not have to ape and commit the same mistakes committed by their sisters in the West. Feminist movements in capitalist and pro-capitalist societies have special significance being complementary to class struggle, human rights and green movements as they encompass the broadest framework across the classes and because women have a naturally favourable attitude tó environment. But the goals set shall have to be different in different nations, sub-nations and cultures, and even ecosystems to involve women at the lowest rung in the forefront with their needs and demands in the bottom-up approach.

Orthodox Marxists hold that unless and until the means of production are socialised the social objectives remain private and consequently women's rights are not to be achieved. This is a restrictive and deterministic position that Marxism as a theory and instrument of social change can hardly accommodate. Socialisation of women's domestic labour is capitalist contribution, which is a welcome change in cultural evolution. But within the capitalist system humanisation of values and cultures across class, nation, sex, religion or other social divisions of varied origin and dimensions cannot take place, unless exogeneously forced upon. There lies the historic role of feminism. human rights, green movement, ethical economics, ecotechnology etc., which have no doubt arisen as the contradictions of the capitalist society itself.

2.2.6 Women in global capitalism, new technology and neo-imperialism. Human civilisation, which is largely technological, is culture-driven, but anti-nature, anti-biology (Dasgupta 1998) and anti-woman too. The new changes in industry and technology are getting more and more gender-neutral as much as more and more labour-dispelling, alienating and demoralising. The impact of these most recent changes on the man-woman relation is devastating—fragmentation and housewifisation of industries from large factories to isolated units and franchises delinking the finance capital from the management and market risks, reducing workers per investment unit, particularly the less skilled and the more generally skilled of them,'raising the working hours to the point of mental and physical breakdown under the guise of five days a week, employing fewer and fewer white-collared employees and (insignificantly few manual labourers) favouring women. At the same time it has became a handy tool to reduce personnel management problems. Also, the specifically skilled employees in new-technology industries, men or women, because of their upbringing and type of cultural education, are denuded of collective bargaining, thinking, emotion, sensibility and attitude to the society at large.

The unholy bondage between the state (read new economic order benefiting largely the superindustrialised countries) and patriarchy with changed content and form loosens only as the state power-based social system itself is challenged by the contradictions from within. This is due to the overgrowth of monopoly capitalism with or without the malignant growth into classical imperialism or of political centralisation into social imperialism. But capitalism saved itself from the New York share market crisis, called Black Friday, and invented the craftiest system so far developed, where it reaches the nadir of subtlety. This is the new global order based on liberalisation, privatisation and globalisation (the LPG phenomenon).

Globalisation is nothing but meganationalisation of trade and commerce, capital and manpower, technology and management, resulting in commercial and cultural transnational neo-imperialism. It has been symbolised into an economic guild mutually protected by an oligarchy of state power. The national state-power from within has become subservient to the transnational economic-power with its new weaponry in technology, warheads, financial manipulative tactics, technology-fetishism-instigated consumer-fetishism, and manipulative management-induced processes. It turns employees into work maniacs. The rapid strides in technology as a new social and economic power at the hands of the commercial and financial establishment has nearly obliterated any need for parallel or back-up developments in science as a means of conceptualisation. Such developments are remarkable in the fields of telecommunications, informatics, robotics, biotechnology etc., wherever there is or can a market be created. It has affected the concept, system and management of education (Dasgupta 1999b). It has damaged family and social life and thus affected women more than men.

The revolutionary proletariat seems to be non-existent in the developed world and in the organised sector even in the developing countries particularly with the rise of new-look industries exploiting the unorganisably isolated white-collar workers, such as in the modern computer manufacturing, application and other franchises.

The capital- and technology-intensive new breed of industries is increasingly asserting itself to crush even the white-collar technocracy and bureaucracy to a set of de-politicised, de-ethicalised, de-sensitised and even de-humanised, greedy and pampered working brains that do not act with emotions as of altruism or collective reasoning. Hence, one cannot look for a collective choice for humanity in any near and foreseeable future. The lower rank of employees in such industries and franchises is subjected to inhuman service conditions in the new sweatshops for unlimited workhours, low wage rates, little job security and little legal and trade union protection, aggravated by the ever-squeezing job market.

Such industries engage as many women as they can in preference to men for their sincerity and ability to do long hours of hard work in an unassuming manner with commitment and loyalty. But the conditions are more difficult to adjust for women than men. While the technology the workers have to work with is increasingly becoming gender-neutral, which facilitates their preference over men's, the long hours of strenuous work tend to stimulate progesterone and consequently, it has been claimed, breast cancer is likely to be predisposed. Therefore, in either way, be they in domestic work or in wage labour, even under the dispensation of new technologies, the suffering of women continues.

The worst of this trend is taking place in the poor and developing countries, which has been strengthened by the LPG promoted by the World Trade Organisation (WTO). The current tendency is to isolate industries to franchises, segregated sectors, subunits, diversified units, and even family units operating in residential establishments. There has been a gradual delinking of finance and investment capital, increase of 'flexible workforce' into which both women and men suffer apparently equally. Even there also women are at greater disadvantage than men are. The industries so affected at present are particularly in computer and electronics manufacture, garment, food processing and various other automated industries. In consequence, the traditional labour-intensive industries are forced into the red without redeployment.

The superprofit of the industrialised world arises from militarism and exploitation of women's labour (Custers 1996), which is an oversimplification of a complex drama. A system of neo-colonial global economy has emerged to which the entire non-industrialised world has been coerced into acceptance in the name of 'win-win logic'. But actually it favours the countries with greater and stronger political and economic power, capital and technology, which only the superindustrialised countries are having and shall continue to strengthen further. The gap in technology and economic power and consequently the political power is ever widening. New sweatshops are emerging as in the post-World War I Europe particularly Germany, in the garment industry. The finance capital is earning profit without any bother of personnel management downstream and no risks whatsoever. The finance capital is shifting the risk and management to franchises located suitably in the poor and developing countries, however asking for strict quality maintenance. Even that is not free from contradictions. Some of these transnational industries are looking into the occupational interest of the workers in their franchises for upholding their goodwill. Little wonder that they have the interest to keep the economically small fries, i.e. the franchises under stricter control rather than look into the interest of the workers at the franchises. I have serious doubt, for example, in the interest shown by the West in the rights of the child workers in the developing countries.

III. Current Trends In Feminist Movements

3.. Reformist Feminism

Reformist feminism rightly exposes the link between class and patriarchy. However, it naively aims at the integration of women into the highly questionable development efforts in the poor and developing countries. Of course, mere existence of women of the lower economic strata is at a stake and they have no alternative for their own subsistence and that of their families. In spite of the reformists' concern for the developing debt crisis in the underdeveloped world, they are out to cooperate, co-opt, graft and subjugate women's movements in the poor and undeveloped countries to that of the elitist movements in the developed countries. Such movements are often for unrealistic and incompatible goals. Some MNC's manufacture women-unfriendly hormonal contraceptive implants. Women activists in India thwarted some such systems. But they highlight the sexual division of labour operating at extreme disadvantage to women of the poorest strata, extreme loan and aid dependence and debt traps in the poor countries leading to their pauperisation with every fiscal year. They also show with concrete data how poverty compels the rural poor women to take up heavy menial domestic and other hired and odd jobs at a very low wage rate and for longer hours than regular men wage earners. Such jobs have to be taken, even more inconveniently, away from their hearth and home.

As in Bangladesh, the notionally superior Mehr system (the promised alimony to the wife on divorce) among the Muslims is giving way to women-disrespecting dowry system in practice among the Hindus. In Bangladesh, displacement of women's wage labour has been effected through the mechanisation of rice processing. Similar situation has happened in India too with the introduction of husking machines and other grain proceesing machinery with the intensification and mechanisation of agriculture.

3.2. Anarchist Feminism

Anarchist feminism arose as an antithesis to orthodox and patriarchal Marxism. Custers (1996) labels Maria Mies, Veronica Bennholdt-Thompson and Claudia von Werlhof (1988)as anarchist feminists, although they themselves do not claim so. They had put forward a curious argument, strong in premise but wrong in inference, that the housewives the world over and peasants in the poor and the developing countries produce work outside the market economy, their wage value remaining concealed. These women and the peasants perform 'non-capitalist' tasks, i.e. the values so created go unnoticed and unaccounted. They therefore likened the women's domestic labour to that of the subsistence farmers in the poor agricultural economics (Malos 1980). Custers (*loc. cit.*) also has a valid point when he argues that women cannot be equated with the subsistence farmers because they also earn (I add, if and when) wage labour like men. I further add that the generalisation by the anarchist feminists of the equation between subsistence as a form of existence of peasants and housewives of the world can however be redrawn and restricted between the peasants and the housewives of the poorest strata of the poor, undeveloped and developing countries. Housewives developed in the West with industrialisation in the early nineteenth century, which is now non-existent as much as that the word has gone into disuse in these countries. The identity of the women of the poor and undeveloped countries and 'housewifisation' of industries (Mies *et al.* 1978) is a new development that the new LPG phenomenon has generated and is interesting to examine from varied perspectives including the man-woman relations. (See Section 2.2.5)

3.3. Socialist Feminism

Socialist feminists believe in the need for proletarian struggle without any special and separate women's movement outside the ambit of the proletarian struggle (Stites 1977). They view 'housewife' as a part of the labour reserve together with their male counterparts. The housewives belong to the unorganised sector with high exploitation marked by low wage rate, long workhours, weak legal guarantees. The volume of the reserve labour force is increasing all over the world including among the poorest social and economic strata in the highly industrialised world. They exposed the trend of decentralisation or informalisation (=housewifisation) of industries according to and as a demoralised expansion of the Japanese and Dutch models of turning workaholics into work maniacs and the commercial advantage of super surplus profit generation. Sexual division of labour has presented women to a subordinate place in the hierarchy of wage labourers (Leydesdorff 1977). The trend has only been strengthened by the LPG phenomenon and, I am afraid, worse is yet to happen.

3.4. Radical Feminism

During the first feminist movement itself, Kathe Schirmacher emphasised the economic productive character of housewives who preserve, distribute values, and also create new values—'the value of values', the human beings. Radical feminism propounded by Zila Eisenstein and Kate Millet arose during the second feminist movement during the sixties. They held that patriarchy is the determinant social relation and that 'every means of power in society' including statecraft is 'entirely in male hands'. They charged the government and the industry to appropriate profit from the domestic labour and argued for a common battle against all men for the removal of such discrimination and demanded monetary recognition of household tasks pro rata with the factory workers and particularly for the reproductive labour, the exclusive job of women. The slogan however did not question the sexual division of labour *per se*, neither the isolation of housewife from the economy, nor the society itself. The outlook was too narrow to encourage or stimulate any women's movement, and was of no relevance to the poor not only in the developing countries but also those in the industrialised world.

Margaret Benston (1969) asserted that 'Roots of secondary status of women in fact are economic'. She opposed the view that the family belongs to the superstructure, and is not an economic unit. Woman in the industrialised world itself, as Benston observed, be she a wage-earner or a housewife, has to put 'an irreducible minimum of necessary (domestic) labour of 15-20 hours a week, and a woman with small children 70-80 hours a week. In the poor and developing countries, women and even men domestic workers and child labourers are at plenty to be engaged even by the lower middle class who thus develops a stake in the status quo, and natural revolutionary linkage with the proletariat is lost. Women and girls so engaged fall easy prey to sexual harassment, aggression and perversion by males of easy virtue. Women, Benston (*loc. cit.*) further argued, produce 'use values' for home consumption. But she failed to see that sexual division of labour and wage labour structures are inseparably linked. Women and only women do work as the most 'comprehensive labourers', combining all forms of production. With increasing mechanisation, automation and electronic revolution, the gender discrimination in domestic and industrial labour is on the wane. But the facilities will take a long time to reach all people. We will note how even industrialisation has caused misery to the poorest women in the villages of the poor and developing countries. In the socialised production system the family lineage of labour operates. With industrialisation the domestic labour, traditional women's jobs, is increasingly being passed to the industry itself, where mostly women work as the poorest wage earners. However, the benefits of this industrialisation will be difficult to reach the poor women irrespective of development across nations.

The occupational health hazards of these women do not bother the owners as much as they are compelled by their principals for the quality of the products for their choosy customers overseas, protected by stringent environmental and health laws.

Even in the socialist and post-socialist states, women's share of domestic work remained as usual in the capitalist societies, although legal rights were established with state patronage. Housewives produce surplus value and help accumulate capital. They are productive both in value creation through the 'socialised production cycles' (family lineage of labour) (Della Costa, in Mies 1986). She kept housewives including the proletarian women outside the women's movement and the fight against capitalism and patriarchy could not be waged together.

Women's two-fold exploitation as 'the producer of labour power' and 'the producer of commodity' was accepted at the Conference of Socialist Economists, London (1977). But the domestic labour in the society does not take either the social form of value producing labour as Dalla Costa (1986, cit. Custers 1996) was the first to point out during the first feminist movement itself.

3.5. Struggle for Empowerment

How to mobilise a united front of labourers on economic issues—women and men, organised and unorganised, factory or franchise, wage and non-wage—is a million-dollar question. The emancipationists' argument that the women should join the wage labourers' cause and their liberation would be slowly achieved is, to be kindest to them, a sectarian view. Women's participation in political and trade union struggle has always been poor because of their being bonded to domestic duties; woman leadership is a curiosity, almost always stepping into the shoes of the father or husband. Party leadership is more difficult to secure for a woman than for a man. Reservation for women in the assemblies and the parliament in India is being vehemently debated within and across the political parties. Leadership within even communist parties is difficult to reach for women. Women generally are kept tied to 'feminine duties' and those who join the politics are compelled to act in men's way. For that matter, in every field of outdoor activity women have to join, and excel, if at all, according to men's rules of the game.

Entitlement to not minimal or marginal but decent livelihood, social wealth, and to social customs and laws without bias or prejudice, is more important for the downtrodden women than empowerment, which preferentially benefits the more privileged women.

A Bengali poet, Mallika Sengupta, raises the question, 'Comrade, shall we remain as the dedicated temple-maidens at the throes of revolution?'

IV. Existentialism And Feminism—A Critique Again

During the Second Feminist Movement (1960's onward) Simone de Beauvoir's (SdB) 'The Second Sex' (SS) and 'Autobiography' were held as the Old and New Testaments. SdB defines feminism as the fighting on specifically feminine issues of class struggle (Mahon Joseph 1997). Herbert Marcuse also viewed revolutionary student power outside class struggle during the sixties in France in particular. These show merely the weakness of the contemporary class struggle vis-à-vis the strength gained by capitalism in its newer and newer crafts.

4.1. SdB and Marxism

SdB denounced Marxism as a determinist theory of history. But she accepted historical materialism and remained extremely hopeful of socialism to be the ultimate force to remove women's subjugation. She also intended to revise SS with a socialist perspective. She seemed to have a temporary agenda for the contemporary feminist movement.

Her criticism of classical Marxism veers round two principal arguments: (i) the turn-over of primitive communism to private property is not adequately explained; (ii) it does not explain why private property should necessitate enslavement of women. She argues that (i) the human, man in particular, had pre-conceived notion of women as 'The Other', and aspired to dominate women, (ii) Engels, Bebel and others subsumed 'the oppression of women under class oppression, and reduced sexual antagonism to class antagonism', which is, to SdB, a misconcept.

Her reading of Engels is absolutely incorrect. There need not be any biological basis for class division. As Engels (OFPPS) sees it, women's oppression has an economic dimension. Housework — the labour contribution of women — is seen as a purely private service that the married woman performs for her husband and children, and even inlaws. It is not remunerated too, nor seen as a form of or contributory to social production. Thus, there are two alternatives: (i) to recognise housework as a contribution to social production, or (ii) to encourage all women to participate in paid labour. With industrial revolution, the option (ii) opened up. To quote from Engels, 'if she carries out her duties in the private service of her family, she remains excluded from public production and unable to earn; and if she wants to take part in public production and earn independently, she cannot carry out family duties.' Yet option (ii) is preferable to him. '...the first condition for the liberation of the wife is to bring the whole female sex back into public industry, and this in turn demands that the characteristic of the monogamous family as the economic unit of the society be abolished'. Further, Engels regards the abolition of the monogamous family as a necessary but not a sufficient condition of the married women's liberation. Again, it is not the abolition of monogamous family *per se* that is called for but only the monogamous family as the economic unit of the society. Monogamous family as an economic unit presupposes economic dependence of the wife, and therefore inequality of the female spouse is the outcome.

By proletarian marriage, Engels (*loc. cit.*) refers to the extent to which the economic basis of marriage is fundamentally altered, where there is good deal more to marriage than economics, so that 'no basis for any kind of male supremacy is left in the proletarian household, except, perhaps, for something of the brutality towards women that has spread since the introduction of monogamy'. Domestic violence crosses all thresholds, including class — a point that Engels did not miss. The only moral basis of marriage is clearly pointed out. '...if affection definitely comes to an end or is supplanted by a new passionate love, separation is a benefit for both partners as well as for society.' He looks forward to 'a generation of men who never in their lives have known what it is to buy a woman's surrender with money or any other social instrument of power; a generation of women who have never known what it is to give themselves to a man from any other consideration than real love or to refuse to give themselves to their lover from fear of the economic consequences.' (All quotes in this part of the paragraph from Engels, *The Origin of Family, Private Property and State*; OFPPS). Thus, overall, SdB and Engels had identical views on women question. Engels concludes with a paean to relationships premised on mutuality and love. So, too, does SdB. But she rightly insists that there will always remain a core of irreducible differences between the two sexed individualities. As she puts it, 'women's eroticism, and therefore her sexual world, have a special form of their own and therefore cannot fail to engender a sensuality, a sensitivity, of a special nature' (SdB in SS).

The abolition of the family *per se* is neither feasible nor desirable. Commensurate with the current value system, there is no alternative unit of human societal structure in sight. As the USSR came to be a reality, it had difficulty keeping its promises to women, which did not surprise SdB. She rebuked Engels, ' We know how often and how radically Soviet Russia has had to change its policy on the family according to the varying relations between the immediate needs of production and those of reproduction.' (SdB, cit. Mahon Joseph 1997). There is multiple irony that SdB, a trenchant critic of Engels, should expect so much from the USSR. But the fact remains that what the USSR achieved in establishing women's right in a short time was unprecedented in human history. SdB justly seeks equality through difference, a recognition of differences in equality — an acknowledgement that equals can be different. However, as the history of Marxism suggests, I believe, Engels remained so overwhelmed by Marx throughout his life that he hardly ever produced any political or philosophical document, barring *The Dialectics of Nature or* OFPPS, which bear his imprint and take an independent position.

Sex, in human, ideally, is the culmination of a personal drama and cannot be reduced to a personal service, a social task, a family or societal goal under a code of reproduction. It militates against the survival or social instinct of human, a highly emotionalised and characteristically humanised being. However, modern men have to reconcile between the two dimensions of sex – biological and cultural.

4.2. SdB's Philosophy of Feminism

Philosophically, SdB distinguishes between (i) the subject itself (as the absolute, man) and the object (The Other, other than oneself, woman), (ii) transcendence (activity, freedom from biological state and animality, creative, innovative, as man) and immanence (passivity, submission to biological life, uncreative and repetitive, as in woman), and (iii) actions (related to transcendence, to set goals, to win the world, to create, to achieve self-realisation, to lay foundation for the future as in man) and functions (related to immanence, no goals set, nothing to achieve, no self-realisation, nothing to look forward to but only to serve biologically pre-determined tasks, such as for woman). Women's liberation is to continuously reach toward the male behaviour pattern as a free and autonomous being, individual, according to her possibilities. Recognition of biological factors, her disadvantages (and why not, advantages!) are essential but not sufficient to understand a woman. The biological differences get grounded as a concept as 'the humans set themselves' and 'find themselves caught up'. Levi-Strauss asserted that 'passage from the state of nature to the state of culture' is marked by (hu)man's ability to view biological relations as series of contracts, duality, alternation, opposition, and symmetry, whether under definite or vague form, consolidate not so much phenomena to be explained as fundamental and immediately given credence to social reality.

4.3. SdB and the Female Prototype

SdB identifies more vices in woman than in man. 'One is not born, but becomes a woman'—is a SdB cliché. The female prototype is a cultural construct. That is what makes her self and lets her feel and consent to be The Other. Parenthetically speaking, biologically, the human is neither born a male nor a female but a juvenile, genetically pre-determined while yet to be fully differentiated morphologically, anatomically and physiologically to be, in most cases, a male or a female (See Section 5.1). She has ably highlighted the frustrations of the typical modern women of the 20th century—the alienation they face since early childhood itself—and tragically 'end up in alienating themselves from themselves'.

Biologically, SdB's argument that 'The female is the victim of the species.... She is under the iron grip of the species.' is a partial truth. Macmillan (1982) finds in her observation a Cartesian dualism between body and mind, and between biology and individual. SdB strongly asserts that biological differences 'are insufficient to explain why woman is The Other; they do not condemn her to remain in this subordinate role for ever.' She strongly pleads that woman should be understood on the basis of her possibilities rather than on the basis of her limitations. SdB was therefore caught in a Hobson's choice between domestic conformity and derided and ostracised womanhood. She proved herself an apologetic feminist—a position that is not forced upon women by the rule of nature.

Men confronted the biological conflict of sexual dimorphism in two contradictory solutions: (a) social, economic and cultural subordination of women, and (b) assigning a cult status and then developing it into a moral, mythical, mystical and symbolic notion around motherhood. While the biological and material man cultivates subordination, the ethical cultural man takes solace in motherhood that sublimes his biological and material-cultural self. SdB missed this masculine contradiction and compunction.

Is man also 'a victim of the species'? Undeterred sex is often viewed as a male privilege and a tool of male dominance and domestic violence. It has its disadvantages and dangers. Sperm production is highly energy consuming, period of sexual activity is unproductive and most unsecured (such as from a predator), and competition for females generates conflict among males (Diamond 1992). His genetic and psychological make-up condemns him to sexual laxity and indiscipline; which arises for his biological pre-determination to mate finding and competition for females, unregulated bodily readiness for sexual act, sexual ability in spite of ageing, uninhibited semen production since adolescence till near-disability, prostrate enlargement as a result of sexual suppression only to promote desire and other related uncomfortable hormonal maladjustment. This is a small compensation for freedom from child bearing or breast-feeding. Need I emphasise again that it does not make a modern man's case to sexual laissez faire?

4.4. SdB's Critiques

Cottrell (1975) finds in SdB's thesis a Sartrean existentialist doctrine of absolute freedom. The apotheosis (deification) of masculine values is accompanied by an impassioned indictment of injustice, cruelty and egotism. Firestone (1971) and Elshatin (1981) criticised SdB's male-dominated scientism and technological authoritarianism (such as viewing artificial baby food as a means of women's liberty from breast-feeding). Elshatin (*loc. cit.*) rejects both the views as crass biological reductionism that the heart of women's oppression lies in her childbearing and rearing roles. (All references in this paragraph cited in Mahon Joseph 1997.)

I submit that if the feminists care a naught for the biological differences they would quarrel with the facts of nature and miss the real target, i.e. the cultural differences imposed by men. They would also ignore the legacy that the source of men's cultural strength lies in biological differences, where men would have to be counteracted only on the grounds of ethicality. SdB's notion of 'an independent woman' is a euphemism for a woman without the naturally assigned biological role, which is necessarily linked to the survival of the species. Rather, let both the victims of the species start a new game on equal terms and why not let a woman share an emotionally enjoyable experience with weal and woe, as much as a man does.

SdB has been criticised by many in her admitting no motherhood instinct, the instinct of desire for a child in woman and the maternal devotion. Her view is far from the truths of biological evolution. Modern evidences suggest that even desire may be gene-controlled.

To SdB, marriage is obscene. This is not acceptable. Marriage fails more as an individual failure (particularly in economically and socially upper class societies), than as a social institution across classes. In traditional societies as in India, marriage for a woman ends up being a doting wife and a dutiful daughter-in-law, achieving the male-desired blend of a *devi* and a *dasi.* Societal traditions strongly affect individual relations and marriages sometimes evidently fail. Some people argue that because Indian society is traditional in its value system it ensures a stronger tie—holy tie—in a marriage. Indeed, the tie is of a *devi-dasi* prototype value system. With changes in economic and social factors such ties are breaking, which we find more in upper echelons of this society than in lower rungs. Failure of marriage in subaltern societies is a result of many factors including their patriarchal acculturation from the apex of the pyramid downward. No doubt as an institution it is yet to be culturally and morally perfected. Stoltenberg (1990) hopes that sexual union rather than sexual possession and usurpation will become the social norm. Humans can feel that their body is intrinsically and harmoniously systematised 'to the resonance(s) of eroticism'. Men must realise that orgasm is not one-sided but 'mutual, equal, reciprocal, profoundly communing'.

The socio-cultural factors like dowry system, oppression by husbands and in-laws (a feudal legacy, insitutionalised in many societies through firmly established customs and even so-called religious-textual approvals), and the personal factors like notions of emotional independence and even sexual freedom outside marital bondage, etc. are difficult to solve. So, there is some truth when SdB tells in frustration that woman becomes a service provider for sex, a mutilated mistress and a maniac housekeeper. For the last point, Mahon Joseph (1997) argues the incorrigibly 'squalid habits and indifference' to women's efforts by the husband and other members of the family makes the women constantly feel condemned. It turns housekeeping, a rewarding activity, a satisfying artistry and a pleasant task into a Sisyphean torment by undoing whatever is done neat and tidy. I confess, I am no exception.

Femininity is not entirely but largely a cultural construct, principally a male construct. A cultural misconstruct can only be culturally deconstructed, and has to be healthily reconstructed for human good, while the biological fact of differences at its root cannot be. Marriage will remain the predominant institution of sexual bondage in spite of failures galore, demoralisations and aberrations including rebellious ideas and practices against the notion of sex or marriage itself. It can be culturally modified, biologically substantiated and culturally sublimated, with full conscience and cognisance of both the partners in each and every case and in the social conscience as a whole. And that is the golden way to adaptation—gradually or macromutationally, transcendentally or by punctuated equilibration what-so-ever.

The 'independent woman' as advocated by SdB multiplies her tasks as both a female and as a man, and suffers from inferiority complex. For the androgynous society of the future, I do not see an independent man or woman to be the ideal for that is not the 'blauplane' acceptable to individuals. Overall, it is also unsustainable for the human species. An androgynous society is to be logically, socially, morally based on an equal sharing of tasks without culturally enforced division of labour, so determined more than biology demands. There shall have to be unhindered opportunities, which will lead to a comprehensive societal development or further evolution of the species and a new cultural ecology of the species may emerge in the third millennium.

Technology eases reproductive and domestic burden and attendant risks but has as yet found no total answer to its elimination. Technology often reverts itself from earlier quick-fixes to more natural problem-solving as it happened with persistent commercialist persuasion for 'baby food' for about half a century as an alternative to breast-feeding, which has now come back to square one (which SdB found as a technological tool to women's liberation). Not only is it said to be without an alternative for the baby but also good for the mother too.

Beyond reproductive biology, psychological, emotional, educational and cultural support by the mother to the children in the nursery and the formative years of personality development has received considerable weight of argument and evidences in recent years.

Humans have a prolonged gestation period as among the higher protohumanoids but have unparalleled long childhood under the aegis of the mother, the family and the society to reach biological and psychological adulthood. It is so needed to complete the process of complex development need of humans. But the debate has been raised from among the socio-biologists if humans have genetically acquired it. Can or should technology or culture prevent the process? Social responsibility at this phase is essential but not enough as a substitute for the matter. Be it in the feudal, semifeudal, capitalist or socialist societies, options to technological innovation have to be voluntary for women, which they never had been, and shall be a collective and ethical social choice not to be imposed by any society, far less its women.

SdB held that men are infinitely more human than women. Not all men do or can transcend nature, and only some of them can achieve absolute, or any transcendence, if at all. Both women and men need to target transcendence. Rousseau's contention may be re-stated as that not only women but also men should also respect the biological constraints of women.

SdB argues for the negative thesis that the biological or genetic factors do not causally determine female nature resulting in subjugated female status. But she fails to make a case for the alternative thesis that culture carries out the functions as assigned in other theories, to biology (Kaefe 1983). The substance of the argument should be that neither man should view nor a woman should find her body as an obstacle to transcendence. Socio-biologists claim to see a strong foundation, in this line of argument, in the genetic truth as some unevolved human genes have been traced to the 'lowliest of creatures' as there are evolved genes characteristic to humans. For instance, 60 per cent of the insect *Drosophila* genes and 70 per cent of the worm *Caenorhabditis* genes have been located in humans. They act in harmony and there is no reason to suspect an evolutionary competitive exclusion of the unevolved genes. Human ethology has a biological past, which anthropocentrists and cultural sociologists tend to scale down.

To transcend, as SdB held, a woman does not have to alienate herself from her being—an unnecessary and ordinarily unachievable bother (nevertheless with the Cartesian duality conflict introduced). But it remains a fact that modern society recognises a woman for her masculine achievements alone—which is simply not done, in an equal society. For example, modern difference feminists argue that maternity is fundamentally 'active' (SdB believed the opposite—that it is functional). It is not to be regarded as a patriarchal debasement of women's activities.

SdB accepts the 'Darwinian orthodoxy' of progress of evolution from simple to complex as generalisation for all evolutionary processes in the organic world or in the societal sense of the term. (It may be noted that the concept of progress of evolution from lower to higher is not Darwin's, but of some later Darwinian enthusiasts (Dasgupta 1999b, Gould 1982). The cybernetic concept of problem solving in evolving newer structure-function relation is a concept a little too distant for Darwin. The protagonsists of anthropocentrism will better understand that it is Darwinism under the scientific banner of which, religious creationism and religious fundamental thesis that man without a biological past was created unique to the Great Design was fought.

The argument that female biology seems problematic to man and in male terms (Mahon Joseph 1997) is cogent enough to blow off much the wind out of SdB's sails. Women do not live from cycle to cycle alone but menstruation, pregnancy and other roles have positive features on her body and mind (Evans 1985).

While SdB believes in amelioration and redemptive power of a different education for women, what is singularly lacking in her social action thesis is to ask for wholesome male behavioural changes and a systematic social change (Evans 1985). That should be the common goal of feminism, howsoever distant it may seem to be. Evans (1985) stands out as a social philosopher as she sees that education at some point has to confront the problem of social structure outside the classroom.

Okely (1986) does not find SdB's 'biological reductionism' — an uncritical generalisation of animal behaviour to explain the primary cause of women's subordination. I am with SdB in seeking the biological basis being at the root of patriarchy. I am also with Okely (1986) that because of the highest communicative achievements of the species human sexuality is far distinct from animal sexuality. Human experience, emotion, understanding and sensibility are very much personal, sublime, exceptionally fine-tuned, and may attain newer and newer heights, what no animal has ever achieved. This is precisely the reason why cultural re(e) volution may bring about a great change in man-woman relation.

Both Firsetone (1971) and SdB import some neutral but orthodox and dualist philosophical notions and distinctions that boil down to an inferior status for female biology and fail to see the 'social constructions that embody historical and cultural values' (Gatens 1991). The value-laden character of a theory smacks of values of a given culture only to devalue woman and scale down the factors for her subordination, both nature and culture (Mahon Joseph 1997). It is unfortunate for a philosopher of SdB's merit. She was one of the first few to draw a clear-cut distinction between woman's biological sex and the way that sex is lived in culture (Mahon Joseph 1997). Le Doeuff (1991) says that SdB changed the phallocentric masculinist Sartrean existentialism into a tool of feminist inquiry, adding new values — neither utilitarian nor normative. SdB does not chastise woman, not even man, nor does she offer a positive role model for women, not even the blueprint of a collective, feminist movement. For she decided not to break out of the cocoon of the pathologically misanthropous Sartrean ethics and existentialism — an individualist philosophy that it is, and there she fails as a social philosopher in her own right.

SdB's optimism in the emancipatory power seems naive, and ought not to have been so obvious (Moi 1994). But Moi (*loc.cit.*) cannot quarrel with facts that the status of women changed overnight with the first socialist revolution across all levels of social and economic hierarchy at the behest of the government. Total equality has never been achieved and it deteriorated too fast with the fall or 'democratisation' of governments in the socialist world. That is indeed a different story. It remains to be argued if cultural evolution promoted by state power can be anything more than transient and concomitant.

Moi (*loc. cit.*), however, rightly argued that SdB underestimated the potential political impact that feminist movements can make upon the governments, the intelligentsia and the enlightened public in democratic societies. SdB has unnecessarily and tautologically projected childbirth as transcendental for women. But most women regard this mere 'facticity' as valiant achievement, which is due to the symbolic hyperbole that the society attaches to womanhood or motherhood. If this criticism is valid it is no less valid to argue that Moi (*loc. cit.*) has also unnecessarily denounced this socially reproductive womanly function as too biological event not worth social cognizance. SdB does not help in integrating socialism, biology and feminism — a pointer this article is addressed to.

SdB is logically torn between (i) the tragic ambiguity of human's and woman's existence — a feminine duality, (ii) society relegates woman to mute domestication and reproduction but entrusts socially fundamental task of child rearing on the woman, and (iii) a socialist ethics for justice together with liberty and women's individual task of fighting against socio-cultural mutilation without denouncing individuality. SdB has done no wrong in distinguishing between biologically constructed body and socially constructed psyche (Mahon Joseph 1997).

Moi (*loc. cit.*) figures out the contemporary debate on women's liberation movement between two schools. First are those who accept the strategic use of intellectual and political separatism in order to achieve a truly egalitarian society. Second are those who are convinced that women's interests are best served by the establishment of an enduring regime of sexual difference in every social and cultural field. Instead of looking for the conflict, I find that it calls for a synthesis between the two as long-term and short-term objectives, respectively.

SdB remains, in outline, a difference feminist longing for an androgynous world where sexual differences are not masculinised but seen with mutual respect, because of the highest communicative achievements of the species (Della Costa and Janes 1972).

V. Socio-biological Viewpoint

5.1. Sexual Dominance

Sexual dominance is viewed as a component of social dominance systems. Theorisations are made from evolutionary and behavioural socio-biology, archaeology, anthropology and psychoanalysis. Excluding the view that there is no sexual dominance, there are two contradictory concepts. In the enslavement concept, the food-gathering child-breeding-feeding woman invented agriculture and man invented the plough, the woman enjoyed equality. In hunting-gathering society, as prey dwindled, women were both protected and victimised by the male and enjoyed better status as reflected in matriarch and mother goddess. The queen theorists view women as gentle queens in the world of men through love. We have seen through the previous sections that reality cuts across all theories so far propounded. Women did shape human destinies while they were subordinated in most societies. Over the ages, feminists pleaded to be accepted as humans, seeking voting rights to equal rights in all spheres of life.

Hierarchical dominance is a characteristic of stratified society. Is hierarchical dominance also a biologically determined feature of human relationship? Does it operate regardless of sex? Or, are the males genetically determined to dominate females? Kenneth Boulding (1976, cit. Elise Boulding 1996) related sexual dimorphism to dominance. Biologists hold active nucleus donors as males and passive nucleus receptors as females. Isogametic and isogametangial fertilisation resulting in true zygotes was long left out in sexual evolution. Oogamous fertilisation where the male contributes only the nucleus and the female contributes both nucleus and cytoplasm has remained the dominant system. Irony has it that while nature has given the more significant role for survival to females the relative biological relief to males has rendered them an opportunistic position to dominate over the females. Is it also predetermined?

How different are women from men? From Aristotle, the worst misogynist philosopher of all times, to the racists with Victorian veil biological differences between man and woman have been prejudiced, and have remained anti-Darwinian and unethical. Darwin held that biological differences between man and woman arose from natural and sexual selection. And we know that sexual selection is due to geographic and reproductive isolation, and it is not only instinctive preference but also culture-driven, especially in man. Radical feminists argue that instead of biological differences social and cultural determination of sexes have become important, which have to be targeted against for feminist movement. True, but we emphasise that social and cultural determination of relative gender status have become possible because of biological differences.

Paul Broca (1824 –1880) of Paris carefully measured 292 male and 140 female brains and found that female brains weighed 181g or about 14 per cent less than male brains. Later corrections for height reduced it to about 113g. Manouvner's (1880) corrections for weight, i.e. "sexual mass" positioned women's brain as weightier than men's. Montessori (1913) claimed that women were intellectually superior but physically weaker than men.

Testosterone (T), the Hormone of Desire, is the definition for maleness and has become a metaphor for manhood. It is the male hormone, linked with a gene in the Y-chromosome, and starts getting expressed in the foetus itself. It is produced both in the testicles and ovaries with the help of subcutaneous tissues as well as in the adrenal glands of both sexes. An average man has about 300-1000 nanogram per decilitre of blood plasma, while an average woman contains only 40-60 ng per dl. Even a teenage boy may have as high as 1300 ng per dl! A man has three flushes of T, first in a few weeks after conception, second within a few months after birth, and third at puberty. With the first flush, the male foetus is instinctually conditioned to respond to its subsequent flushes. Without abundance and repeated flushes of this maleness expresser, the male would revert to a female. It develops both body and brain, deepens a boy's voice, playing a major role in building the masculine physique, such as strong jaws, large bones and well-pronounced cheek bones, boosts metabolic rate, promotes more muscle than fat compared to a woman, and a host of other changes. Men in long-term marriages have their T-levels falling. Women need T to stimulate her sexual interest, to provide strength, to defend herself and take risks. Women at menopause and still later increasingly drop their T-levels. Such women lose sexual desire, face depression, anxiety, moodiness, insomnia, fatigue, decreased sensitivity, difficulty in concentrating, etc. A combined dose of oestrogen and T corrects the problems and restores a post-menopausic woman back to her self. Women with polycystic ovaries hypersecrete testosterone show maleness problems like facial hair. Pregnant women given progestin, a synthetic analogue of testosterone, may deliver tomboyish daughters. It stimulates energy generation, strength, sexual desire, and affects man's attitude and mood, conditions them to taking risk— physical, criminal and personal, often ill-advised ones like sexual affair or uttering a lie, or even taking raw physical confrontations. It makes them least cautious, impulsive, drastic in decision-taking, and greater involvement in violent and criminal cases. It seems to affect family ties promoting more than one partners in sex, divorce rates, and body building cult. T-levels are related to baldness, heart disease, prostrate cancer and some kinds of infection. According to Matt Ridley, in her *The Red Queen* (2000), finds young boys to be more hyperactive than young girls, better in physical tasks, and girls in verbal, boys preferring action-oriented programmes and girls preferring relationship-oriented entertainment. Women are more stability-seeking and family-oriented. Of no less significance to our discussion is the fact that testosterone level is dependent on environment such as sports and hot exchanges and brawls. The environment should include culture. T levels are not correlated to economic power. Professional women are claimed to have higher T-levels than housewives. Blue-collar workers have greater T-levels than white-collar ones. As economy becomes less physical and more cerebral, high-T men may be more cornered and dominated. An androgynous society will rely less and less on biologically determined T-levels but more and more on culturally regulated T-levels.

For over a century male protagonists have emphasised the sexual differences to justify a lower status of women. With the same logic they were so worried about "mulattoes" (offspring from black and white marriages) that they perpetrated hate and isolationism against coloured people, relegating blacks to inferior a status to white women's (all references in this paragraph cited in Gould 1980). The mindset still prevails. Watson of DNA structure fame and now with a human genome project, in a Cold Spring Harbour Lecture (2000), has made wild conjectures on the human Pom-C gene which controls several hormones including melanin and other functions, suggesting that blacks are sexier than whites.

Socio-biologists relate sexual dimorphism to behavioural dominance. The patterns in primates are compared with and speculated to have evolved to humans. Gibbons living in a friendly habitat with a few predators are sexually least dimorphic, live in small families without aggression, and their males share child rearing. Their monogamous couples may spend years without sex. A gibbon female comes into heat only when the youngest child grows to be sufficiently big. Once conceived female gibbon avoids sex. Baboon males are twice the females in size and weight, live in dangerous Savannah full of enemies, exhibit strong male dominance. Baboon females can feel monthly period of ovulation, can meet hundred of males during the period but otherwise remain sexually disinterested. However, new findings suggest that there are baboon communities without dominance. Rowell (1973, cit. Elise Boulding 1996) argued that hierarchy/dominance is a pathological response to stress. Chimpanzees, closest cousins of humans, more brainy and skilled, are halfway dimorphic, live in half-arboreal half-terrestrial environment, have male dominance. Their sex is not paired, free and uninhibited within community while they are fairly casual about both sex and dominance (Barlow and Silverberg 1980, Branden and Burian 1984, Cavalli- sforza and Fredman 1981, Diamond 1992, 1996, Trivers 1985).

Humans are minimally dimorphic except with secondary sexual characters, being more like gibbons. Human sexual desire is not period-bound or limited between adolescence and menopause. Concealed ovulation in women, so Diamond (1992, 1996) believes, is the only explanation for unjust human behaviour. This has resulted from extreme helplessness of human babies, late weaning and longer dependence of human young on mother (and thereby on father too in modern societies) long after weaning. Cavewomen's child rearing must have been extremely trying.

So the necessary strategy for pregnant women and weaning mother must have been to keep her sexual desire alive and to satisfy sexual urge in her mate so that he would not desert her for a new mate. He would share the roasted meat with her at the end of day's hunting when he would not have to search and fight for a new mate. Prolonged childhood in human necessitates long survivability for mother. Yet every new child adds problem for its survivability in terms of mother's death at delivery, enhanced food insecurity and less chance of a healthy child. However, reproductive rate increases with lower survivability. Conception is a sort of investment security in for the future. Motherhood instinct is necessitated by and grows out of increasing security for the baby. Conflict also arises with increasing children's number, which leads to greater risk for survival for the new and older children. This implies problem solving through increasingly fewer conceptions to avoid a small gain taking a great risk.

Prolonged security need for mother and undeterred sexual urge in father had developed strong family bondage albeit at the cost of unfair sexual dominance of men over women. Besides a species of bats, no males can breast–feed their babies. Human males can bear as an exceptional phenomenon and produce milk only under certain pathological or stress situations. Women can continue to lactate through breast-feeding without conception. Even in birds where chicks can be brooded by fathers, the investment of conception leads to strong motherly instinct. Nature has chosen females of all species for bearing as the complete female reproductive process. The act of bearing and rearing becomes a highly specialised biological function for women as an exclusive endeavour for the survival of the species. Biological role of males is transient and social role of fatherhood is more culturally imposed than biologically determined in men.

Further, women have earlier menopause than primate females. In about ten years, bearing capacity is totally lost, while wild animals can bear till a very old age or even until death. This instance of human sexual biology is extremely rare among animals. This phenomenon goes against the principle of reproductive success favouring evolution. There is a strong ecological reason for that. A species adopts r-selection or K-selection strategy or a mix of the two for survival. The r strategists have high fecundity and low survivability among other characteristics. The K-strategists have low fecundity and high survivability among other characteristics. Humans have high survivability, which makes them K-strategists. But human communities in socio-economic distress have lower survivability than those who are better off, and show relatively greater fecundity. A comparison of rates of birth, death and growth over time in different communities, nations and regions, and relating them to socio-economic variables will corroborate our view (Sen 1991).

Socio-biologists agree that the environment, food security, enemy status determine life style, social behaviour and natural selection. Determinants of dominance are community size, age, androgen-stimulated levels of aggression, physical and mental strength, skill, self-confidence etc. Dominance is genetically determined and environmentally influenced. Hunting became a male specialisation through course of time.

Dominance systems operate across most of the modern economic, social and political hierarchies. All social interactions create power imbalances. Oppression survives and flourishes through compliance of the oppressed, including that in man-woman relation from families to all social states. Withdrawal of compliance characterises all liberation movements including women's, without removing but only manipulating dominance structure.

5.2. Alternatives to Dominance Systems

There are two alternatives to dominance systems:

A. Egalitarianism: Equality is extraordinarily difficult to achieve—least in diads (two-unit associations) than in triads or still higher associations. Equality can be ensured by contribution of something "extra" in two ways. First is reciprocity, distinguished in three types: One, reciprocity multiplier, two, generalised reciprocity, And three, social reciprocity to a third party (Kenneth Boulding 1973, cit. Elise Boulding 1996). Second is a type of complementarity relations such as between leaders and emotional supporters. Egalitarian systems need large reciprocity multipliers. The best is achieved when dominance alternates as resources and situations demand.

Social drift explains why equality is unstable, but can flourish only with egalitarian principles.

B. Altruism: Opposed to dominance, altruism extends one's fitness at the expense of another through kin selection. Gould (1980, 1982) considers that kin selection is a rare phenomenon. Kin as a group cannot be the unit of natural selection. Altruism is not sex-linked, but culturally conditioned. Alloparenting is an altruism. Altruism by oppressed-coerced groups or individuals, such as women, is pseudoaltruism. Altruism does not lead to equality or change dominance behaviour pattern. Women mostly have adapted to dominance structure. At the same time, women are highly skilled to convert their power to derive a special and privatised underside power and authority over their men.

5.3. Family Roles and Marriage Bonding

Family remains outside social dominance but reflects these structures historically through the evolution of society. Patrilocality is more adaptive to household formation. Male dominance began with patrilocality but was contradicted by altruism, egalitarianism within and across households. Within such a system women developed a special set of interstitial roles outside the hierarchy and dominance in developing social bonding, conflict resolution, crisis management from interfamilial to international alliance structures through history. Inter-kin marriages were made to redistribute resources, ensure peace and acquire status utilising women's exceptional adaptive behaviour in alien cultures. Some ethnographic accounts show higher status of women in some traditional societies (Martin and Voorhies 1975). Levirate marriages (man to marry brother's widow) and sororate marriages (woman to marry deceased sister's husband) were institutions created for similar advantages.

Other factors like sex-and-temperament relation; territoriality (crowding elicits aggression) and societal evolution (dominance increases with transformation from nomadic to urban society because of loss of space) have been highlighted by different authors from time to time to relate sexual dimorphism to social and male dominance. Similarly, sex ratio is considered important. More women lead to male dominance, less women to higher status for women (Guttenberg and Secord 1983), while Cavin (1985) holds the opposite view. Social attitude to women may be significant — women viewed as wives bring about lower status, while women viewed as sisters elevate higher status for them (Karen Sachs 1979).

To resolve women's unpaid and status-unrelated work roles efforts still continue. Scott Burns (1975) estimated that household economy is a third of total economy. However, recognising the same in monetary terms with units of time spent invites more problems than solves (all references in this paragraph cit. in Boulding, 1996).

5.4. Weakness in Neo-Darwinian Sociobiology

Richard Dawkins (1976, 1981, 1982), the premier sociobiologist, has been criticised most commonly for his premise of genes being "selfish", which biological macromolecule cannot have volition of its own. He probably does not mean so. Selection cannot occur at the level of genes because they are expressed at the level of individuals. More seriously, his assumption that gene is the unit of selection is impossible because selection cannot operate without being expressed. Only individuals not their parts can be selected. To find a role for genes as units of selection, Dawkins would have to assume 'a caucus of genes' to be the unit of selection, which is more atrocious an idea. Dawkins's argument calls for an assumption of one-to-one adaptive mapping, a single but changed gene making an individual or species adaptive, which is well nigh impossible. Philosophically, as Gould (1982) argued, Dawkins's approach is atomistic, deterministic and reductionist. More recent sociobiological or neo-Darwinian findings and arguments centre around this basic premise, while we must eagerly wait for more substantial evidences and arguments (Barlow and Silverberg 1980, Branden and Burian 1984, Himmelfarb 1986).

VI. Evolutionary-ecological Strategy of Survival

6.1. K-Strategy or R-Strategy

In communities, nations and regions with higher growth rates in different points of time, women are relatively treated unfairly, more for their functional role of reproduction of species than for anything else. Women's entitlement, education and empowerment remove this problem substantially (Dasgupta 1999 c).

6.2. Unity Without Diversity

Unity in diversity is an idealist philosophy, a poet's dream, and a mystic myth. Biological or genetic diversity across species is very important, and shall not be allowed to erode. In an interbreeding community, due to geographic and reproductive isolation as well as other means (those of which apply more to simpler organisms). Separate gene pools develop into species from such non-interbreeding populations over a long time, which no longer interbreed. As some reproductively isolated gene pools enjoy certain, but never completely, relative adaptive advantages over other gene pools and result, in their turn, into new species. In human, geographic and cultural isolations lead to reproductive isolation. Reproductive isolation is a strong evolutionary process of speciation. While culture dominates over biology and nature in nearly every other area, it is culture which has imposed reproductive isolation in human in its more recent history. Ethically, should we allow species diversification to continue in *Homo sapiens*? Diversity toward isolated gene pools among human communities is better removed. It breeds contempt and conflict, and acts against integration. Extensive cross-cultural marriages are a means of genetic mix-up of recognisably different morphologies as in ethnicity, and colour, and wide differences in religion, language, cultural norms, etc. It would permit retaining entire genetic diversity in *Homo sapiens.* Widely acceptable egalitarian and altruistic behaviour norms would prevail. An ethically and ideally more progressive human culture would emerge without biological and cultural barriers (Cavalli-Sforza and Fredman 1981, Cook 1980, Dasgupta 1999c). But that is a goal to be achieved over a pretty long time.

VII. Survival Instinct and Ethics

"The spectre of an unbridled technology is a manmade monstrosity and any application of technology should be checked by the control and balance of wisdom while only the tool is scientific." (Dasgupta 1983). Many of the culture-driven institutions which humans have forced upon themselves are not only anti-nature and anti-biology, but also half the population of the entity itself that makes the species. Only the survival instinct will engage the species into using the biological or ecological tool. The survival instinct can be boosted by egalitarian and unilaterally altruistic expanse of heart and mind, which can be sustained by widest possible anthropocentric and intergenerational concern. "It is ironical to see that a concern for the future of the primitive man had bred the urge to destroy nature and, now, a concern for posterity alone can save nature and its most endangered component man." (Dasgupta *loc. cit.*).

Men need to understand the interchangeability of roles of men and women in a home and the society. Sexual division of labour was the need of the pre-technology society. Gender values and characteristics are reinforced and perpetuated with the process of socialisation as children are brought up as boys and girls. Gender ideology is a different set of ideas and values in each culture and in each community, concerning the relation between men and women, which all the members are convinced about, although there are no logical explanations for these ideas. Recent evidences from psychology also suggest that children acquire their role from an "inborn understanding", which later grow into father and mother archetypes. Gender roles are strongly established for about 60,000 years, and it is not an easy task to break away. Gender behaviour is a manifestation of the dynamics of power that defines man-woman relations. This asymmetric power structure has to be changed. Studies also reveal that women prefer to stick to feminine roles and keep away from challenging tasks. This is not merely "achievement anxiety" as viewed by psychologists but a biological feminine attribute. A survey in the 80's in 40 Bengali-medium Kolkata schools over 83% among 1200 middle-class girls wanted to be good wives and mothers in future, and most of them gave priority to good looks and beauty care.

Vivekananda said, "Just as a bird cannot fly with its one wing only, a nation (read humanity) will not march forward if the women are left behind." Social ambidexterity—as in an androgynous society—in which both women and men have the analytic and intuitive sides equally developed (Margaret Mead 1967) evokes hope. Sex role equality will lessen differentiation. Men must understand that "women are the creators, users and guardians of biodiversity" (4th UN Conference on Women and Development). World Bank (1993) declares that women are better performers, more responsible in repaying credits, put in more care for children during hardship, endure longer working hours, leave large share of their income to the family than for self. Gillard *et al.* (1990, Science News report) reported that women have a very holistic approach to life both in home and community as part of an ever–changing network of complex interrelationships. They have better leadership skills, they are better communicators, etc. In the new millennium further cultural and economic progress in possible only with such realisation (Mitter 1986). Men are generally unenthusiastic about this. Women in general are accustomed to male dominance while a few want to reverse the dominance structure (Macmillan 1982). A slow yet steady realisation on both sides is indeed taking place. Gender equality is a distant goal as long as men strive to be masculine and women brought up and preconditioned to be feminine aspires to be masculine. Only laws and politics cannot remove gender bias. As a short-term programme, women empowerment is very essential at all levels cutting across social and economic hierarchy, not merely at the highest levels.

VIII. Synthesis

Ecosociology integrates New Ecology into New Sociology, which strives to place human both as a biological and sociocultural entity, gifted with the highest levels of intellectual ability, conscience and ethics, capable of understanding the depth and expanse of the knowable cosmos across space and time. Marxism still remains a correct method of social philosophy. Seeking for a unified field of ecosociology integrates universality of historical materialism and dialectics with subalternism and other modern philosophical thinkings as of Popper, Foucault, Derrida, etc. for a contemporary and comprehensive social philosophical standpoint across time and place.

Unless the natural, i.e. biological determinist differences are assumed to have favoured men to subjugate women is accepted, there is no alternative and valid explanation as to why women could not have dominated over men since even before the rise of patriarchy or, maybe, ever in the past. The biological differences between men and women include their instinctive, physiological including hormonal nature, and even the psyche. In post-technology human societies, need for food or security has largely lessened, except in traditional societies. Through cultural evolution, women now seek more for love and care than food or security including sex for herself, rather than as a provider of the same for men. The cultural force of subjugation of women could be strong because it is founded on biological differences. At all micro-and macro-levels the biological differences continued to favour men. The biological differences instilled in men and women a highly biased cultural value system and could increasingly manipulate everything over time. This biological determinism need not continue to prevail culturally in view of the cultural and intellectual evolution of human.

With the rise of capitalism patriarchy received its first jerks from within the system itself. Matriarchy as a social institution dwindled to some values like the motherhood mysticism depending on the stage of the culture. The development of private property and patriarchy were coincident with the class society. Oppression on the basis of sex and class was first consequential, then concomitant and in either situation, dialectically interlinked. Women's total subjugation and unquestioned male authority is drawn within the purview of the state and is established by civil and criminal, property and personal laws. Social practice ensures male control over her body, mind, psyche, culture, emotion, sensuality and sensibility.

Women gained little newer relative advantages but suffered from newer relative disadvantages compared to the contemporary men. For instance, with industrial revolution and rise of capitalism, the sudden need for additional and reserve labour and procreation of labour for future, was met biologically as well as socially, i.e. by raising women's status. The most conspicuous newer relative disadvantage was the degradation of the value about woman. Commercialisation of women's body as a public commodity was noted for the first time in history. Besides technological appliances and social innovations in child rearing and kitchen activities relief was also provided through nannies and maids drawn from the most deprived in the social rung. They are the women again to suffer most! Here women subjugate women. But violence and oppression by in-laws is merely an extension of patriarchy.

Capitalism led to nuclear families, de-collectivisation, alienation and isolation of all descriptions. Marriage remains a contract highly tilted in favour of man. Conflicts arise about legalised and surreptitious forms of subjugation. Development of economic wealth has changed the face of the world but neither the heart nor the brain. The inequalities between man and woman have narrowed down, if at all, only at the individual level.

Feminist movements are complementary to class struggle, as much as the human rights and other anti-establishment movements are as they encompass the broadest framework across the classes. But the goals have to be different in different nations and cultures, and even ecosystems to involve women at the lowest rung in the forefront.

The new changes in industry and technology are getting more and more gender-neutral as much as more and more labour-dispelling, alienating and demoralising. The impact of these most recent changes on the man-woman relations is devastating. Housewifisation of industries has favoured women employment but became a tool to reduce personnel management problems.

Transnational monpolism is characterised by social and cultural neo-imperialism. To which entire non-industrialised world has been coerced into acceptance in the name of'win-win logic'. It is the new global order based on liberalisation, privatisation and globalisation (the LPG phenomenon), symbolised into an economic guild mutually protected by an oligarchy of state power. It is turning employees into work maniacs. Working-women are more vulnerable to occupational health hazards and are hard-pressed, leaving little of life beyond workplace. Working-women in such industries are physically and psychologically shattered in this new dispensation.

Sociobiologists relate sexual dimorphism to behavioural dominance. Humans are minimally dimorphic except with secondary sexual characters. Evolution of sexual behaviour is too complex a phenomenon to draw linear conclusions. Human sexual desire is not period-bound or limited between adolescence and menopause. Concealed ovulation in women is the only explanation for unjust human behaviour. This has resulted from extreme helplessness of human babies, late weaning and longer dependence of human young on mother (and thereby on father too in modern societies) long after weaning. Prolonged security need for mother and undeterred sexual urge in father had developed strong family bondage albeit at the cost of unfair sexual dominance of men over women. Sex life is not entirely forced by survival for reproduction of species. Human has transformed sex into a fun and a solemnity through its variety and diversity, which has led human to evolution. Sex may be as important as his walking on two legs or freeing the hands, or having the largest brain.

Sociobiologists agree that the environment, food security, enemy status determine life style, social behaviour and natural selection. Determinants of dominance are community size, age, androgen-stimulated levels of aggression, physical and mental strength, skill, self-confidence etc. Dominance is genetically determined and environmentally influenced. Dominance structure may also have evolved from mother-offspring relation to adult eroticism, expressed as fathering and mothering roles of adult males and females, and male dominance and female surrender, respectively. Changing concepts and practices of parenting and home making continuously modifies this master-slave relation.

Thus, behavioural dominance is not exclusively genetically specified but can be produced by the social drift or multiplier effect, forced by environmental constraints or female helplessness. Cultural variations in behaviour patterns originate from infinite variations in settings. Generalised male dominance is not necessary and inevitable as a cultural requirement, as it may vary from no dominance to severe dominance, which is related not to sex but social activity and skill.

There are two alternatives to dominance systems, egalitarianism and altruism. Equality can be ensured by contribution of something "extra" by means of some kind of reciprocity. Altruism extends one's fitness as the expense of another through kin selection. But kin selection is a rare phenomenon. Neither species nor kin, but individual is the unit of natural selection. Altruism is not sex-linked, but culturally conditioned. Altruism by oppressed-coerced groups or individuals, such as women, is pseudoaltruism. Altruism does not lead to equality or change dominance behaviour pattern. Women mostly have adapted to dominance structure. At the same time, women are highly skilled to convert their power to derive a special and privatised underside power and authority over their men. Women developed a special set of interstitial roles outside the hierarchy and dominance in developing social bonding, conflict resolution, and crisis management from interfamilial to international alliance structures through history.

Evolutionary-ecological strategy of human survival should be set at K-selection, more of survival than of reproduction. Human is at the steering of his own evolution, and should not give into biology or culture, without intelligent use.

Cross-cultural marriages without any inhibition would permit retention of genetic diversity without permitting phenotypic differentiability, in order to end mutual contempt and conflict between communities and cultures, but encouraging cooperative livelihood.

Sexual division of labour was the need of the pre-technology society. Gender ideology is a different set of ideas and values in each culture and in each community, without any logical explanations. There may be an "inborn understanding", which later grow into father and mother archetypes. Gender roles are strongly established for about 60,000 years (may be more, as recently claimed by some Australian findings of a *Homo* sp. there.). And it is not an easy task to break away. Gender behaviour is a manifestation of the dynamics of power that defines man-woman relations.

Sociobiology of sexual dimorphism shows that the extent of behavioural differentiation in most human societies is environmentally and culturally determined. Environmental determination operates through for adaptation. The subordination for women historically has not done society much good. The androgynous society in which both women and men have the analytic and intuitive sides equally developed evokes hope. Sex role equality will lessen differentiation. Men must understand that women are creators, users and guardians of biodiversity and development. Women are better performers, more responsible in repaying credits, put in more care for children during hardship, have longer working hours, leave larger share of their income to the family than for self. Women have a very holistic approach of life both in home and community as part of an ever-changing network of complex interrelationships. They have better leadership skills, better communicators, etc. In the new millennium further cultural and economic progress is possible only with such realisation. Men are generally unenthusiastic about this. Women in general are accustomed to male dominance while a few wants to reverse the dominance structure. A slow yet steady realisation on both sides is indeed taking place. Extensive cross-cultural marriages are a means of selection of culturally acceptable behaviour norms, which tend to egalitarian and altruistic with latest social and economic trends. Gender equality is a distant dream as long as men strive to be masculine and women brought up as feminine aspire to be masculine. Only laws and politics cannot remove gender bias.

Epilogue

"History of human civilisation is the history of the purity of human love and living, while what is purity of love is debatable. ... An ideal is highly valued merely because it is unfortunately achievable for a limited few, not for the laity at large. Making an ideal a social objective brings forth suffering for people.... But that is human characterisitic again to seek for an ideal of humanity greater than the preceding to be realised through people's suffering and ordeals. When this greater ideal serves its social role, a still greater ideal is set from the garbage of the already decomposed preceding ideal. This is how good sacrifices itself for the better. This alone is the path of human liberation."—*Sarat Chandra Chattopadhyay.*

References

Bardhan, K, 1993. Social class and gender in India. In: *Gender and Political Economy: Exploration of South Asian system* (Clark, Gillard E, Brough E, Duffierd B., eds.). New Delhi, Oxford University Press.

Barlow W, Silverberg J, eds. 1980. *Sociobiology Beyond Nature-Nurture?* Boulder, Co., Westview Press.

Barston Margaret 1969. The political economy of women's liberation. Reprinted in: *The Politics of Housework* (Ellen Malos, ed., 1982). London, Allison and Burstry.

Betzig L L Borgerhoff Mulder M, Turke, P.W., eds. 1988. *Human Reproductive Behaviour: A Darwinian Perspective.*, Cambridge, Cambridge University Press.

Boulding Elise 1996. *The Underside of History. Vol. 1. A View of Women through Time,* Chicago, University of Chicago Press.

Boyd R Richerson P, 1985 *Culture and the Evolutionary Process,* Chicago, Chicago University Press.

Branden R N, Burian R M, eds.1984. *Genes, Organisms, Populations: Controversy over the units of selection.* Massachusets, Cambridge, MIT Press.Burman Erica, ed. 1998. *Deconstructing Feminist Psychology,* New Delhi, .Sage Publications.

Callicott J Baird. 1989.The metaphysical implications of ecology, 51-64 pp. In: *Nature in Asian Traditions of Thought: Essays in environmental philosophy* (Callicott JB, Ames RT, eds.). Delhi 110 007, Sree Satguru Publications, A division of Indian Books Centre, First Indian Edition 1991.

Cavalli-Sforza L L, Fredman M W. 1981. *Cultural Transmission of Evolution,* Princeton, Princeton University Press.

Cook J. M. 1980. *The Evolution of Human Consciousness.* Oxford, Oxford University Press.

Cottrell Robert. 1975. *Simone de Beauvoir.* Frederick Unger.

Custers Peter. 1996. *The Debate on Women's Labour: Historical and theoretical perspectives*, Calcutta, Ratna Prakashan.

Dasgupta M K. 1983. The ecological crisis — Groping for a solution, *Everyman's Science* 18 (6), 170-175.

Dasgupta, M.K., 1995. Sustainability re-viewed: Toward systems agriculture with an ecological perspective. In: *Sustainable Agriculture in Sub-humid Tropics* (Dasgupta, M. K., ed.),.

Dasgupta, M.K., 1998. Technology, agrotechnology and environment: Historical, cultural and societal issues. 69-81pp. In: *Selected Readings on Environmental Awareness and Education* (D. Dasgupta, ed.), Sriniketan, Visva-Bharati, Palli-Siksha Bhavana.

Dasgupta, M.K., 1999a. Challenges to agriculture Y2K: Shall we be caught unawares? 41-47pp. In: *Agrotechnology and Environment* (D C Ghosh, ed.), Sriniketan, Visva-Bharati, Palli-Siksha Bhavana, ASEPAN, March

11, 1999.

Dasgupta, M.K., 1999b. Deconstructing and reconstructing university concept, system and management. 125 – 131 pp. In: Proceedings of First Indian Educational Science Congress (D K Sinha et al., eds.), Visva-Bharati, Santiniketan, 28-30 Dec, 1998, 145 pp.

Dasgupta, M.K., 1999c. From Darwin to Sen: Evolution, ecology, economics and ethics for entitlement to earth. 49-51pp. In: *Frontiers to Plant Protection,* Vol. II (M K Dasgupta, ed.), Visva-Bharati, Palli Siksha Bhavana, Dept of Plant Protection, Sriniketan.

Dawkins Richard. 1976. *The Selfish Gene.* Oxford, Oxford University Press.

Dawkins Richard. 1981. In defence of selfish genes. *Philosophy* 56, 556 – 573.

Dawkins Richard. 1982. Replication and Vehicles. In: King's College Sociobiology Group, *Current Problems in Sociobiology,* Cambridge, Cambridge University Press.

Della Costa Mariarosa, Selma James 1972. *The Power of Women and the Subversion of the Community.* Bristol, .Padua.

Diamond Zared. 1992. *The Third Chimpanzee.* Los Angeles, California University Press.

Diamond Zared. 1996. *Why is Sex Fun?* Los Angeles, California University Press.

Dworkin Andrea. 1974.*Woman Hating,* New York, EP Dutton.

Dworkin, Andrea. 1987. *Intercourse.* Secker and Warburg, Arrow Books.

Eisenstein Zilla, ed. 1979. *Capitalist Patriarchy and the case for Socialist Feminism,* New York, Monthly Review Press.

Elshatin Jean Bethke. 1981. *Public Man, Private Woman,* Princeton, Princeton University Press.

Evans, M. 1975. *Simone de Beauvoir, A Feminist Mandarin*, Tavistock.

Firestone Shulamith. 1971. *The Dialectics of Sex,* London, Jonathan and Cape.

Gatens M. 1991. *Feminism and Philosophy.* Polity Press.

Gould Stephen Jay. 1980.Is a new and general theory of evolution emerging? *Paleobiology* 6, 119 –130.

Gould Stephen Jay. 1982. *The Panda's Thumb,* New York, W. W. Norton & Co.

Hartman Heidi. 1986. The Unhappy Marriage of Marxism and Feminism: Towards a more progressive union. In: *Women and Revolution* (Lydia Sargent, ed.), London, Pluto Press.

Hansen Kathryn.1988. The *Virangana* in North Indian history, myth and popular culture. *Economic and Political Weekly*, Vol. XXIII, *Review of Women's Studies* (April 30), WS 25-32.

Hartung, J. 1985. Matrilineal inheritance: New theory and analysis. *Behavioural and Brain Sciences* 8, 661-688.

Himmelfarb, Gertrude. 1986. Social Darwinism, Sociobiology and Two Cultures. In: *Marriage and Morals among the Victorians,* New York, Knopf.

Irigaray I. 1993. *Je, tu, nous.* London,.Routledge.

Irigaray I. 1996. *I Love You.* London,.Routledge.

Kaefe Terry. 1983. *Simone de Beauvoir: A study of her writings*, Harrup.

Kishwar, Madhu. 1986. Arya Samaj and Women's education: Kanya Mahavidyalaya, Jalandhar, *Economic and Political Weekly*, Vol. XXI, *Review of Women's Studies* (April 26),WS 9-24.

Kuhn Annette, Ann Maria Wolfe, eds. 1978. Feminism and Materialism, London, Routledge and Kegan Paul.

Le Doeuff M. 1991.*Hipparchia's Choice: An essay concerning women, philosophy, etc.*, London, Blackwell.

Leibowitz S. 1986. The origin of the sexual division of labour and the development of the first human societies. In: *Woman's Work, Men's Property* (Stephaine Coontz, Peta Henderson, eds.), London, Vesco Books.

Lefebrre H. 1992. *Critique of Everyday Life,* Vol. B, London, Verso.

Lewenhak Sheila. 1980. *Women and Work.* Glassgow, Fontana Paperbacks.

Leydesdorff Selma. 1977. *Hidden Labour — Forgotten Labour,* An exploration into the history of women's labour around 1900, Amsterdam, Van Gorcum.

MacMillan Carol. 1982. *Women, Reason and Nature.* London, Blackwell.

Mahadevan K., ed.1989. *Women and Population Dynamics. Perspectives from Asian Countries.* New Delhi. Sage Publications.

Mahon Joseph. 1997. *Existentialism, Feminism and Simone de Beauvoir,* London, Macmillan.

Malos Ellen, ed. 1980. *The Politics of Housework,* London, Allison & Busby.

Mies Maria. 1986. Indian women in subsistence and agricultural labour (assisted by Lalitha K and Krishna Kumari), Women, Work and Development, No. 12, Geneva, ILO.

Mies Maria, Bennholdt-Thomson Veronika, Von Werhef Claudia. 1988. Women, the last

Maria, Bennholdt-Thomson Veronika, Von Werhef Claudia. 1988. *Women, the Last Colony,* London, Zed Books.

Milkman Ruth. 1985. *Women, Work and Protest*—A century of women's labour history,

London, Routledge and Kegan Paul.

Miller, Geoffrey. 1989. *The Mating Mind: How sexual choice shaped the evolution of human nature.* Heihnmann.

Millet Kate. 1971. *Sexual Politics,* London, Hart-Davis.

Mitter Swasti. 1986. *Common Fate — Common Bond:* Women in Global Economy, London, Pluto Press.

Moi, Toril. 1994. ***Simone de Beauvoir:*** *The Making of an Intellectual Women.* London, Blackwell.

Nayar, PKB. 1989. Kerala women in historical and contemporary perspective. 205 –221 pp. In: Mahadevan, K. 1989.

Okely, Judith.1986.*Simone de Beauvoir: A Re-Reading.* Vivago.

Omvedt Gail. 1983. Household labour, Marxism and patriarchy. A series of three articles. Calcutta, *Frontier*, June.

Reed E. 1979. *Woman's Evolution,* New York, Pathfinder Press.

Richards Robert John. 1987. *Darwin and the Emergence of Evolutionary Theories of Mind and Behaviour*. Chicago, University of Chicago Press.

Robinson, Sandra P. 1985. Hindu paradigms of Women: Images and Values, In: *Women, Religion and Social Change* (Yvonne Yazbeck Haddad, ed.), Albany, State University of New York Press, 181-215.

Ruse Michael. 1985. *Sociobiology: Sense or Nonsense?* 2nd edn., Dordrecht, Reidel.

Ruse Michael. 1989. *The Darwinian Paradigm: Essays on its history, philosophy and religious implications* New York. Routledge.

Ruse Michael, Wilson, E. O. 1985. The evolution of ethics, *New Scientist* 1478: 108-128.

Sargent Lydia, ed. 1986. *The Unhappy Marriage Between Marxism and Feminism,* London, Pluto Press.

Sen A. K. 1991. Gender and cooperative conflicts. In: *Persistent Inequalities* (Tunker, J., ed.), New Delhi, Oxford University Press.

Sen Ilina. 1988. Class and gender in work time allocation. *Economic & Political Weekly*, August 13, 1702 pp.

Stites R. 1977. *The Women,s Liberation Movement in Russia: Feminism, Nihilism and Bolshevism,* 1860-1930. Princeton, .Princeton University Press.

Stoltenberg John. 1990. *Refusing To Be A Man,* Fontana.

Trivers R. L. 1985. *Social Evolution.* Benjamin-Cummings, Menlo-Park.

Wilson, E. O. 1975. *Sociobiology: The New Synthesis*. Harvard University Press, Cambridge, Massachusets.

3

Women's Question: The Three Distinct Viewpoints

Dr. Aparajita Mukherjee

There are three distinctly different basic viewpoints towards the problem of empowerment of women. The first viewpoint is what we may call the liberal democratic viewpoint, the second viewpoint is what is known as the radical feminist viewpoint and the third viewpoint is the Marxist viewpoint with all these viewpoints having different shades. In the liberal democratic view of the problem, it is basically the problem of achieving democratic rights for women, achieving equal rights with that of men and ensuring their legitimate share in the process of development and power structure, within the bounds of the existing socio-economic framework. The broader variant of such a viewpoint recognises the need to establish women's identity as independent individual human beings within the family and in the society outside the family. Such liberal democratic viewpoint towards women's problem was born some 200 years ago with the rise of the principles of 'equality', 'liberty' and 'fraternity' and the recognition of individualism as the sole motive of human existence. The idea of women's liberation based on this particular viewpoint was thus the direct result of advent of capitalism in Europe, the French Revolution and Rennaissance. The emergence, survival and growth of capitalist system of production necessitated this new culture of individual freedom and liberty, because expansion of capitalist system of production required conditions for unrestricted growth of the individual capitalist. It required unrestricted right to enter other country's market to get access to cheap sources of productive resources including labour. At that early stages of its development the system needed ever expanding supply of cheap labour. It therefore became essential for the system of production to free the erstwhile serfs from their chain of feudal subjugation and connect them to the free market for labour. In the face of ever expanding demand for labour it was essential to ensure unlimited supply of cheap labour so as to prevent real wage rates from rising. The newly developed concept of liberty and freedom was combined with the concept of 'laissez faire' i.e. the unrestricted freedom to achieve maximum self satisfaction by individual agents of the society within the bounds of capitalist framework. As a corollary to these concepts and principles which arose directly from the necessity of maintaining and expanding the capitalist system of production, women also were to be made free to participate in the social process of production to offer themselves as supplier of labour power in the labour market. With this right to associate oneself to the social process of production came the demand for a host of rights, the right to education, the right to suffrage, the right to choose one's own life partner in marriage and so many other rights, and finally the aspiration to liberate oneself from the customs, traditions and values of the old society which for ages had acted to subjugate the independence of women's personalities. The subjugation of women, the lack of their rights and power are viewed as problems arising out of the socio-cultural superstructure of the erstwhile feudal society which, though inconsistent with the values and culture of modern society, nevertheless, still continues to plague modern society as vestiges of the old society. To a liberal democratic person thus, women's liberation in this sense is an essential condition for development of modern civilisation. It is no wonder then that the modern society gives rise to so much concern about women's democratic rights. The different branches of modern education system include studies and research on the problem of women's degradation. Women's secondary position in society which is not only revealed in every sphere of social and private activities of life but also in languages used, in literature, in economics, politics and social power structure - is carefully studied and researched. New laws are introduced on divorce, remarriage maintenance of wives by husbands, rape and various other issues related with protection of rights of women. But inspite of all these, the fact remains that even in most developed capitalist world women's position remains as insecured as ever. The tremendous development of technology and human capability achieved in the twentieth century, the rapid onward march of modern civilisation have actually failed to change women's position. Women's education, their newly achieved democratic rights to divorce, remarry, participate in social production have not reversed their secondary position in society and family; all these have not changed the sexual division of labour in which women are typically considered as primarily housewives irrespective of their role in the social production process. All these new laws and rights have not removed her degradation. The question then arises : What is the way out, how can women's empowerment be achieved ? is it through education ? is it through economic independence ? is it enacting laws and rights that would ensure women's freedom from subjugation and degradation ? There are actually no definite answers to these questions to the liberal democrat. The new realisation that emerges is while one is to study and research into the innumerable ramifications of women's degradation in all spheres of life, one must investigate the root of women's oppression, the root of her secondary position in society and family.

The radical feminist viewpoint to the problem of women's empowerment places the origin of the problem in the system of partiarchy. According to this approach the concept of patriarchy should be used as a central concept of analysis with which to understand the nature of women's oppression. The use of the concept of partiarchy in theoretical analysis of women's oppression gives rise to a new dimension of the concept, partiarchy means not only the rule of the father but the rule of men and as such is seen as a universal 'mode of power relationship' and domination. According to this line of argument patriarchy is all pervasive as it penetrates class division, different societies and different historical epochs. It is considered as primary oppression because it predates class oppression. The specific variation within patriarchy over different historical epochs are considered to be less significant compared to its general truth. The radical feminist describes the present day society as patriarchy, to mean that men wield political power over women and this amounts to the fundamental political division in society some even go to the extent of describing patriarchy as the state of the present day society in which the rule over women by men is more rigorous, more uniform and more enduring than class stratification. Patriarchy is viewed as a fundamental system of domination that is analytically independent of any mode of production. According to another shade of radical feminism the root of patriarchy is to be sought in the biologically determined division of labour between men and women in the process of reproduction of the species.

Patriarchy is also looked as the 'exploitation of wives' labour by their husbands which takes place within the family based on the institution of marriage which is essentially a labour contract between the husband and wife and exhibits a 'patriarchal mode of production'. According to another group of modern-day feminists partiarchy is the power of males which is institutionalised in nuclear family; sometimes patriarchy is also defined to cover two aspects, namely, the control of women's fertility and sexuality in monogamous marriage and economic subordination of women through the sexual division of labour.

The radical feminists' approach to the problem of women's oppression is unsatisfactory for the reason that while they view patriarchy as the root of women's oppression, they do not provide any definite clear meaning of the term patriarchy neither do they provide any answer to the question : what the root of patriarchy itself is. Moreover, the radical feminists' identification of man-woman contradiction as the fundamental political division in society is obviously untenable. Since it means man and woman should be taken as belonging to two completely separate and fundamentally different camps with antagonistic relationship. The radical feminists' approach to the problem thus suffers from one-sidedness which places males as the enemies of the females. This misconception arises from the failure to locate the root of patriarchy in the historical process of development of society alongwith its ideologies and culture; while patriarchy is often identified as the culture and ideology of civilised society, the root of its existence in the material basis of the society remains unidentified.

In fact, if the concept of patriarchy is used to mean a system of subjugation of women which encompasses so many varied forms of males, domination over women, male control over woman's sexuality and fertility, his control over her personality and existence as human beings then it cannot be viewed simply as an ideological concept but also as an economic and social concept. The questions which become relevant are that : how the different forms of patriarchy are interrelated with social relations of production, how the changing modes of production change the forms of patriarchy without destroying its existence. It is evident that the concept of patriarchy as a form of organisation of labour in the household is inadequate without at the same time, locating how the sexual division of labour and the social relations generated by the reproductive role of women are structured in such a way that relations between the sexes are relations of domination and subordination. Thus further development of the concept of patriarchy is called for in order to be able to explain the interaction between the relation of production and relation of human reproduction. Biological determinism seems to be too inadequate in the theoretical understanding of the family and of human reproduction in relation to subordination of women. Instead it is required to explain how patriarchal oppression of women in the family is crucially connected with the need to control their fertility and sexuality and how it is connected with the need to control wife's labour in the precapitalist producing families and in the working class families under capitalism.

To the Marxists the problem of women's subjugation, the lack of recognition of her personality and independence in family and society are not simply matters belonging to the socio-cultural superstructure of feudal society which perpetuates in the modern society as vestiges of the old society. To the Marxists the origin of woman's subjugation, her total degradation and lack of rights is to be sought in the process of development of private property rights system and the class society. The dialectical materialist analysis of the historical process of development of society from its pre-class origin through its varied class-based forms exposes the nature and origin of the women's problem with all its ramifications.

To the Marxists the process of development of patriarchy as a system is closely interwoven in the process of development of private property rights, development of class exploitation and the rise of state as an instrument of class exploitation. The structures of oppression on the basis of sex and on the basis of class are two processes which are dialecticaly interlinked, like the structure of oppression on the basis of nationality, race, caste and religion, each of which originates at particular stages in the history of class exploitation and is dialecticaly interlinked with the structural process of class exploitation. The structure of oppression on the basis of sex originated at a particular stage in the development of productive forces, social division of labour and exchange which also served as pre-condition for the growth of class exploitation.

From Engel's formulation of the origin of family, private property and state it follows that the biologically determined special role of women in the process of reproduction of the species, instead of causing their degradation actually gave them the special power of dominance over the community; but that special power of dominance lasted only as long as the society was based on collective system of production, consumption, division of labour, exchange and distribution.

The communities were big families - each constituted of persons related through blood. Division of labour within these communities was based on sex - women performing child care and other activities like cooking, making utensils, weaving etc. i.e., all the activities which could be performed within the area of the communities alongwith child care, and males performing hunting, rearing of cattle pets, collecting food and saving the community from outside attack. But this division of labour was not at all a strict division imposed by the society nor did it degrade women's position in society - because women's activities from rearing of children to hunting were collective and social activities; since communities were identical with households as basic unit of production and consumption, since survival of the community was the most serious question and reproduction of the species received highest importance among all other activities. It is within this primitive communal system of possession and performance of all economic and social activities that there was indeed no contradiction between individual and private on the one hand, and collective and social on the other. According to Engel's it is this communal household system alongwith the special capability of women for bearing children, which was in fact the basis of women's power in the stage of matriarchal society. All activities were not only social in nature but also were performed under the direction and control of women as important members of society. Even bearing and rearing of children were social concerns which automatically precluded the possibility of male control over women's sexuality and maternity. The division of labour based on sex, hetereosexuality and women's special power of child bearing - none of these served as important basis for male domination over the female, as long as 'individual' and 'social' did not arise as two separate and contradictory aspects of human existence.

According to Engel's findings the early stage of matriarchal society was based on clan marriage. Naturally for the children born out of clan marriage paternity remained unidentified, only maternity could be determined. As a result, a child was naturally a mother's child and belonged to the clan of his/her mother. Determination of children's identity was made on female lineage. The transition from group marriage to pairing marriage did not change the situation as long as community household system was not disturbed. The pairing marriage was based on complete freedom of separation for either partner and the marriage relationship was completely unstable. With every break-up of the relationship it is the male partner who had to leave the community and go back to his original community with all the weapons and instruments used by him, while the female partner remained within the community which was her original community, with the children and utensils and other things used by her, jointly with other women of the community.

The transformation of the society from the stage of food gathering to the stage of cattle raising and food producing brought about some new contradictions within the society. The development of productive forces not only brought about new modes of livelihood but also newer and newer instruments of labour used by males. Males' personal possessions of important productive instruments increased in number and quality. But the system of pairing family uptill then allowed the males to leave the clan with every break-up of marriage, with all his personal possession of taken with him, leaving possession which gave rise to the first sense of private property rights on weapons and instruments of labour used by males, as a direct negation of the sense of collective rights and collective enjoyment within the communal social system. The question of inheritance became more and more important with every increase in the number and quality of these personal possessions. With every increase in the wealth of society, it was male's power that increased and the question of inheritance of the productive instruments under personal possession of males by none other than their own male offspring became all the more important. As a result of further development of the productive forces and increase in male power, the system of pairing marriage which enabled the males to identify their own children, came in direct contradiction with the collective system of possession of society's wealth, the community household system and the matriarchal system of identification of the children. Again, the question of inheritance of male possession by his own children was in direct contradiction with females' right over children, their right to control their own sexuality and maternity, and above all their right to break-up marriage. All these contradictions were sought to be resolved with the transformation of the society based on communal-household system of production and consumption into one based on personal-family-based household system of production and consumption. The basis for individualistic family household system had already been created through private control and possession of productive instruments including cattle. The increase in the degree of division of labour, introduction of newer and newer forms of productive activities and exchange, further consolidated the basis for personal family-based household units as basic units of consumption and realisation of private property rights.This transformation brought about complete reversal of women's position in the community. Cooking, weaving, collection of drinking water and fuel, pot making and child bearing - all the activities which could be performed within the four walls of the household now lost all its earlier social character and turned to be private and individual duties, while the activities which could not be performed without the cooperation of other members of the society, retained their social character. All of the first kind of duties which could be performed along with rearing of children, and which were related with individual consumption, satisfaction and enjoyment, became strictly the duties of the women - while all the second type of activities became strictly male duties. In this way the two different kinds of labour acquiring two strictly different characters, namely 'private' and 'social' led to complete reversal in the relative positions of men and women in society. Women's social role became more and more insiginificant. This degradation of women's position along with male's right over his children brought about epoch-making change in the family system, with the pairing families transforming into monogamous families. The ever-increasing male power of control over the productive instruments of society gave them the infinite power over their private household also. To ensure that all his personal possessions be inherited by none other than his own male offspring, after his death - strict monogamy was imposed on women. They lost all their previous rights to control their own sexuality and maternity, their right to dissolve marriage was also taken away, having lost all their rights over social wealth which they previously used to enjoy collectively with other members of society, the women lost their rights over their own bodies, and they came under strict male control confined within the four walls of the household. Though polygamy was never prohibited for males, women came under strict rules and regulations and values of monogamy became imposed by society. She became completely isolated from the outside world, all her desires and happiness came to be subjugated to male desires and happiness. She became mainly a tool for the creation of her husband's heir and even as a procreator of the new generation, her role was recognised as secondary and less significant compared to that of her husband. A patriarchal system of possession and inheritance was strictly imposed. Monoganous family households thus became the essential institutional framework within which males' infinite control and women's total subjugation to male power could be effected.

Marxian dialectical method of analysis of history thus posits the origin of patriarchy not merely in the division of labour on the basis of sex - because such division of labour existed even in the matriarchal society; rather it posits patriarchy at a particular stage in the history of development of productive forces which gave rise to the existence of 'individual' and 'social' as two contradictory opposites. The division of labour on the basis of sex became instrumental in the process of rise of patriarchy only when private family household system of possession and consumption became the only form of possession of productive instrument and consumption, as opposed to social and communal system.

Further, it is the family household based on strict monogamy on the female side, which provided the essential framework within which patriarchy and women's degradation is primarily effected.

Further, in Marxian method of analysis, the system of patriarchy and class system are two closely interwoven categories and product of the same historical process of development of society. As the surplus producing capacity of human labour provided material condition for the division of society into slavemasters and slavelabours new conditions for domination on women were created. Women's reproductive capacity now had to be used for the generation of surplus. While the women of the defeated community now could be transformed into slaves who would reproduce slaves, the married wife of the slavemaster produced heirs to inherit the slavemasters' accumulated wealth and power. Thus, strict control of women's sexuality and fertility became serious concern for the slaveowing class. Thus, women's subjugation and the monogamous family system based on it was not only fully consistent with the slave mode of production but it actually served as one of the fundamental ideological social frameworks within which slave mode of production could function and develop. For the possessing class thus, patriarchy provided the essential ideological and material instrument for the perpetuation of class domination.

State and Patriarchy

While oppression on the basis of sex and class oppression are two closely interwoven categories, patriarchy is considered as an essential complementary institution for the functioning of state system.

To the Marxists the irreconciliability of class contradictions gave rise to the formation of state as an instrument for maintaining class authority and class rule of the exploiter upon the society. The legal and administrative system, the judiciary, armed forces and police, the bureaucracy - all are so designed as to maintain and reproduce the specific form of the system of class-exploitation as well as the system of private property rights and its inheritance through generations. On the other hand, it is for the special purpose of maintaining the private property right system and creating conditions for the continual reproduction of the system of inheritance in the male lineage as well as the system of class-exploitations that patriarchy alongwith monogamous family system that emerged as the essential basic framework of patriarchy. Thus, the monogamous family system and the structure of patriarchal oppression became an essential complementary part of the state. Again by maintaining the system of class-exploitation and strengthening the basis of private property right, the state at the same time strengthens the basis of patriarchy with the monogamous family as its basis.

Therefore, patriarchy alongwith monogamous family system with all its essential features characterised by women's total subjugation and unquestioned male authority is drawn within the purview of the state. New ethical values and concepts are created to suit the system of class oppressiosn and perpetuation of private property right system. Heterosexuality was recognised as the only form of sexuality. New concepts continued to be created to regulate women's behaviour. All the newly created concepts of women's fidelity, motherhood and her monogamy, male's authority and woman's total submission to male authority, i.e., all the values and ideas that strengthen the basis of patriarchy and the monogamous family system are strongly secured and maintained by the state. The state and the society delegate women to perform the special roles of wife and mother within the family, as her ultimate objective and end in life. The religious codes of conduct, the values and culture, the dictums and social practices make women's total subjugation absolute and ultimate. Women's degradation, her insignificant social existence, the glorification of the concept of fidelity and motherhood, the absolute male control over woman's body as an individual, continued to provide important subject matters and themes for art and literature that shaped the values, social habits and customs throughout the slave and feudal era. Her whole life in all its phases came under the most cruel social regulations of male-dominated society Newer and newer state laws and religious regulations were created in conformity with these social values and customs. Force was increasingly being allowed to be applied by the society in order to compel women to concede to all these rules and values and internalise them.

Capitalism and Liberation of Women

With the advent of capitalist production system alongwith its socio-cultural superstructure women were introduced to the new bourgeoise, democratic concept of freedom which indicates freedom for economic independence, education, property rights, freedom of choice in marriage etc. But all these freedoms were conditioned not only by the class system but also by the obligation to accept male domination in family and society, male lineage of identity and inheritance and above all the monogomous family system based on patriarchy as the essential basic unit of society.

Capitalist society however is inherently averse to unconditional freedom for women due to several reasons : First, while capitalist system necessitates women's participation in the system of production, it can never ensure complete development and utilisation of women's capacity. In the early stage of capitalist development, conditions favourable to women's participation in social reproduction process were created. But as capitalist production system developed into monopoly, concentration of capital and cut-throat competition among oligarchical firms made cutting down of production and employment a regular feature of the system. As a result in the latter stage, i.e., in the stage of imperialism, development of productive forces was obstructed and its utilisation became limited. Thus, women labour could not be used except as a reserve army of cheap unemployed labour force, specific kind of labour for so-called women's work, cheap labour used in small-scale and family-based industries and unorganised domestic labour.

The capitalist mode of production itself thus stands in the way of full-fledged participation of women in the social process of production. Another important fact is that women's participation in outside activities cannot free them from their traditional responsibilities of household duties including child care. As a result a large part of women's energies and mental and physical capacities remain confined to these duties which stand in the way of the development of their mental faculty. Moreover, the capitalist system does not do away with the system of male lineage of inheritence and identity and father's natural guardianship of children. All these make women's role unimportant and secondary in the social process of production, and insignificant even in families. The important social function that women perform in bearing and rearing of the new generation, goes unrecognised in bourgeoise society as it happened in all other previous societies based on private household system.

Third since capitalist system is a system of private property rights and class exploitation, like all other previous class societies it also perpetuates partriarchy as an ideological and material instrument essential for its own existence. But the changes that follow from the essential nature of the economic and cultural system of the new modes of production create some serious contradictions whose resolution goes beyond the scope of the system. First, the capitalist system brings out women from within the bounds of the household and connects them with the outside world; but it cannot create unlimited scope for the effective utilisation of their full capacity. Because of the inherent limitations of capitalist production system itself, the role of women in society remains secondary and notwithstanding the social benefits of women's work, the work remains greatly undervalued. Secondly, the right to break up marriage comes in direct contradiction with the patriarchal system of inheritance and identity through male lineage and system of bringing up of children as a private responsibility. The new rights which women achieve through struggle, along with the system that allows them to be educated and economically self-sufficient, creates conditions which enable women to break marriages and thus to shake the stability of the family system. Though marriage in a developed western society is marriage of 'free' choice, in practice it is a marriage of convenience; the vulgur materialist values of bourgeoise society upholds crude monetary calculations, in place of personal feelings, as the basis of all human relations. As a result in the advanced stage of capitalist development the families always are to face the possibility of break-up, as an inevitable outcome. The rights to divorce and abortion make this possibility even stronger. In all previous societies, force, either in the crudest form or in the form of culture, ideology, state laws, social customs and so many other forms, had been actually used to maintain the institution of family as the essential basic institution of society. Capitalist society also requires such institutions for its own survival. The bourgeoise state apparatus, through its law and judiciary, the social customs, values, culture and ideology strongly maintain these institutions. But the democratic rights which it promises to women, at least in principle, tend to shake the very basis of the system by shaking the stability of the family system. Thus, women's democratic rights in the full sense of the term is inherently inconsistent and contradictory with the capitalist mode of production. The system with all its apparent promise of democracy remains as autocratic and oppressive of women as all previous systems based on private property rights and class exploitation.

In Lieu of Conclusion

Women's question thus is not merely a question of democratic rights for women. It it much more than that. The problem is rooted deeply into the basic structure of society based on private property rights. The Marxist ideology on this question suggests that the problem cannot be totally solved unless and until the means of production are truly socialised but also the social objectives in place of private objectives become the main motive of human existence. This suggests not only the abolition of the system of private property rights along with the system of inheritance through male lineage but also socialisation of household and child's upbringing. This, it is beliveved, will transform the families from being centres of male domination over females to true democratic institutions, based on love and personal feelings, in place of crude material calculations. The exponents of communism envisage such an ideal system, though in reality the socialist countries miserably failed to reach anywhere near these ideals. One or two examples of failures, however, cannot prove that the theory itself is wrong. At least one can say we have no other practical alternative solutions to the problem before us.

References

1. Althusser, L. (1971). 'Ideology and ideological state apparatuses' in *Lenin and Philosophy and other essays*, London, New Left Books.
2. Engels, F. (1972). *The Origin of Family, Private Property and the State*, London, Lawrence and Wishart.
3. Marx, K. (1973). *Grundriste : Foundations of the Critique of Political Economy*, Penguin, Harmondsworth.
4. Marx, K. (1970). *Capital* Vol.I, London Lawrence and Wishart.
5. Millet, K. (1971). *Sexual Politics*, London, Hart - Davis.
6. Roisin Mc Douough and Rackel Harrison (1978). 'Patriarchy and Relation of Production' in Annette Kuhu and Ann Marie Wolpe edited *Feminism and Materialism*, Routletge and Kegan Paul Ltd.

4

Rabindranath and Gender Politics

Sultapa Bhattacharya

"The English are strong, Bengalis weak; the English are brave, Bengalis cowardly; the English are hardy, Bengalis soft; etcetera, etcetera. If differences in rights arising from these natural differences are deemed proper, then why do we make such a fuss over the minor differences in the rights enjoyed by the English and the Bengalis ? If it is judged proper to consider the woman the slave and the man the master, then it will only be proper to judge it fair to consider the Bengali the slave and the English the master".

It is apparent from the parallel drawn between the English-Bengali relationship and the Man-Woman relationship in the above extract, that Bankimchandra recognised the Man-Woman relationship as a *political* one, at least in his work, *Samya*. In this work, at any rate, Bankim did not accept that differences in rights arising from differences in nature were justified. He did not accept either the Bengali = Slave, English = Master or the Woman = Slave, Man = Master relationship as justified. This third section of *Samya*, from where the quotation above has been extracted, was published in 1875. Although Bankimchandra himself later declared that "*Samya* was all wrong", this section, published in the journal *Bangadarshan*, may well have influenced young Rabindranath.

Like Bankimchandra, in the 19th Century Rabindranath too draws parallels between the English-Bengali and Man-Woman relationships, although from a diametrically opposed direction.

"If we Bengalis say that the selfishness of the English is at the root of Bengali subservience, then this is merely the unthinking wailing of the weak. The English could never have asserted their selfishness, if we had not been weak to begin with. Therefore, the fundamental consideration is not [English] selfishness, but [Bengali] weakness. The root cause of all forms of domination is weakness". *(Sadhana, 1891)*

Just as Bengali weakness is at the root of English dominance, the natural weakness or inferiority of the woman is at the root of male dominance. It is not correct to hold men responsible for this state of affairs. Thus, wrote Rabindranath in his polemical exchanges with Krishnabhabini Das. That the man-woman relationship is a political relationship was recognised by Rabindranath. Just as he had protested against the merely verbal, and thus ineffective, railings of the Bengalis against the English, so too had he protested against the feminist speeches of Ramabai and writings of Krishnabhabini. In his opinion, "human beings have to tolerate certain necessary forms of dominance. If these are always felt to be forms of dominance and subservience, it only goes to prove our real subservience. If these are treated as *dharma*, then we can find our independence precisely within such dominance". (Letter written in response to a lecture by Ramabai and published in the journal, *Bharati,* in 1889.) It is for this reason that Rabindranath found "the recent outcry against male-dominance" improper and unjustified.

Rather, in his opinion, accepting male-dominance as *dharma* leads to the "realisation of the greatness of the feminine character". The name of this *dharma* is *"pati-bhakti"* (which term can be translated as "husband-devotion", meaning the unquestioning loyalty of the wife to her husband.) Rabindranath has drawn parallels between *pati-bhakti* and *raj-bhakti* or *prabhu-bhakti* (i.e. devotion to the king or master). "If *prabhu-bhakti* is taken as *dharma*, then there is no loss of humanity in the servant. The same can be said for *raj-bhakti*". But the master-servant or king-subject relationship is one of dominator and dominated. The triumph of the dominator lies in successfully concealing the nature of this dominance from the dominated. The metaphysical idealisations of religion are extremely successful in concealing the nature of such dominance. From such an idealising viewpoint, Rabi, of *Panchabhuta*, says of the *"punyaha"* ritual, "one owns the land. Someone else pays him rent for the land. This bare contract is sought to be beautified for the sake of the embarrassed human soul". Srotoshwini says, "when there is high and low in the world, which is not to be destroyed unless creation itself ends, then the existence of an unbreakable bond between the high and the low makes it easier to bear the burden of the high".

Srotoshwini's utterance is a statement of Rabindranath's political beliefs of this time. Just as the dominated needs idealisations to bear the burden of being dominated, so too does the dominator need idealisations to "carry the weight" of his dominance. It is from this idealising perspective that Rabindranath found Beauty in the "unbeautiful faces of the ignorant farmers" of his family's *zamindari*, and could write, "the docility I see here is a docility that has divine sanction. It is not surprising that Rabindranath will introduce "woman" in his consideration of the "beauty" of farmers in this essay entitled "Palligram" from *Panchabhuta*. "I have already said that such beauty depends on permanance. ... In human society, Woman is comparatively the most enduring; Man has always been restlessly influenced by many kinds of work, many situations, many transformations; woman has *reigned* enduringly as Mother and Wife, no revolution has disturbed or divided her. Thus, is woman so beautifully intermixed with the very essence of what constitutes society".

In this essay, one finds the following dichotomies :

Village	City
Belief/Permanence/Beauty	Skepticism/Restlessness/ Glamour
Woman	Man

1. It is noticeable that this essay celebrates "permanence". "When, after having endured for a long time, debate, reason, knowledge gradually become a permanent part of Tradition, of a belief-system, only then do they become beautiful". If one has to label Rabindranath's political beliefs at this time, it seems most justified to call them "Liberal", and supportive of the status-quo.

In *Panchabhuta*, there are two women among the five protagonists, Deepti, and Srotoshwini. Deepti is somewhat aggressive, while Srotoshwini is gentle. The writer's sympathies are with Srotoshwini, his antipathy towards Deepti is all too apparent. It may well be that these two characters were based on two women of the Tagore family who were close to Rabindranath, namely, Sarala and Indira. Rabindranath is said not to have been too fond of Sarala whose conversation and laughter were considered loud. Indira, whose every gesture was mild and gentle, was Rabindranath's favourite. Could it be Rabindranath's antipathy towards Sarala, however mild, may have been due to her insistence of independence, an insistence which led her to take a job and move to distant Mysore.

2. Women's education was a much discussed and debated issue in late 19th century Bengal. That the British had no hesitation in spelling out the real reasons for the introduction of educational reforms in India is apparent from the Charter Act of 1854. Apart from the needs of governance, another major reason for such colonial education was to keep intact the growing Indian market for goods and commodities produced in

rapidly industrialising England. The British had never wanted the economic self-sufficiency or the intellectual independence of India. In the debates about women's education one finds strong echoes of this. What are the aims of women's education, what should be the syllabus for such education - there was no dearth of debate and discussion on these issues. And women, too, participated in these discussions. In the Tagore family, there was considerable emphasis on women's education. Women of the house, whether daughters or wives, went to educational institutions, sometimes English governesses would be employed to educate the women of the household. All this has been written about and is well known. However, it is clear from the descriptions of the educational arrangements that there were considerable differences in the way men and women were educated in this family - a fact not often pointed out.

What was the aim of women's education for the Tagores? The introduction to the autobiography of Rasasundari Devi was written by Jyotirindranath Tagore. There, he complimented her on the grounds that her perseverance and desire to acquire knowledge was driven by her need to study religious texts. Jyananandini Devi wrote in *Bharati*, "keeping the house in beautiful order, grace in her dress, increasing the happiness of the family, caring for the unwell, arranging for and cooking meals, and the proper rearing of children - the woman who masters such essential knowledge and then goes on to learn other things for the improvement of her mind, others' pleasure, or the benefit of the nation" is to be complimented. What this list omits is the need for education that will make women self-reliant. Krishnabhabini, in her essay "Shikshita Nari" had written of circumstances that would require self-reliance on a woman's part and spoken of the usefulness of education in achieving this end. And it is precisely this that had led to Rabindranath's attack on her views.

Sanatkumari Chaudhurani, a close acquaintance of the Tagore family, has spoken of the need for women's education in her essay "Ekaal O Ekaaler Meye", published in *Bharati*. She had, in her essay, spoken several times of the need for education in ensuring a good marriage for a young woman, but had entirely omitted to mention the emancipatory potential of education for women. Rabindranath discussed these two essays, Krishnabhabini's "Shikshita Nari" and Sanatkumari's "Ekaal O Ekaaler Meye", in a piece he published in *Sadhana*. If we read these essays today, Sanatkumari's piece will appear rather lightweight when compared to the logical arguments put forward by Krishnabhabini in her essay. Yet, Rabindranath had unstinted praise for Sanatkumari's essay and offered strong adverse criticism to Krishnabhabini. The way in which gender politics is tied to the discourse regarding women's education is wonderfully illustrated in this essay by Rabindranath. Criticising Krishnabhabini, he wrote, "She who is born a mother at Nature's command must acquire education not to sell but to distribute [freely]". Then, is it proper for a *man* to sell education ? He who distributes his knowledge freely, and does not sell it, is considered the true *Brahmin*. So, why this stricture meant particularly for women ? Alongwith the spread of women's education, the role to be played by educated women was also being defined by a male-dominated society.

Rabindranath's strictures often seem to be the official pronouncements of that patriarchal society. "Our opinion is that Mothers, Aunts, Sisters should raise our children properly by giving them food and education up to a certain age. This is their duty . . . . That the children's book under discussion is the work of an educated woman is a cause for particular happiness. I have already said that the imparting of education to children is a major success of women's education". (From a review of Hemlata Devi's book, *Bharatbarsher Itihaas,* published in *Bharati*, 1898.

3. Of course, Rabindranath has also defined the role and duty of women outside the realm of education. "There are some ugly women in this world who cannot arouse a feeling of beauty even when they are bedecked in a thousand fineries". ("Sahityer Satya", in *Sadhana*, 1891.) It is for this reason that even Chitrangada has to borrow beauty and feminine charms to seduce and conquer her beloved. Apparently, the relationship between Chitrangada and Arjun is not one of dominance and subservience. It is not parallel to the master-servant or king-subject relationship. But, in actual fact, even this relationship is heirarchical, it possesses hidden boundaries and observes unspoken interdictions. It may be said that the very alphabet of heterosexual love contains this hidden interdiction - there is no possibility of a life for a woman which is independent of a man. In enabling Arjun to transcend the boundaries of Chitrangada's physical beauty and see, and love, her real, unadorned self, Rabindranath is transcending the limits of late 19th century Bengal, where Bankimchandra's heroes and heroines remain transfixed by physical beauty. Yet, even Chitrangada wants to remain beside Arjun, in giving herself to him is her existence justified.

However, Rabindranath also says that there is no possibility of fulfilment in a *man's* life, which is independent of a woman. Man remains trapped in his self-created prison, in his male pride. Only Woman can set him free. This is very different from the age-old Indian concept of *moksha* which is predicated on the renunciation of *Kamini* and *Kanchan*. In *Valmikipratibha*, the disguised Saraswati brings Ratnakar from greed to music; *Prakritir Pratishad's* young girl wants to return the *Sanyasi* from renunciation to life; *Bisarjan's* beggar-girl Aparna is finally successful in bringing Raghupati from the temple of power and pride to the ordinary path of real life; and Nandini brings the king outside his net, gives him life instead of a mechanised existence, in *Raktakarabi*. But an opposite picture is also present in Rabindranath's works. *Chaturanga's* Sachis, or Ananda in *Chandalika*, consider staying away from women an integral part of their quest.

There is, in fact, no contradiction in these apparently contradictory pictures. Patriarchy sees women and men through the Nature-Culture dichotomy. For patriarchy, on the one hand, Culture is the fruit of consciousness, whereas Nature is unconscious, primitive, primal. On the other hand, patriarchy sees, in modern civilisation, culture as urban and artificial where Nature has remained rural and natural. Woman, seen as Nature, can hinder Man by binding him to her primitive unconscious self. Here, she is Man's obstacle. Again, Woman, seen as Nature, can rescue Man from his urban, artificial self. Here she helps Man's fulfilment.

This Nature-Culture dichotomy carries an unexpressed power relation, for culture has developed through dominating/supressing Nature in human civilisation. When women and men are seen in terms of this Nature-Culture dichotomy, there remains unstated this same power relation. Rabindranath's works are not free of this dichotomy, nor can we expect them to be so. For who can deny history ?

No writer can escape her or his literary inheritance, not even the greatest of geniuses. Men and women both have to accept socially defined roles. These roles define the limits of the emotional configurations that have been composed over many eons. Self-aware human beings want to transcend these socially-defined gender roles. This leads to a dialecties of conflicting desires.

In Rabindranath's works, we have seen the playing out of conventional gender politics, yet, he has also successfully overcome the limitations of this politics. That is why there are so many strong female characters in his works,even in those written in the 19th century. In his story "Shasti" Chandra finally sees the "demon-husband" instead of the "divine-lord". In protesting against the tyranny of her husband, Shashikala gives up her life in the story "Didi". "*Maanbhanjan*" has Giribala renouncing her kin status in protest against her husband's heartless insults and tortures. In the 20th century, especially from the time of *Sabujpatra*, Rabindranath articulates the voices of feminine protest in a new key. Then it is no longer protests against a husband's tyranny. It is then that we hear, in the voice of *Streer Patra's* Mrinal, or *Jogajog's* Kumud, the desire for emancipation in a woman which is not dependent on a man. The infinite possibilities of a woman's existence are given utterance in many of the poems of Rabindranath's last years. We have seen Woman throw off the demure, domestic wifely form in a poem like "Sabala", a story like "Aparichita".

Not just this, even his discussions of the politics of the man-woman relationship undergo a fundamental change from the 19th to the 20th century. In a discussion published in 1927, Rabindranath wrote, "For whatever physiological or psychological reasons, women have to depend on men for their livelihood. Men want to take advantage of this situation to extract whatever price they fancy for this dependence. A man who is dependent on another man for his livelihood has to give up his independence to the extent that he depends on someone else. In fact, even more than the degree of his dependence. It is over this issue that there is today, in Europe, a conflict between capitalists and workers. And the same conflict is going on there between women and men".

It is noticeable that Rabindranath is no longer asking women or workers to accept theiir burden with the help of religious idealisations. Rather he is protesting the oppressor's unfair assertion of his demands. "Men boast of dominance because dominance is a part of barbarism . . . . It is precisely because the British have conquered India that it is so difficult for this external [imperial] power to wholly understand India. A man who judges a woman by measuring her against the list of his rights of dominance over a woman is a man who manifests the worst form of barbarism . . ." It is best natural that Rabindranath's political beliefs will change in the course of his long career.

Perhaps another parallel may be involved in this context. Rabindranath never supported the armed revolutionary movement to overthrow the British *raj,* but helped individual revolutionaries, nevertheless. These revolutionaries took inspiration from his songs and poems. Similarly, he may not have been a supporter of feminism, especially of feminism in our country, but when there was a conflict between women and society, he was always supportive of women. And even today, there is nothing to compare with Rabindranath's writings when it comes to raising the feminist consciousness of our country.

(Translated from the original article in Bengali by Samantak Das)

5

Revolutions : Parampara : Women

Rama Kundu

I

Jane Flax, in her article '*Re-Membering the Selves*' (1987) spoke of the possibility of reading three parallel histories into every culture : 'his', 'hers' and 'ours' among which 'his' and 'ours' often tend to become equivalent. Indeed, if we consider important historical movements and revolutions across time and space, the indifference shown to the 'she'—either in policy matters or in action—seems striking. 'She' remains voiceless, imperceptible in the saga of male 'sound and fury', though it is often 'she' who has to bear the brunt at times of war the 'breaking(or making) of nations'. Yet what does she achieve after all her suffering and sacrifice ? A case in point is Bangladesh. The noblest and saddest martyrs for the cause of a free Bangladesh were the women there. But how many of them could even go back 'home' when independent Bangladesh was born at last ? The bitterness and pain that seeps through Tasleema Nasreen's writings also holds up a small mirror to us to see whether after all the bloodshed and suffering the woman's position has improved or deteriorated ? Due to her protest against the unfairness that Tasleema was branded, threatened and finally had to go on a lonely exile.

Bangladesh is no isolated phenomenon. More than two centuries ago the French Revolution had celebrated the victory with slogans of fraternity, there was no separate charter for the sisters, nor was there promise of any new rights. Linda Kauffman in *Gender and Theory* (1989) has shown how neither the rationalism in England nor the revolution in France did bring about any change in the woman's situation in the respective countries : "Just as women's position did not change, and the feminist voices fell silent in the trap of Enlightened Reason's dominance, so too the Revolution in France merely confirmed "Reason's iron hold on the social order" and whatever hope or conviction thus might carry for men, "for women, at least, the Revolution represented no such release from servitude".

These two apparently unconnected examples from twentieth-century Asia and eighteenth-century France are tips of the iceberg that has remained undisturbed and pervasive through millenia. Not only in the remote pre-Christ and post-Christ centuries but also in the post-Renaissance history till date, the question of women's dignity, right and social position has not come under purview of even pioneer philosophers or leaders—messiahs of revolutions.

Machiavelli is one of the earliest modern pragmatic thinkers who replaced religion-oriented political morality by pragmatic utilitarianism; yet in one respect Machiavelli shows no shift from the orthodox stance. A full chapter of *The Discourses* (this chapter is not so widely discussed as the others)—is devoted to prove 'How States are ruined on account of women'. Here the writer maintains that the woman, by means of her sexuality and corruption, may so tempt the man that he may lose his rationality and confuse personal affairs with state affairs therefore, in the area of state activities the woman is an undesirable, potentially dangerous element who is to be kept at bay. Machiavelli represents here an ancient heritage which rules across the globe and casts its shadow over countless pagan, Christian, Arabian, Indian, Far Eastern myths. For example, it is Helen, not Paris, who is held responsible in the male-written discourse for the destruction of Troy; it's Eve, not Adam, who is blamed for "man's first disobedience" and subsequent woes. In the Hindu's *Manusmriti* the woman figures as 'the doorstep to hell'; and the *Arabian Nights* festers with adulterous licentious, treacherous *femme fatales*.

Machiavelli also contends that a statesman is not to be judged by what he does within the four walls of his home, whereas a woman is to be judged only by the standard of personal/domestic morality. This dichotomy held good for the European psyche till the other day as was evident from the prolonged refusal to grant women the franchise.

In some of the former colonies under European imperialism women had snatched franchise as part of the freedom struggle, though this was by no means the common pattern. Gandhiji had invited Indian women to join the freedom movement, and had declared that public life became "purer" with their arrival in the field. Other leaders in our times or any other do not appear to have shown such respect to women. But after independence the democratic constitution of India dribbled before the issue of women's rights, and quickly came to an understanding through the backdoor with orthodox religion-oriented superstitions and customs. Thus there remained a separate set of 'personal laws' for each community, which were based on the respective religion of the community concerned, and according to each of them the woman's status and rights were inferior to and less than those of the male citizen of the same community. Thus, a new born modern egalitarian society robbed half of its citizens of equal rights. However, in view of the ways of the wide world and the sequences of the great world revolutions it does not really seem that strange.

The impact of Rousseau's thoughts on the French Revolution is commonly acknowledged. His idea that 'man' was born free but chained to society was an inspiration for the freedom-loving mind. But how did Rousseau think about women ? In *Emile*, Rousseau said that women were perpetual slaves to their own sex impulses, and therefore could not develop the kind of rationality necessary for participating in "formal political culture"; the appropriate place for all women was within and all men had social responsibility.

The epoch-making influence of liberal thinkers like Hobbes on modern politics is common knowledge. Pateman in her book *The Sexual Contract (1988)* shows how Hobbes's theory of 'social contract' starts by accepting the sexual contract. In *Leviathan* 'family' includes a man with his children and slaves, where the father/master is the supreme authority. When a man conquers another male/female he gets a slave. What remains unnoticed is the basic difference between the male slave and the female; the subordination of the female involves sex slavery from whose complicated trap she will never be able to come out. Is it possible that the memory of this ancient pattern of helpless subordination/slavery still conditions the woman's response in such a complex way that she easily comes to adjust with inequality, and to remain protestless and contented in spite of injustice? Betty Friedan (*The Feminine Mystique* 1963) feels disturbed at the evidence of this operation of the millenia-old memory within the feminine psyche, which she located in woman's "identity-limiting nostalgias of place". On the other hand, pushing the woman off the wider social arena into the 'safe' home, the men, the residents of the social contract-based Leviathan or 'unruined' (by women) state, fight for sovereignty over their own respective lands.

Modern social thinkers are but continuing this heritage. Christin Sylvester in her book *Feminist Theory and International Relations in a Postmodern Era* exposes this irony : "Women always figured in modern social theory awkardly". As example she alludes to the classical Marxists who use to say : "Women producers laboured in ways that were not susceptible to technological modernization and so this category of persons was outside history". This idea is that in the context of the revolution of production relations women are irrelevant since the area of their labour is unorganised and unmodern; so history will be created by men, as children are created by women. The step to the Marxian utopia is the abolition of private ownership over the means of production. For the bourgeoisie his wife is just another means of production. So the utopia would achieve the abolition of the family and its replacement by 'community of women' (*Manifesto of the Communist* Party, Ch.2.). Here Marx's argument is vague and self-contradictory. Once he says, community of women has all along been there and the Communists were aiming nothing new; again he says, since "our bourgeoisie...take the greatest pleasure in seducing each other's wives", the present bourgeois marriage, therefore, is but "a system of wives in common". And again : "It is self-evident that the abolition of the present system of production must bring with it the abolition of the community of women springing from that system, i.e., of prostitution both public and private". If the married woman is a means of production owned by her husband and at the same time a consumer good, the revolution is supposed to abolish only private ownership. But does not necessarily change the role/status/identity of the woman or leave her branded as just another article/means of production, and/or a consumer good ?

Since Marxism identifies class as the source of all problems, the woman's special problem remains ignored. Hence, a section of modern feminists finds Marxism uncongenial to women's interest. As Heidi Hartmann says : "The marriage of marxism and feminism has been like the marriage of husband and wife depicted in English common law; marxism and feminism are one, and that one is marxism'. Recent attempts to integrate marxism and feminism are unsatisfactory to us as feminists because they subsume the feminist struggle into 'larger' struggle against the capital. To continue our simile further, either we need a healthier marriage or we need a divorce" ('The Unhappy Marriage of Marxism and Feminism').

Indeed, no so-called revolutionary 'ism' has ever given an appropriate voice to the aspirations of women for dignity and fulfilment. Though Mao-Tse-Tung was supposed to be a man closer to the 'good earth' than Marx, he too did not envision women in pioneering revolutionary role; neither did he specially consider the question of her dignity or assertion as woman. He had just seen them as a vast protential labour force, and a shrewd calculation seems to inform the programme : "Solving the labour shortage by arousing the women to join in production" (*Quotations* 1955). No wonder, she continues in the same supportive role through the 49 years of revolution. During the first phase of revolution when there was no birth control, she had to shoulder the endless burden of bearing and rearing as the 'means of production'. Today after the introduction of one-child policy female foetus is being killed; after giving birth to female child the mother is often maltreated and deserted by her husband. This is the woman's position in a communist country after almost half-a-century of revolution.

In Russia, after seventy years of revolution in the name of Marx and Lenin, Gorbachev had dared to take the bold step of Perestroika. But it is interesting to note how even from this courageous, modern, liberal programme the woman remains exiled. The third section of the second chapter of *Perestroika* is not so widely discussed : "....We have discovered that many of our problems...are partially caused by the weakening of family ties and slack attitude to family responsibilities This is a paradoxical result of our sincere and politically justified desire to make women equal with men in everything. Now... the question ...(is) what we should do to make it possible for women to return to their purely womanly mission". Even a visionary and liberal like Gorbachev seems to represent here the gender-biased milieu and does not seem much different from some orthodox patriarch a millenium ago. This only shows how deep the roots of orthodox notions are regarding women. This is the Taliban voice.

It may seem curious that the rising religious fundamentalism in India and abroad today speaks in a tune not much different from Gorbachev in this matter. Indeed, all the religious movements that have taken place so far, conservative or liberal, including radical movements like Christianity, Buddhism, or the Ramkrishnaite cult, have always resulted in further damaging the woman's status.

Examples come crowding in and there could be an endless list, including the protestant upheaval in England, the industrial revolution of Europe, the scientific revolution that started in the seventeenth century and *et al.* Not a single of these cultures recognised the woman as an individual in her own right. Christine Sylvester analyses these various movements in her book in order to show how the attitude regarding the woman's status and rights remains basically unchanged after all the social-political-economic-religious exercises in utopia.

"The modern world is one in which western people called women have a domestic script to follow, a household place in which to follow it, and a set of *rabid* aesthetic and cultural guidelines *for success* that 'scientific' studies help to bolster . . ."

It is apparent from the above bird's eye survey that the third world women as well as her first world counterpart have been excluded from all dreams/visions of 'great' thinkers; because the bastion is not anywhere outside; it has been embedded within the collective unconscious over milennia across the globe. Considering from this perspective one feels like asking how revolutionary the revolutions of the past really were. If society can ever emerge from this heritage of gender-bias that will be the greatest revolution of history. In the meantime, to speak in Sylvester's words : "We will remember that recognition is a hard-fought battle when one is among the excluded".

II

Parampara : Woman : The Indian Scene

The battle becomes a thousand times more difficult in the case of a tradition-bound society like India where ancient social customs or *parampara* however unjust they may be, are still upheld by the general public, and where rejection of the same requires tremendous courage. Last year we celebrated the bi-centenary of Raja Rammohun Roy who is remembered, among other things, for his extraordinary work as a champion for the woman's cause. That the woman also needed happiness, peace, security was an assumption that went against the ancient *parampara* of the Indian Hindu Society of Roy's time, as it was, and is, against the grain of any religion-oriented society. To think about the women in the above terms, and to attempt to do something for them meant a dangerous departure from the norm. Roy had staked life-property-reputation-peace in order to adopt a few programmes for women which were extraordinary considering his time. What Roy had started was carried further ahead by another great man, Vidyasagar, and a number of idealistic young men of the time who were inspired by these noble examples. A far-reaching consequence of this process was that women of a layer of the Indian society got some scope at last, and by utilising that scope, slowly emerged in course of two centuries, -- first in handful then in bulk in the various fields of higher education, professional works, pursuit of scientific/other studies, creative arts, politics, social work, research, business administration, mountaineering, even writing world-famous books. Yet this is only an illusory picture of only one facet, or the tip of the iceberg. The huge submerged reality remains cruel and ugly. The unpleasant truth is that the perception of the society regarding women has basically undergone no radical change in vast areas of life. To cite just a few evidences : advanced technology is being used, not to promote scientific rationalism, but to detect and kill the female foetus; dowry is steeply on the rise in spite of legislations, and bride-burning too is common.

Discrimination against and contempt towards women continue to prevail in social attitudes and get translated in individual and social action. Burnt brides die unwept. Rarely does a rape victim get legal justice; the norm is pervasive social condemnation often leading the victim to suicide. The husband is generally obsessed with age-old notions of proprietory rights over his wife and her servile status. In case a marriage breaks up the divorcee woman finds it hard to fend for herself and the child (if any) amidst sneering unsympathy and contempt. In the poorer strata food,education, health and all the privileges are still the male child's prerogative. Women placed at different rungs of our multi-layered society have to confront different kinds of problems. The professisonal woman, the housewife, the urban poor, the rural poor, each category is being affected in some way by the tradition-bound society, and the dehumanization of the woman continues at all levels.

Orthodoxy has always been a strong force in our society, and terms like Parampara/Sanatan Dharma/Shariat are still dangerously appealing in this subcontinent. The revived religious fundamentalism of the recent decades, alongwith the growing criminalization of society and political opportunism may pose real threats to women's rights and status here like the Taliban experience in Afganisthan.

For the modern woman of the subcontinent the struggle is far from being over. Not fringe benefits, or piecemeal solutions; she has got to throw overboard the tradition itself that inhibits her, cripples her, and hypnotizes her to get herself fitted into myths of self-sacrificing self-effacing women. It is perhaps an assuring sign that in the 1990s some young women writers of this subcontinent, including Tasleema Nasreen (*Nirbachita Kalam*,1992), Githa Hariharan (*The Thousand Faces of Darkness*,1992), and Arundhati Roy (*The God of Small Things,*1997) have been challenging the very validity of the tradition that shackled and crippled the woman, preventing her to have 'a story of her own' (Hariharan), her "Locusts Stand I" (Roy).

Reference

1. This section on 'Revolutions' is a summarized form of my article 'Revolutions and the Exile' (*The Radical Humanist*, New Delhi, Oct. 1997) which gives further details and more information on the subject.

6

Society, Women in Bengal and Brahmo Samaj: Historicity and Present Relevance

Aruna Mukherjee

Society is a web of human interaction and interrelations. It renders mutual service to men and makes them acquainted with one another. Family is the first and the smallest unit of the society based on biological interdependence of men and women. Each by itself is incomplete and seeks fulfillment with the help of the other. Thus, man and woman can be termed as two wheels of that chariot which keeps society moving. There is fundamental difference between these two sexes which can never be eradicated so long as mankind continues to exist. However, this very fundamental difference has become a deciding factor of the fate of women in society for centuries.

In the tribal phase of the society the status of woman was very low. She was being used as a possessed item. She was merely a slave to the men-folk of that society. The men during this period were mainly barbarians. They lived on hunting alone. The technique of hunting was inaccessible to women. This required immense physical strength which women naturally lacked.

The position of women became slightly better when the pattern of livelihood changed from hunting to cultivation. Women started controlling the fields and thus became the sole controller of food. Men were forced to change their attitude towards them. This period was known as high kinship phase. Women during this period attained a position which she never recaptured in the course, of all subsequent evolution.

In the late kinship phase again the scales dipped unequally low between man and woman. The idea of acquiring wealth as a means of exchange, became once again concentrated in the male hands. This enabled them to regain domination over women. Once again they were reduced to the status of the minors.

The industrial revolution brought major changes in the life of women. It had thrown open before them various careers. She regained her economic freedom which gave her initiative not only in the domestic field but also in the public field. However, this condition prevailed only in the developed countries specially in Europe. The women of the economically and industrially backward countries like India were still subject to hardship and servitude. The light of renaissance was far away from them even during the late eighteenth century.

Though the British came to India in the sixteenth century, they could firmly establish their presence only in the mid-eighteenth century. Since their victory lap started from Bengal, the socio-economic and cultural life of Bengal had undergone a big stir during this period.

Bengal like all other provinces of India was then under the spell of illiteracy, superstitions and blind faith of an orthodox society. The society was completely unaware of the great revolution that changed the life of the Europeans. The men and women were still in the medieval stage where woman was a subject to her master doing only household and other such duties which men never thought of sharing. However, there were exceptions in some of the higher castes.

The incoming of the British in Bengal brought a fresh wave of European ideology which roused the society from their medieval torpor and gave a rude shock to their cherished ideas and institutions. In every sphere of life they met the challenge of a new culture which forced them to revise their orthodox ideas and to make a reevaluation of their old concepts. A greater section of the Bengali society gave up their attitude of uncritical deference to authority, tradition and customs and became the pioneers of almost all movements for social and political reforms.

Though the above picture was very true for the male section of the society, women were still living under the most abject form of social subservience. Among them the married class was the most deprived ones. The husband and other members of the family were all her masters. She was treated worse than the inferior animals. If she happened to incur the displeasure of her husband, she could be cast aside by him any moment in favour of a more fortunate rival. The law afforded no protection against such a fate. The fate was even worse after the death of her husband. She was burnt alive against her will in most of the cases along with the dead husband. This cruel custom was given a religious coating since religious parametres were never questioned in society. Such was the level of ignorance till the end of the eighteenth and the beginning of the nineteenth century.

But there is always a silver lining whenever such dark clouds of injustice engulf society. Raja Rammohan Roy appeared on the scene as a saviour of the women of Bengal. He was the pioneer of religious movements and social reforms and was a brilliant product of the impact of western education upon Indian culture. A true humanist and a reformer, he wanted to raise the society from the slough of superstition and despondency. With this object he founded the Brahmo Samaj in 1828. It was a theistic organisation open to all who believed in the unity of God and discarded the worship of images. His idealism was based upon the universalism of the Upanisads. Rammohan defended the legal rights of females, advocated their right to education and enlightenment and above all devoted all his energy to save them from cruel death.

In 1812 and 1813 a number of regulations were issued by the then Governor General Lord Moira, which partially restricted the customs of 'Suttee' (compulsive immolation). These regulations were issued in a collected form in 1817. But to everyone's surprise it was found that during these years (1815-1817) a total of 1,328 widows had been burnt alive in Calcutta itself and nearby areas. The publication of the regulations by the Government created a commotion in the orthodox Hindu Society and a petition was sent to the Governor praying for their abrogation. This petition evoked a counter-petition from Rammohan Roy and his friends in August, 1818 where the following text was there : "Your petitioners are fully aware from their own knowledge and from authority of credible eye-witness, that cases have frequently occurred where women have been induced by the persuasion of their next heirs, interested in their destruction, to burn themselves on the funeral pile of their husbands . . . . All these instances, your petitioners humbly submit, are murders according to any Shastras, as well as to the common sense of all nations".[1]

Rammohan Roy truly understood the agony of women and thus appealed on their behalf : "Women are in general inferior to men in bodily strength and energy, consequently the male part of the community, taking advantage of corporeal weakness have denied to them those excellent merits that they are entitled to by nature, and afterwards they are apt to say that women are naturally incapable of acquiring those merits. But if we give the subject consideration we may easily ascertain whether or not your accusation against them is consistent with justice".[2]

Rammohan however did not confine himself only to lectures and writing articles on these issues. He formed a vigilance committee with his friends and always kept a regular vigil on whether any force was employed during 'Suttee' and also if the other requirements of the law, as laid down in the regulation were fulfilled. Thus, this intense fight went on till Lord W. Bentinck took the final decision on the subject in December 1829.

One more aspect is worth mentioning here that of Rammohan's concern for the Hindu inheritence law in which he showed how the ancient rights of the female on property were encroached. In one of his articles published in 1822 he decried polygamy and described the miserable condition in which widows lived, indirectly proving thereby that their self-immolation in many cases was an escape from greater misery perpetuated on them after their husbands' death.

The stalwarts of the nineteenth century Bengal renaissance were all connected with the Brahmo Samaj. The work begun by Rammohan was carried forward by people like Devendra Nath Tagore and Keshub Chandra Sen, a very powerful preacher. Keshub Chandra's fervent devotion, wonderful eloquence and missionery zeal carried the influence of Brahmo Samaj even outside Bengal. Everywhere the Samaj played a notable part as a reforming and uplifting agency.

Another pioneer of Bengal renaissance was Iswar Chandra Vidyasagar. He himself was not a member of the Brahmo Samaj but had good connections with the Samaj in many ways. He was a member of the Tattwabodhini Sabha. Iswar Chandra also fought for the cause of women. Widow remarriage and education were the two things for which he devoted his entire life. He was also against child marriage and polygamy. In his fight for these social injustice the Brahmo Samaj stood by his side.

Literacy and education of women in Bengal apparently were started by the Buddhists. Though in the Vedic age women had access to education only the daughters and wives of saints were among the few lucky ones who received education. But in the period when the Brahmins dominated the society women lost all these rights and were not allowed to utter even the very word 'OM', whereas, Buddhist women ('Bheekshunis') were allowed to perform as priests. They could read all the Shastras. The Yogini were also educated in the early eighth century. Laksimkara, a yoginies was one of the highly educated woman of eastern India of that period.

These are only few examples of educated women of Bengal. In fact, female education was not at all popular in the eighteenth century society. The Vaishnava community was the only one where some educated ladies were present. Literacy and education were obligatory for the Vaishnava devotees for reading of Bhagavata Purana and recital of poems and songs from 'Padavali'.

Female education was formally introduced in Bengal during the British rule as a necessary step for securing a supporting background for the education of boys. The idea behind was that a literate mother is a boon to the family. She can bring her child up better and can give him early education. Thus, some educational institutions came up in the city of Kolkata where girls could get their preliminary education till they attained marriageable age. This programme was not very successful in the villages as the village girls were more occupied with household and other jobs.

The contribution of Brahmo Samaj towards female education in Bengal was mainly connected with the social system through which they were able to change the values and attitudes of the common people regarding this very issue. The Tattvabodhini Sabha set up by Debendra Nath Tagore did the work of stimulating intellectuals and in awakening a concern for social welfare. The members of the Sabha were almost all great intellectuals of Bengal of the 1840s and 1950s. They contributed enlightening articles in the journal Tattaavabodhini Patrika. Akshay Kumar Dutta and Ishwar Chandra Vidyasagar were also members of this Sabha. Debendra Nath's association with these gifted thinkers and men of action had some effect on the evolution of the Brahmo creed. A number of his followers, including men like Ramtanu Lahiri became founder members and active workers of the 'Samajonnati Vidhayini Suhrid Samity' and 'Sarbashubhakari Sabha'. Their main concerns were social reforms and uplift affecting women in particular and the spread of female education.[3]

For spreading the idea of education among women some drastic steps were necessary which changed the prevailing customs and values. The Brahmo Samaj took the lead in this direction. When Debendra Nath Tagore had Keshub Chandra Sen ordained as a minister of the Samaj in April 1862, Keshub's wife was present at the ceremony. This was unusual even for the Brahmo Samaj for so far only men attended public prayer meetings. Keshub was responsible for starting 'Brahmica Samaj' in 1865. The ladies here met to have discussions or to listen to lectures. In 1866 an arrangement was made so that women could sit behind screens in the hall during prayers. In 1871, some Brahmo wives accompanying their husbands occupied seats in the open portion of the prayer hall hitherto meant only for men and since this led to a bitter controversy, a compromise was effected by keeping reserved seats for women in the general area. In 1878, Manorama Majumdar, wife of Girish Chandra Majumdar conducted the prayer of Brahmo Samaj in Barishal. Since that time Brahmo women have regularly officiated as ministers in religious services. In 1889 two Brahmo ladies attended the session of the Indian National Congress held at Bombay as delegates. One was Swarna Kumari Devi, Debendra Nath's daughter and the other was Kadambini Ganguly, the first Indian woman to qualify as a doctor.[4] The incidents mentioned above show that there was a gradual transformation of attitude towards women by the society where the women had started reestablishing their socio-cultural identity in a definitive way and according to the changing social scenario. This can no doubt be termed no less than a revolution in the society from the perspective of women participation in the social life of Bengal.

The most important landmark in the history of female education in Bengal was the foundation of a school in 1849 by John Drinkwater Bethune. He realized that unless and until girls from higher class families were ifluenced to join the schools the mission of female education would not flourish. His mission became successful when the enlightened Brahmo families came forward to help him. Thus, girls from Tagore and other renowned families joined the school. Soudamini Devi, Rabindra Nath Tagore's eldest sister was one of the first students of this school. The founder of the school was not from the Brahmo Samaj but the pupils and the governing body members were mostly from the Samaj. Gradually the school became very popular and was raised to the status of a college. The college laid the foundation of higher education for the women of Bengal on a firm ground. It is interesting to note that the first lecturer appointed to Bethune College was a highly respected member of the Brahmo Samaj. Most of the women teachers who were graduates for the first four decades were all from Brahmo families.

Two significant steps were taken by the Brahmos as early as 1860, one of these being 'Antapur Stree Siksha' or a programme of study which could be performed at home by women. They appeared in examinations at respective homes where sealed question papers were supplied to them. The other step was the publication of a journal named 'Bamabodhini Patrika' for the enlightenment of women. This journal also encouraged them to contribute articles for it.

Thus, gradually the social reform and female education movement started spreading beyond Calcutta to other parts of Bengal. Many associations sprang up to promote this noble cause. Though all these associations were not directly connected to the Brahmo Samaj they were very much influenced and supported by the members of the Samaj, like Bipin Chandra Pal, Sundari Mohan Das, Dwaraknath Ganguly, Ananda

Mohan Bose, Shib Nath Shastri and many others. The first 'Hindu Widows' Home and school in Bengal was started by Shashipada Banerjee. 'Sevabrata' (the name of the Home) was located at Baranagar. This Home existed for nearly forty years since its inception.

Along with the male members of the Samaj, the Brahmo women also worked for the cause of women's emancipation from social evils and exploitation. This was an ideal situation when men and women were fighting for the same cause. This accelerated the programme of women's education throughtout Bengal and its neighbouring States also. The Eden School of Dacca was set up in 1878, the Bankipur Girls' High School in Patna was established by Aghore Kamini Devi (Dr. Bidhan Chandra Roy's mother) in 1892. The Maharani Girls' School in Darjeeling fulfilled a pressing need in that District. The initiative there was taken by Suniti Devi, Maharani of Cooch Behar and the eldest daughter of Keshub Chandra Sen, and Hemlata Sarkar, daughter of Shibnath Shastri. The latter served as Headmistress and advisor there for forty long years.[5]

The spread of education in a wider section of the society and other socio-religious reforms brought drastic changes in the marriage ceremonies of the Brahmo families. The system of 'Sampradana' or making over the bride to the groom by her father was replaced by the exchange of vows by the parties to a marriage. Thus, the legal status of woman was raised to the same level of the groom. She was no more taken as an inanimate object having no wish, say or feeling of her own. The exchange of vows cleared one more obstacle in the way of the development of society, the practice of child marriage. Unless and untill both the parties attained enough maturity mentally and physically to understand the meaning and importance of such vows there could not exist any marriage. "Brahmo marriages according to a reformed ritual from which the idolatrous portions of orthodox Hindu rituals were expunged, began to be celebrated from July,1861. Since then the number of reformed marriages began to multiply and almost evey year witnessed the celebration of one or two of them. The progressives among the Brahmos took another bold step in 1864. The intercaste marriages started that to an accomplished widowed girl of a different caste. The ceremony of mutual vows made the ceremony more western than eastern.

In 1868 the legal validity of the reformed marriages was raised by the other sections.This led to an agitation and became a matter of bitter controversy. "One good however came out of this controversy. The legal insecurity of the reformed marriages was made manifest. One of the contested points in the controversy was the proper marriageable age of Indian girls. Mr.Keshub Chandra Sen at once set himself to work to settle the point. In April 1871 as President of the Indian Reform Association he addressed a circular letter to some of the leading medical authorities in the country, both European and Indian, asking for a statement of their opinionon the subject. The majority of these gentlemen declared sixteen to be the minimum marriageable age for our girls." After much debate fourteen was fixed as the minimum marriageable age for the Indian girls in the new bill which was brought forward on 19th March 1872 and was passed into law as Act III 1872 after three days. This was indeed a crowning glory for the social reformers of the Brahmo Samaj. It abolished not only early marriage but made polygamy penal and sanctioned widow and inter-caste marriages.

Thus after much fight and long waiting the dreams of Raja Rammohan Roy and Vidyasagar were fulfilled. The war launched against social evils and injustice could thus be eradicated for the time being only by enforcing certain Acts and laws. But the question still exists whether the fruits of the reforms are fully available to every woman. It is no doubt a fact that ours is still a male dominated society and there are various examples of the role of women being deliberately downplayed in spite of many social restrictions. To cite a few examples, apathy towards inter-caste marriage or widow marriage, the rituals performed by a daughter in case of the death of her parents, right of worshipping deities, legal ownership and inheritance of properties and to top it all, the girl child is still considered as a liability in comparison to a male one. The son is still considered to be the social baton carrier of a family which is not substantiated. Very interestingly registration of marriages, advocated by the Brahmo Samaj to safeguard the interest of women, is still not a very popular practice in society in spite of the fact that no one can deny the importance of it legally, socially or otherwise. So the problem remains, the attitude towards equality, reverence and acceptability of women in our present day society have not really reached to the stage that the Brahmo Samaj protagonists dreamt of.

Thus, the social reform movement initiated by the Samaj still has plenty of relevance and needs to be reactivated. We are yet to place our women in their ideal status for which blue prints are to be prepared for the implementation and execution of the Brahmo Samaj objectives and to reorganize them with reference to the present day society. Thus, the Brahmo Samaj can provide us with very specific social guidelines in reorientation of social attitude towards women even today.

References

1. *History of the Brahmo Samaj by Sivnath Sastri*, Second edition, 1974, Calcutta, p. 31.
2. *Ibid.*
3. *Bethune College Centenary Volume*,1980, Calcutta Article. "The Brahmo Samaj and Women's Education in 19th Century Bengal" by A.K. Dutta, p. 144.
4. *Ibid*, pp. 145-46.
5. *Ibid*, pp. 151-52.
6. *History of the Brahmo Samaj* by Sivnath Sastri, Second edition 1974, Calcutta (p. 158).
7. *Ibid*, pp. 155-56.

Bibliography

1. *Tattwakaumudi* ed. by Amiya Kumar Banerjee (1900-2000 volume Bengal,1398), "Bharatiya Paribare Narir Maryada"—article by Kshama Mukherjee, p. 101.
2. *Ibid* (9th-1200th Vol.) 'Bharat Barsha Nari Mukti Yuga Yuge'—article by Dr. Madhushri Ghosh (p. 41).
3. *History of Bengal*, Ramesh Chandra Mazumdar, Vol. II & III, 1966 and 1975, Calcutta.
4. *Ram Mohon O Takalin Samaj O Sahitya* - by Probhat Kumar Mukherjee, 1972, Visva-Bharati.

7

Looking Beyond the Individual: Interaction of Structural Factors and Agency in the Empowerment of Women

Bandana Purkayastha

The discourse on *Women's Rights* as *Human Rights*, at the international level, has been a powerful force in moving women's issues from the realm of the private arena to the formal global political stage.It has also revealed fissures in our understanding of what these *women's* issues are and what different groups consider to be empowering to women. Such differences are not surprising. After all thousands of activists around the world bring a variety of cultural backgrounds and experiences to bear on the debate about how to work for women's empowerment. Nevertheless, given the language of the debate (primarily English) and who has access to institutionalised structures for disseminating selected views most widely (usually white middle class activists and scholars in western societies) the discourse on women/human rights is increasingly being framed in terms of individual *vs.* cultural group rights. In this chapter I focus on some of the conceptual contours of this debate and argue that insisting on this dichotomy strengthens other social hierarchies and hurts the cause of most women.

My primary argument is that defining empowerment in terms of individual rights is insufficient to address the multiple causes of women's subordination. I use the recent work of Susan *Moller* Okin as an exemplar of the arguments on individual vs. cultural group rights to discuss the strengths and limitations of the dominant perspective. I argue that the seemingly neutral individual rights model carries within it restrictions on access to rights depending on whether an individual fits the hegemonic standard of race/caste, gender, religion and class. Drawing on cases from India and the US, I advocate working for individual and cultural group rights. My conceptualisation of culture groups moves beyond groups identified on the basis of religion or language and such other pre-given ties and envisions socially constructed communities which are created and recreated within specific contexts. Both affliative and filiative bonds are recognised for defining such cultural groups.

Paths to Empowerment. Bookman and Morgan(1988) state that women's empowerment has commonly been associated with the ability to assert oneself, strive for upward mobility, or attain the psychological state of being powerful. However, the ability of individuals to do these things is dependent on cultural norms and institutional arrangements that regulate their lives. Given the historical separation of the home and public worlds, which has been the cornerstone of the modern state (e.g. Glenn 2000, Pateman 1989), women's movements have focused on examining, challenging and changing the rules and roles that have kept women's needs and achievements outside the purview of the public world. The current emphasis, at the international level, on women's right to move around freely, work outside the home, to bodily integrity, and freedom from violence rise from concerns about the rules and roles which govern everyday lives of women.

The movement for equal rights has been the primary thrust of changing the rules governing women's position in societies. Women's right to vote and access education have been among the most significant issues considered to be crucial for women's empowerment. As a result of centuries of ideological resistance and political action (e.g. Basu,1995), most independent countries grant some recognition to women's rights, although the exact rights vary considerably between societies (Seager and Olson,1986). This emphasis on equal rights led some scholars to distinguish between practical interests of women (meeting needs for food, shelter etc.) and strategic gender interests (challenging patriarchal structures in society) and to denote the latter as more imporant for women's empowerment (Molyneux,1985; or Moser,1993 on how this classification was used in development projects funded by the UN).

However, the primary discourse about women's empowerment-the idea of empowerment through gaining equal rights-has always been challenged by radical feminists who have felt that a separate set of rights were required for the full empowerment for women (see review in Jones,1985 or Shiva,1988; Gilligan,1982). According to this view, equal rights simply allow women the right to complete for masculine achievements. Equal rights do not attend to the rights necessary for attending to activities traditionally associated with women's roles. The equal rights movements won women the right to get the same education and apply for the same jobs and vote, but 'family' issues such as childbirth, child-care, support, nurturing and sustenance of less able family members were all left outside the purview of 'real' work and 'real' societal needs.

In many ways the redefinition of women's rights as human rights address some of these latter, specifically women's concerns. The 1979 Convention on the Elimination of All Forms of Discrimination Against Women (CEDAW) addresses issues such as pregnancy and maternity related health and leave issues, as well as affirmative action for women in education and employment. The 1993 Human Rights conference at Vienna addresses gender based violence including defining rape as a war crime. The 1995 Beijing conference addresses women's right to say no to sexual intercourse.

Thus, two main strands of thought-as rights equal to men and as rights specifically attending to the needs of women-continue to enrich the larger cause of women's empowerment. But as more and more women around the world are able to speak out at a global level, debates continue about the meaning and scope of terms such as women or empowerment. The individual vs. cultural group rights discourse is one among many such debates.

Rights of Individuals. In many ways the recent writing of Susan Moller Okin exemplifies the efforts to frame the ongoing discussion on women's rights as human rights in terms of 'individual vs. cultural group rights' issues. Her work is also relevant here because she frequently uses Indian examples to illustrate her arguments. I will focus primarily on two recent publications - 'Is multiculturalism bad for women?' (1999) and 'Feminism, Women's Rights and Cultural Differences'(1998) - to illustrate the strengths and weaknesses of the approach where cultural group rights [1]are seen as detrimental to individual rights of women.

[1]Okin's definition of cultural groups rests upon the idea of minority cultural groups within the US or Europe and the source societies of such groups in the world stage. From the examples she provides, it appears that she defines such groups in terms of primordial characteristics so that all non-white and non-Christians fall within this category. Except where noted, the terms 'minority group' or 'cultural group' will be used in this sense.

Okin (1998) presents a strong case for making women's rights central to the conceptualisation of human rights. She correctly argues that like the earlier process of defining citizenship based on a male subject and his experiences (e.g. Jones and Jonasdittir,1985; Pateman,1989), the thinking about human rights, at present, reflects a similar gender bias. The human rights discourse and institutionalisation reflects an assumption about separate public and private worlds. Since, the UN Human Rights Commission was established in 1946, human rights have often been conceptualised on an understanding of the individual in the public sphere (see Das,1999; Sacerdoti,1983). Yet this privileging of an individual's rights in the civil and formal political sphere lead to a renewed emphasis on men's experience alone. Women are often victimised in their homes, and focusing on the state alone leaves unattended these other arenas of human rights violations. She argues that 'respecting' cultural differences is often a euphemism for denying or restricting human rights to women. She points to India's granting of civil rights to religio-cultural groups as a clear example of how women's individual rights are violated when cultural groups are given formal rights.

In the multiculturalism essay Okin (1999) continues her arguments that women are best served if cultural groups are not given any political rights. Okin notes the increasing demand by groups—indigenous populations, minority ethnic or religious groups and formerly colonised people - to seek rights against states. She points out that whenever groups are given cultural rights—which mostly equate to rights within the domestic arena such as right to determine laws of marriage, divorce, child custody, division and control of family property and inheritance—these group rights have a greater negative effect on women than men. Thus, she argues, if minority cultures are allowed group rights, the power of the elite within the groups is strengthened and women remain in subordinate positions. She describes women as victims of regressive norms of gender transmitted by families and cultural groups across generations. She emphasises that most religions and minority cultures are far more patriarchal compared to Western majority cultures hence they are part of the problem for women. Okin argues;

In the case of a more patriarchal minority culture in the context of a less patriarchal majority culture, no argument can be made on the basis of self respect or freedom that female members of the culture have a clear interest in its preservation. Indeed, they might be much better off if the culture into which they were born were either to become extinct (so that its members would become integrated into the less sexist surrounding culture) or preferably, to be encouraged to alter itself so as to reinforce the equality of women. (Okin, 1999, pp. 22-23).

Okin's concern about the level of power accessible to women in smaller cultural groups cannot be easily dismissed. The history of women's movements record the bitter struggles within communities as different groups tried to define tradition and culture in their communities. For instance, Karlekar (1994) and Kumar (1993) describe the struggle over women's education in India in the late 19th and early 20th century and shows how orthodox Hindu (Brahmin) community members were able to define 'tradition' for the British Women's history in the US reveals similar struggles over the right to vote or access education during a similar time frame. Examples of contemporary struggles are available from both countries as well. In India, some of the most widely publicised events include the struggles over a Muslim woman's maintenance or glorification of sati among sections of the Hindu community in Rajasthan (see Das 1999, Kishwar 1999, Pathak and Rajan 1989, Rajan 1993). In the US, the contemporary struggle to uphold abortion rights is an ongoing conflict with conservative members of society. Similar accounts are available from other countries (e.g. Basu 1995, Moghadam 1994, Seidman 1999).

While Okin accurately describes the dangers of strengthening the power of the elite within groups, her statements about gender interests and minority cultures requires further examination. Her taken for granted conceptualisation of cultural groups as 'minority groups and/or religions', her assumption that cultural groups do not change unless they are encouraged to do so by western societies, and her conceptualisation of rights as extended to individuals in western societies, carries within them a different set of regressive positions for the vast majority of women.

Re-examining the individual rights vs. cultural rights argument.

Patriarchy vs. matrix of domination

Are a common set of women's/human rights likely to be empowering to all women? The assumption of a universal and common set of women's interests has long been an issue of contention among different groups of scholars and activists. For instance, Okin (1998) has been extremely critical of Chandra Mohanty (1991) who argued that the assumption of common sources of subordination simply marginalises Third World Women whose lives do not match the western white, middle class norm. Okin argues that raising such divisive issues is detrimental to women in general because, in her experience, women around the world have identified patriarchy as the common cause of their subordination.

Whose opposed to this essentialist position argue that hierarchies affecting women and men of different groups work relative to the normative standard of masculinity, i.e. race/caste, class and gender hierarchies *intersect* and *interact* to materially affect women in diverse negative ways (e.g. Connell 1995, Ferree, Lorber and Hess 1999, Hill Collins 1990, Menon 1999, Ray 1999). More importantly, this matrix of domination perspective emphasises that restrictions women encounter often rise from their membership in subordinated groups and it is not possible to separate the experience of gender from the experience of race or class (or age, religion or caste) position (West and Fenstermaker 1995). From this perspective it is difficult to separate the individual woman from the conditions of subordination that arise because of the marginalisation of her cultural group by majority society.

Just as the history of women's activism indicates struggles within cultural groups, these histories also show conflicts among women of different culture and groups. The rejection of British feminist Eleanor Rathborne's offer of help by Indian women leaders of the All India Women's Conference in the earlier part of the 20th century represents a clear division of interests based on their respective positions as colonisers and the colonised (Kumar 1993). Hurtado (1996) describes how women of color in the US use 'urban guerrilla tactics' because neither conventional politics adopted by liberal feminists nor free-spirited approaches of radical feminists attend to the issues such as the historical and contemporary loss of their children (to slave owners or due to state sponsored violence). Or in more recent times, collections on women's movements' around the world (Basu 1995, Moghadam 1994) point to economic and religious marginalisation within hegemonic cultures as important factors in understanding what subordinates women in specific locales. The women and development literature similarly point to the large scale dislocation and eroding of women's status because of how the global capitalistic world system operates and marginalises them (e.g. Chang 1997, Meis and Shiva 1993, Shiva 1988, Tinker 1990). These historical and contemporary accounts point to a plethora of interests as women are positioned differently within the global latticework of race/class/gender structures that protect the privileges of the white middle class against the wants and needs of people in other groups (Zinn 1994).

Some of the key themes of the 'women's rights as human rights' plank reflect these white middle classes, biases. For instance, a core demand is for a woman's right to work outside the home - yet little attention paid to countless racial minority women who perform back-breaking labour outside the home and who prefer to have the legal right to attend to their families. The lessons from the life histories of slave women in the

US offer a stark lesson about why the right to work cannot be conceptualised outside the history of minority groups and their experiences within the legal framework of majority society. Having been deprived of the fundamental right and institutional opportunity to form families for generations, black women sought to become homemakers when slavery was abolished - an empowering choice given their previous history of having no right to nurture family relationships (Mullings 1994). Similarly immigration laws in the US - race based restrictions such as the Asian Exclusion Act or the current quotas on family reunification (Ancheta 1997, Espiritu 1997) - which prevent or delay women from forming families, because of their racial classification in the US, indicate that the right to work cannot be separated from the question of who has access to 'basic' rights such as forming families.

Both India and the US provide many examples of dissonance for working class women of different races/castes as well. Ilina Sen's (1990) collection on working women's movement's in India or Ann Bookman and Sandra Morgan's (1988) collection on working women in the US emphasise how 'equal rights' enshrined in the Indian or US constitutions often do not reflect the practical needs of women who are marginalised by their class, race, caste and other social structural hierarchies. Although it has been taken for granted that needs for basic amenities of life such as food water, shelter, or ability to have families are 'practical' rather than strategic gender interests (Molyneux 1985), for many women such practical interests reflect real strategic gender interests (Kaplan 1982, Moser 1993, Ray 1999). For many women of the working class "empowerment is rarely experienced as upward mobility or personal achievement . . . rather feeling powerful is constrained for them by ways in which their gender, as well as race and class, limit their access to economic resources and political power" (Bookman and Moran 1988, 4). For these women, empowerment is a collective, rather than individual state of being. Hence marginalised women often resist homogenisation and centralization of power in order to claim the right of their communities and themselves to decide on courses of action that attend to their strategic interests. The fisherwomen of Kerala, or the informal workers of the SEWA union, or the women in the Chipko movement in India, or black women activism for access to higher education, or Chicana workers' efforts to unionise in the US (see Sen 1990 or Bookman and Morgan 1988) are examples of struggles of women resisting such matrices of domination.

Other women/human rights issues include the right to move around freely, to bodily integrity, and freedom from violence. These freedoms are often denied to women through normative standards on roles within specific culture-groups. But these rights are also denied through definitions in immigration laws where women are rarely allowed to migrate on their own right as women (Kay 1988) and jailed or harassed to prove their 'purity'. The 1875 Page laws in the US that required all Chinese women prove they were not prostitutes (Espirtu 1998) or the more recent virginity tests conducted in Britain to assess the validity of marriages of women from the Indian subcontinent are equal impediments to the freedom to move around freely, to bodily integrity and freedom from violence. These freedoms exist as a relation between men and women within groups but also at inter-group and inter-societal levels. As long as the sexual control of *minority* women is adopted as a means of subordinating and controlling their community, such as the rape of black women in the US (Mullings 1994), or Santhal women in India (Kumar 1993) or women in the former Yugoslavia (Meznaric 1994) race and other hierarchies matter alongwith gender interests in conceptualising women's empowerment.

Attending to race and class as central axes for understanding gender, therefore, suggests a different model for human rights. The woman in the model is not merely an individual, she is also a member of a group with restrictions or opportunities associated with the position of that group within a particular social or global order. Although Okin conceptualises regressive cultural norms within minority cultures as the main impediment to women's empowerment, the argument presented here suggests that both majority and minority cultures are not unique, closed groups, but are part of the same racial structure which privileges and 'normalises' the white experience and marginalises all others. This argument suggests working for individual and cultural group rights because we need to address the matrix of domination rather than patriarchal discrimination alone.

Erasing Agency

Okin's rejection of cultural group rights appears to be think of women within minority cultural groups as victims of sex role socialisation. She expresses wariness about "the different roles cultures impose on their members" (1999, 12) and argues that most cultures (from which immigrants come to the US and Europe) have more negative standards towards women compared to western cultures. Such a sex-role victim model has been criticised because it erases all women's agency and capacity for change (e.g. Ferree, Lorber and Hess 1999). More importantly, historical evidence from different countries suggest re-examining the validity of this argument.

When we read minority women's histories, we often find both strong women and women victimised by the socio-political-economic system within which they lived. These histories frame women in their cultural groups as strong change agents even when their actions do not conform to white, middle class notion of individual women's empowerment. Sen's (1999) account of women in the jute industry in Bengal who attacked the mill owners with brooms, or Kumar's (1993) account of hill women who attacked alcohol shops instead of the men who abused them are instances of alternate paths to empowerment. Similar examples are available in the US, Pardo's (1995) account of how Mexican American women protested the location of a prison in their community or Japanese American women who recreated community bonds even during the Japanese Internment during World War II (Geshwender 1992, Glenn 1986) are testament to how women become change agents. These women use their 'traditional roles' to redefine the parameters to include activities which are more empowering to them and their communities. Dill (1994) describes black (and other ethnic) women's community work in the US as key to the survival of their communities. She points out that instead of being the docile recipients of orthodox strictures about their roles, black women have become the "core around which group solidarity is constructed" (Dill 1994, 242). In a similar vein, Hill Collins argues that black women have often hidden behind a mask of behavioural conformity to nurture a "private, hidden space of black women's consciousness, the inside ideas that allow black women to cope with, and in most cases transcend the confines of race, class and gender oppression" (1999, 92-93). The examples from the Indian Independence movement, where women's roles as mothers and sisters included harboring terrorists or picketing those who bought foreign goods is another example of empowerment through role expansion (Kumar 1993).

By perpetuating the idea that cultural groups should be encouraged to alter themselves to fit western notions. Okin perpetuates the myth that western societies serve as the standard for understanding women's empowerment. Her arguments, including the advocacy for the demise of cultural groups, are eerily similar to earlier colonial arguments about why the savage natives (in many part of the world) had to be civilized by benign Western influences (see for instance Nandy 1994, Sinha 1998,

Schwartz and Ray 2000). Minority/culture groups are described as closed, unchanging, and non-progressive thus making invisible the majority cultural norms that ascribe or withhold labels such as progressive or traditional. Centuries of activism by women in different societies - activism which has targeted changes to empower women in a variety of situations are erased in this victim discourse (e.g. Basu 1995, Davis 1982, Forbes 1996, Hill Collins 1991, Hurtado 1996).

Many scholars have contested the role of western societies in *constructing* the image of the subordinated woman (Mullings 1994, Sinha 1998). For instance, Sinha (1998) describes how the politics of knowledge construction negatively affects Indian women in the US using the example of Katherine Mayo's book 'Mother India'. This book was part of colonial propaganda justifying the continuing presence of the British in India, and Mayo depicted Indian women as infantile sexual slaves who had to be saved from their depraved men. Despite widespread challenges to the data and conclusions of the book in India, it has been re-printed every single decade since it was published in 1926 and it has remained the book which contemporary authors refer to when they talk about Indian women (e.g. Bumiller 1990, Daly 1978). By the time Mayo's book was published thousands of Indian women were active in the national movement, women's rights (to access education, on health issues, inheritance, marriage etc.) were considered to be of national importance, women (and men) had the right to vote, and women leaders had served as the President of the Congress Party. Given the organisation of publishing industry, the voices, speeches, and essays of those contemporary women activists, even those who wrote in English, are extremely difficult to locate in the US. As a consequence the ability of women in other cultural groups to initiate fundamental changes in society remain invisible.

The contemporary experience of many Asian Indian activists in the US show how the categorisation of certain behaviours and attitudes as 'American' vs. 'traditional' robs people of their agency. Shah describes how her progressive opinions are inevitably attributed to her American-ness rather than her Indian-ness (Shah 1994). Dasgupta describes how she was commiserated on having a child - being a mother was attributed to her traditional-ness and lack of choice (Dasgupta and Dasgupta 1997). Other activists describe how their opting to follow a different model of domestic violence activism resulted in their being labeled as a group with diffuse ideology and not following the 'real' path towards women's empowerment (Purkayastha, Raman, Bhide 1997). Pollit (1999) and

Narayan (1997) point out how the ease with which the majority US society is willing to accept 'cultural tradition' as an excuse (based on an ignorance or taken for granted assumption about other groups' lack of progressive ideals) is part of the reason for ethnic women's subordination within their ethnic communities in the US.

In sum, a generalised discourse about minority women victims within regressive cultural groups ignores the multiple ways in which women are subordinated structurally. It also ignores the many ways in which women fight back and alter social conditions to improve their own and their community lives. But when we pay attention to the intersectionality of gender with race/caste, ethnicity, religion and class and how these combine to create a latticework of institutionalised social relationships that unequally allocate resources and control access to rights and benefits (Ferree, Hess and Lorber 1999) we begin to glimpse that arguing for human rights on the basis of gender at the individual level alone (or gender as sex differences alone) is simply not sufficient to usher deep changes in the condition of women.

Fluid Cultural Groups and Multifaceted Empowerment

The history of women's activism around the world suggest multiple sources of their subordination. Thus any conceptualisation of empowerment has to pay attention to the rights of individual women and the rights of women as members of minority groups. This approach suggests there are considerable reasons for being wary of seemingly neutral individual rights. At the same time it is problematic to assume cultural groups are automatically beneficial for women. Working towards empowerment implies balancing these positions.

One influential suggestion about multicultural citizenship, which Okin (1999) challenges in her essay, has been put forth by Will Kymlicka (1995) Kymlicka suggests that cultural groups require external rights such as language rights, guaranteed political representation, land claims, compensations for historical injustice or regional devolution of power to ensure groups have the same opportunity to express their interests as the majority. However, he feels that since cultural groups may impose internal restrictions upon some of their members, there have to be mechanisms to protect those most vulnerable. He advocates rejecting internal restrictions while granting external rights to groups as a way of balancing individual and community interests.

While Kymlicka's suggestion is a step in the right direction, his definition of cultural group requires further scrutiny. When we assume boundaries between cultural groups are clear and are based on 'primordial' ties such as religion, language and or common historical memories we perpetuate the power of the elite in the groups. Recent work by Nagel (1994) or Swidler (1985) indicate how groups with seemingly long immutable histories are often recent inventions based on how traditions are defined and interpreted depending on the political context. The history of colonised societies such as India indicate how fluid, contested meanings of cultural groups were transformed to rigid, unitary definitions of groups because of the needs of enumeration and other colonial bureaucratic procedures (Appadurai 1995). Thus, Hindu and Muslim identities became reified based on elite conceptions of these groups (Agnes 1998).

I would suggest that instead of dwelling on primordial bonds as the way of defining cultural groups, we could draw on women's experinences and define such groups in multiple ways. Thus, if we conceptualise cultural groups in multiple ways - as groups who are ascribed a race or gender status by the majority, or groups which share a language or religion, or groups which experienced a common history of discrimination , or groups based on a variety of other affiliations - we should be able to get away from the pre-given fixed categories which privilege only some aspects of women's identities. Looking at cultural groups as continually created and imagined communities recognise the fissues and fluid alliances that characterise different groups (e.g. Andersen 1983, Taylor and Whittier 1992).

Recognising 'primordial' ties and ties of interest allow us to conceptualise groups as fluid entities, composed of multiple factions, full of conflict, negotiations, harmony and commonalities, and allow us to get away from static definitions. Women's roles within these groups, whether these are defined by cultural norms of the immediate group or as these are codified by state bureaucracy, become palimpsests, open to change. So, the challenge for conceptualising women's empowerment is to look at cases where cultural groups have been given some rights and to assess how, or in what combination, these work for women.

Both India and the US provide a variety of 'cultural group rights' models. Thus, the limited sovereignty of Native Americans, or rights of discriminated groups (sex, race, and caste groups) to affirmative actions in the US and India, civil rights accorded to religious groups in India, or the variety of holidays allowed by Indian states to allow local celebration of local cultural ways of life, and the reservation of one third of the Panchayat seats for women in India are examples of cultural group rights.

Both societies have witnessed an emergence of strong forces in the

1990s challenging such rights. Attacks on equal opportunity rights (described as race quotas in the US), or protest against the invasion of foreigners (Asians in the US, Bangladeshis in India), or religious fundamentalist forces attempting to curtail the religious rights of others (Southern Baptist's vilification of Hinduism, Buddhism, and Islam in the US or the RSS vilifying Muslims and Christians in India) are among the recent examples. Within this context, rights of a group to exist without adopting the majority religion and cultural ethos is often in jeopardy. Rights conceptualise as 'group' rights - Native American sovereignty, personal laws in India, affirmative action - protect the group, to a certain extent, against the will of the majority.

However, the issue of how to protect women against the power of the elite within the group, since they are often committed to maintaining status-quo, is the other aspect of this question. Here I would argue the Indian model provides more opportunities to improve the position of women. Veena Das (1999) points out that, ironically, in one of the most bitterly contested cases about women's status in recent times - the Roop Kanwar sati case in Rajasthan - the judiciary allowed women a new identity within a cultural group by allowing them to voice their opinions about 'traditions'. While the outcome was depressing - these women supported the glorification of sati as part of their cultural tradition - the recognition of women's voices as one of the many voices representing the group, appears to be a significant step in balancing the rights of the individual woman and the right of the women as member-of-a-community.

In instances where cultural groups operate as dynamic communities, local activism (supported by alliances with people outside the group) have lead to progressive results. Weaver (1999) describes how the alliance between a caste council (objectively a very traditional group) and women's groups led by a woman recently elected to Panchayat Council (on the strength of the reservations for women) led to the public humiliation and punishment of a father-in-law who raped his son's wife. By strengthening women's voices as individuals and as members of the group, the political context allowed women to have a definite voice in matters that were of concern to them.

The use of humiliation/shame is an important tactic that women in many Indian locales have used successfully as part of their effort to change their situation. They have drawn on traditional roles - women as keepers of morals -and claimed the right to address any situation that disadvantages them. Maintaining community bonds has been a key method of claiming greater power. Where community is important, shame and humiliation become a key way of sending a message to others about what a group is willing to tolerate of its members, and change is initiated at the level of everyday life. Among other notable examples are the success of women in the Appiko movement against wife beating by drunken husbands (Kumar 1993), Christian women in India who changed 'traditional' divorce laws (Agnes 1998), or the success of women working in the informal sphere in building SEWA, a new affiliative community with a unique legal status (Rose,1992). Without community or cultural group networks, the power of these women to affect any change would depend on the willingness of the majority, to take up their cause, a project that is especially difficult when their proposals are likely to affect the interest of the majority.

The core issue in working towards a multifaceted model of empowerment is that by conceptualising women's rights in multiple ways we strengthen groups and strengthen women in the group. By working for cultural group rights alongwith individual rights we move away from the relentless homogenisation introduced by complex bureaucracies of the economy and state which erode the gains made by diverse women. By recognising fluid groups boundaries we work for rules which are tied to multiple roles and realities within the structure of women's lives. Thinking about empowerment has to be based on an impure gender classification (Geldof 1999) and reflect the complexities of gender as a social relationship.

Similarly, on the international stage, human/gender interests can be defined to best serve the needs of women and marginalised communities. Attending to intersectionality of race, gender, and class suggest that we pay attention to issues of cultural hegemony at the international level as we try to introduce structures supportive of women at other multiple levels. In order to minimise the effect of such cultural hegemony, it is necessary to move away from an emphasis on individuals alone to one on individuals and cultural groups as political entities and think of gender interests based on a clear understanding of the intersectionality of race, class and gender.

Conclusion

Multiple paths and diversity of interests mark women's interests around the world and women's rights as human rights cannot be based on a state of individual rights alone. Instead working for continued empowerment of women requires understanding complex social entities in civic society. The unitary category 'woman' is too narrow for appreciating the diversity of statuses, roles, and power that women experience around the world. It is also too narrow to capture the variety of experiences one woman might have depending on her age, religion, class, sexual preference, marital status and other social and contextual characteristics. Thus, women's rights as human rights has to be conceptualised as a set of multi-layered identities and gender rights attend to the needs of the individual and her position as a member of a group.

References

Agries,F. 1999. *Law and Gender Inequality : the Politics of Women's Rights in India,* New Delhi, Oxford University Press.

Ancheta,A. 1998. *Race, Rights, and the Asian American Experience,* New Brunswick : Rutgers University Press.

Andersen, B. 1983. *Imagined Communities : Reflections on the Origin and Spread of Nationalism,* London Verso.

Appadurai,A. 1996. Modernity at Large : *Cultural Dimensions of Globalization* Minneapolis : University of Minnesota Press.

Basu, A. 1995 (ed.) *The challenge of Local Feminisms Women's Movements in Global Perspective.* Boulder : Westview Press.

Bhattacharjee,A. 1997. A Slippery Path : Organizing Resistance of Asian Women. In S.Shah(ed.) *Dragon Ladies : Asian American Feminists Breathe Fire* Boston : South End Press.

Bookman, A. and Morgan, S. 1988. *Women and the Politics of Empowerment* Philadelphia, Temple University Press.

Bumiller, E. 1990. *May You be the Mother of a Hundred Sons,* New York, Random House.

Chang, L., 1997. The Global Trade in Filipina Nurses. In S.Shah (ed.) *Dragon Ladies : Asian American Feminists Breathe Fire. Boston : South End Press.*

Connell, R. 1995. *Masculinities.* Berkeley : University of California Press.

Connell, R. 1991. Live fast and die young. The construction of masculinity among Young Working Class Men on the Margin of the Labor Market. *The Australian & New Zealand Journal of Sociology,* 27 : 141-171.

Daly, M. 1978 Gyn-Ecology. *The Metaethics of Radical Feminism*; Boston : Beacon Press.

Das, V. 1999. Communities As Political Actors : The Question of Cultural Rights. In N.Menon (ed.) *Gender and Politics in India*. New Delhi : Oxford University Press.

Das Gupta, S. and Das Gupta, S. 1997. Bringing Up Baby : Raising a 'Third World' Daughter in the First World. In S. Shah (ed.) *Dragon Ladies : Asian American Feminists Breathe Fire*. Boston : South End Press.

Davis, A. 1983. *Women, Race, Class*. New York : Vintage Books.

Dill, B. 1994. Fictive Kin, Paper Sons and Compadrazgo : Women of Color and the Struggle for Family. In M.Zinn and B.Dill(ed.) Women of Color in US Society Philadelphia : Temple University Press.

Espiritu, Y.L. 1997. *Asian American Women and Men*. Thousand Oaks : Sage Publications.

Ferree, M. Lorber, J., and Hess,B.(eds.) 1999. *Revisioning Gender;* Thousand Oaks Sage.

Forbes, G. 1996. *Women in Modern India*; Cambridge: Cambridge University Press.

Geldo f.I. 1999. *Against Purity : Rethinking Identity With Indian and Western Ferminisms,* London; Routledge.

Geschwender, J. 1992. Ethgender, Women's Waged labor, and Economic Mobility, *Social Problems*, 39 : 1-16.

Gilkes, C. 1994. "If it wasn't for women... "African American Women, Community Work, and Social Change. In M.Zinn and B.Dill(eds.) *Women of Color in US Society* Philadelphia : Temple University Press.

Gilligan, C. 1982. *In a Different Voice*. Cambridge MA; Harvard University Press.

Glenn, E. 2000 Citizenship and Inequality : Historical and Global Perspectives. *Social Problems*; 47 : 1-20.

Hill Collins, P. 1991 *Black Feminist Thought : Knowledge Consciousness and the Politics of Empowerment* ... London : Routledge.

Hurtado, A. 1996. *The Color of Privilege : Three Blasphemies on Race and Feminism*. Ann Arbor : University of Michigan Press.

Jones, K. 1985. Towards the Revision of Politics. In K. Jones and A. Jonasdittir (ed). *The Political Interests of Gender*. London : Sage.

Jones, K. and Jonasdittir, A. (ed.) 1985. *The Political Interests of Gender*; London : Sage.

Kaplan, T. 1982. Female Consciousness and Collective Action : The Case of Barcelona Signs 7 : 545-566.

Karlekar, M. 1994. Women's Nature and Access to Education in Bengal. In C. Mukhopadhyay and S. Sewymour (eds.). *Women, Education and Family Structure in India.*

Boulder : Westview Press.

Kay, D. 1988. *The Politics of Gender in Exile. Sociology,* 22 : 1-21.

Kishwar, M. 1999. *Off the Beaten Track; Rethinking Gender Justice for Indian Women*. New Delhi : Oxford University Press.

Kymlicka, W. 1995. *Multicultural Citizenship : A Liberal Theory of Minority Rights* : Oxford Clarendon Press.

Kumar, R. 1993. *A History of Doing*. London : Verso.

Manushi : A Journal of Women and Society.

Mazumdar, S. 1989. A Woman-Centered Perspective on Asian American History. In Asian Women United of California (ed.) *Making Waves : An Anthology of Writings by and About Asian American Women.* Boston : Beacon Press.

Meis, M. and Shiva, V. (ed.) 1993. *Ecofeminism.* London : Zed Books.

Menon, N. (ed.) 1999 *Gender and Politics in India*, New Delhi: Oxford University Press.

Meznaric, S. 1994. Gender as Ethno-Marker : Rape, War, and Identity Politics in the Former Yugoslavia. In V. Moghadam (ed.) *Identity Politics and Women : Cultural Reassertions and Feminisms in International Perspective.* Boulder : Westview Press.

Moghadam, V. (ed.) 1994. *Identity Politics and Women : Cultural Reassertions and Feminisms in International Perspective*, Boulder : Westview Press.

Mohanty, C., 1987. Under Western Eyes Feminist Scholarship and Colonial Discourses. In C. Mohanty, A Russo and L. Torres (eds.), Third World Women and the Politics of Feminism. Bloomington: Indiana University Press.

Molyneux, M. 1985. Mobilization without Emancipation? Women's Interests, State and Revolution in Nicaragua. *Feminist Studies* 11 : 227-253.

Moser, C. 1993. *Gender Planning and Development*, New York : Routledge.

Mullings, L., 1994. Images, Ideology and Women of Color. In M. Zinn and B.Dill (eds.) *Women of Color in US Society*. Philadelphia : Temple University Press.

Nagel, J. 1994. Constructing Ethnicity : Creating and Recreating Ethnic Identity and Culture. *Social Problems*, 41 : 152-176.

Nandy, A. 1996. Plural worlds, Multiple Selves : Ashish Nandy and the Post Columbian Future. *Emergences*, 7.

Nandy, A. 1994. *The Illegitimacy of Nationalism*. New Delhi : Oxford University Press.

Narayan, U. 1997. *Dislocating Cultures*. London : Routledge.

Okin, S. 1999. Is Multiculturalism Bad for Women. In J. Chohen, M. Howard and M. Nussbaum (ed.) *Is Multiculturalism Bad for Women*. Princeton : Princeton University Press.

Okin, S. 1998. *Feminism, Women's Human rights, and Cultural Differences*. Hypatia, 13 : 32-52.

Pateman, C. 1989. *The Disorder of Women Democracy, Feminism and Political Theory*, Stanford, CA : Stanford University Press.

Pathak, Z. and Rajan, S. 1989. Shahbano *Signs*, 14 : 558-582.

Pardo, M., 1995. Doing it For the Children : Mexican American Community Activist Border Feminists, In M.Ferree and P. Martin (eds.) *Feminist Organizations Harvest of the New Feminist Movement*. Philadelphia : Temple University Press.

Rajan, R. 1993. *Real and Imagined Women*, London : Routledge.

Ray, R. 1999. *Fields of Protest : Women's Movements in India*. Minneapolis : University of Minnesota Press.

Rose, K. 1992. *Where women are leaders : the SEWA movement in India*. London : Zed Books.

Schwatrz, H. and Ray,S. 2000. *A Companion To Post Colonial Studies*. London : Blackwell.

Seager, J. and Olson,A. 1986. *International Atlas on Women*, New York : Pluto Books.

Sen, I. (ed.) 1990. *A Space Within the Struggle*. New Delhi : Kali for Women.

Sen, S. 1999. *Women and Labor in Late Colonial India*, Cambridge : Cambridge University Press.

Shah, S. (ed.) 1997. *Dragon Ladies : Asian American, Feminist Breathe Fire*. Boston : South End Press.

Shah, S. 1994. Presenting the Blue Goddess : Toward a National, Pan Asian Feminist Agenda. In K.Aguilar San Juan (ed.). *The State of Asian America : Activism and Resistance in the 1990s*. Boston; South End Press.

Shiva, V. 1988. *Staying Alive : Women, Ecology and Development*. London : Zed Books.

Sinha, M. 1998. *Selections from Mother India*, New Delhi : Kali for Women Press.

Swidler, A. 1995. Cultural Power and Social Movements. In H. Johnston and B. Klandearmans (eds.) *Social Movements and Culture*. Minneapolis; University of Minnesota Press.

Taylor, V., and Whittier, N., 1992. Collective Identity in Social movement communities. In A. Morris and C. Mueller (eds.) *Frontiers in Social Movement Theory*. New Haven : Yale University Press.

Tinker,I. 1990. *Persistent Inequalities*. London : Oxford University Press.

US Department of Labor 1997. The Family and Medical Leave Act of 1993 [Computer file]. Available at http://www.dol.gov/dol/esa/public/regs/compliance/whd/whdfs28.htm

Weaver, M. 2000. Gandhi's daughters : India's poorest women embark on a social experiment. *New Yorker,* January 10.

West, C. and Fenstermaker,s. 1995. *Doing Difference. Gender and Society*, 9 : 8-37.

Young, I. 1995. The Ideal Community and the Politics of Difference. In P.Weiss and M.Freidman(ed.) *Feminism and Community*. Philadelphia: Temple University Press.

Zinn, M. 1994. Feminist Rethinking from Racial Ethnic Families. In M. Zinn and B. Dill (eds.) *Women of Color in US Society*. Philadelphia: Temple University Press.

8

Gender Issues in the Perspective of Development

Dipali G. Danda

I

While speaking of India's achievements and failures of 50 years of Independence Amartya Sen appreciated India's success as a democratic polity but according to him, "India has failed to meet it s tryst with destiny on the social and economic fronts... the second field - that of social progress and equity has fared much worse; not quite an immeasurable failure, but certainly a measurable flop". (*The Telegraph*, June 30,1997). He states, that nearly half of the adult population of India, and two-thirds of adult women are still illiterate. Even in the late eighties, about half of the rural girls aged between fourteen and sixteen had not been to any school for a single day in their lives. According to him neglect towards women's interest stands as a barrier to the overall development of the country. Illiteracy, ill health, economic insecurity and the neglect of women's interests and powers not only hurt the deprived, but also make it hard to achieve general economic and social progress. (*The Telegraph*, July 1,1997)

Women as a category even today represent the most oppressed section of human society. Their oppression is very deep-rooted but often unrecognised due to which it is rather difficult to ameliorate their condition. Perhaps for the same reason the contribution of women to human survival is not given due importance although all over the world the number of women in the labour force is greater than that of men. Her work is by and large attached with an auxiliary value generally relegated to the area of domesticity. Hence no contribution of hers in the sphere of production gets due recognition.

Traditionally it is supposed that women and men belong to two different worlds, one is responsible for reproduction and the other for production. Thus, women's productive role goes unacknowledged, on the contrary her faculty of reproduction is over weighed; an issue over which she has least freedom of choice.Women's role is generally perceived as a passive participant in a socio-cultural universe structured by men. Almost in all cultures, more so in the so-called post-agricultural societies, women's contribution is recognised in the sphere of domesticity alone. Her primary responsibility is to look after the well being of others. The set notion for a woman in India is that she is the symbol of sacrifice and self-denial whose whole life is dedicated to the welfare of her children and other family members. Her ideal behaviour is never to question, never to ask anything for her own self. She should be a shadow of her husband as if she does not have any independent existence of her own. Everything in the family or society is for men as they are the bread earners and women are expected to manage everything from behind the stage, keeping herself invisible. In fact, a veil of invisibility surrounds the work done by women. Women are not considered fellow human beings. In India, women are sometimes referred to as 'aurat jaat' and all through this connotation bears a negative load. Hence, the girl child is unwanted. Women are supposed to be physically weak and inferior in intellect. This notion is not limited either to the underdeveloped or the developing nations. Women are discriminated against all over the world. The feminist movement of the West emerged as protest against such discrimination. The subordinate status of women is rooted in the principle of discrimination on the basis of gender which works in the matter of production, division of labour, consumption and distribution pattern of society. All such norms are in favour of men which create a double standard in society that affects the process of socialization.

Inequality thus prevails in the gender relationship by assigning a subordinate position to women and not acknowledging their contribution. Under such circumstances women remain out of any serious consideration for developmental planning. It is high time to have an exact assessment of the situation. What is the degree of participation of women in the matter of production ? Are they really passive participants in the production process and responsible for only bearing pregnancies and reproduction ? It is imporant to highlight all such issues centering around women through systematic studies. Unfortunately, women's study as a new branch of academics is yet to receive due importance in social science. According to Leela Dube, "By ignorning woman as a social actor who contributed to continuity and change in society, the social sciences have seriously impaired their understanding of the total society" (1986 : XI).

Women issues have come into prominence since the decade of the seventies which was declared as the women's decade. Prior to that among all social sciences, Anthropology has considered the women's issues important for study. Lowie's work (1920) on position of women in primitive society may be called a pioneering initiative in this direction. Evans Pritchard's lecture on position of women too, dates back to 1955. Role of women particularly in rural society got reflected through the reportings of anthropologists in South Asia during the fifties and sixties. Village studies conducted during that period provide excellent details of the domestic roles of women in different strata of society. Through them we come to know that many women participated in agricultural production either in the form of family labour or hired labour. As rightly observed by Dube in this context, "the point needs to be made that women have been more visible in Anthropology than in other social sciences. Now, there is a strong advocacy for the need to look into women's lives, attend to the arenas in which women function, and to emphasize women's perception and subjective experiences. In the consideration of the issues where women play an important role such as gender-based divisions of work and articulation between these divisions, an awareness of the need for treating gender as a central variable can give us paradigms that will help towards a better understanding of the social reality. The report of the National Committee on the Status of Women made a special impact on the field of women studeies (*Ibid.*, XII-XIII)".

What do we want to achieve through women studies ? In earlier days the broad objective of women study was to determine women's status in the society. As a sequel, a good number of status studies are now available. Now the thrust has been shifted to "(a) removal of women's invisibility (in social knowledge and some actions); (b) highlighting of problems specific to women; (c) redressal of inequality, injustice and oppression; and (d) identification of the source of powerlessness of women." (Raj,1988 : 892).

Some amount of visibility has been achieved in case of the poor women in terms of their role in production and economic contribution. But the question remains whether visibility is the cause or effect of recognition and empowerment. Does visibility help to reduce subjugation ? Perhaps not. The overall weak position of women is perhaps due to uneven load they carry for human survival particularly in the domestic sphere. Whatever work men perform are given due recognition and valued in economic terms, but women's work are ignored and unrecognised. Thus, a double standard appears at work that bear the influence of patriarchy. To remove imbalance, there is a need for an ideological shift at cultural level in terms of gender relations.

Gender relation, "refers to the relations, of power between women and men which is revealed in a range of practices, ideas and representations including division of labour, roles and resources between women and men and ascribing to them different attributes, attitudes, desires, personality traits, behavioural patterns, and so on" (Agarwal,1994 : 51). Gender relation though primarily means relations between women and men, gender hierarchies also influence the structural relations between individuals of the same sex, the action and attitude of women in a household is often guided by the gender character of their relationship with the men in the household.

II

Issues related to women can be viewed at two levels - specific and general. When specific it relates to feminism or equality between human beings. In such a case women's questions are not taken together with general issues of the society at large. Disregarding her role and relationship with production system, welfare approach is often recommended which gets reflected through health service for women and is mostly confined to maternal and child welfare.

Once women's economic contribution is recognised, women's issues cannot be dealt with separately from the general issues of development. This viewpoint has been emphasized in the Declaration of Mexico on Women's Equality and Contribution to Development and Peace (1975). It states that "the problems of women, who constitute half of the world's population are the problems of society as a whole and efforts and measures aimed at a more intensified integration of women in development can be successfully implemented only if made integral part of overall social economic growth." (Cited from Pandey,1975 : 114-115). During the first two development decades of UN, development strategy was growth with distribution at the macro economic level. The third development decade emphasized the importance of both human resources and people's participation in development process. The development strategy focussed on basic needs at the micro-economic level. For the first time the concept of human resource development emerged. But when it refers to reality, women are yet to be considered as human resource. In the context of Indian social reality, they constitute a great liability. All the development programmes by and large reflect the men's perspective. Thus, women remain in the backdrop and as such have no role to play in the process of development.

Women are an integral component of society. They are at the centre stage so far as the well-being of men and children are concerned. It is therefore, important, if not essential to incorporate women's issues in national planning process. In fact, their full participation in the process of development is a must. Development may be thought in terms of improvement of quality of life of people on the basis of their full participation in the transformation scenario. Cultivation of human dignity is one of its professed objectives. Hence economic growth, gainful employment, cooperation and social equality are the essential elements of development.

Very scanty attention was paid to the women's issues and their contribution to economic development before the epoch making Study of Boserup (1970), based on data from underdeveloped countries of Africa, Asia and Latin America. It has been observed that there is an overall decline in economic status of women all over the world due to lack of proper appreciation of their role and apathy to assess the women's economic role for human survival. "The continual absence of concern for increasing the earning power of women has given women's economic needs a low priority value" (Desai,1986-292). Women are considered as beneficiaries of economic development and not as active participants in it.

Participation of women in development programme usually brings some change in the general power structure. In the long-run, women will be more visible and empowered through their participation in the process of development. Automatically their needs and requirements will be better appreciated. A kind of consciousness about women's development has emerged the world over partly due to feminist movements or human rights movements. The Indian Constitution, particularly its Preamble disapproves inequality and discrimination. But in reality women are yet to share due power. Nevertheless, constraints of the socialization process,based on patriarchal orientation has a bearing on women's psyche for which women themselves are still to go a long way to appreciate their right and just claim. It will take ages for women in our subcontinent to overcome the negative load of culture and ideology. From the heart of the hearts the rural women still today love to remain invisible and dependent though their strength for survival speaks of an unpleasant reality.

III

Recently the lady anthropologists of the Anthropological Survey of India completed a project on women and development. In the context of my deliberation I may refer to some of the findings of that study. The project aimed to evaluate the role of women in rural development, their attitude to rural development programmes. Further, we tried to examine whether women's role and attitudes are constrained by this economic class and the social position.

In village society the human universe appears sharply demarcated as men's world and women's world. Though complementarity exists between these two, the degree of natural interdependence varies. For socio-biological survival, the load on the women's world is relatively more although the contribution made by the women in this regard remains unacknowledged. Thus in terms of gender difference, women appear the exploited lot.

In general, everywhere and in all strata of the society gender related differences are conspicuous in the sphere of distribution of responsibilities and control over resources. In particular, women in poor households often contribute more to the family income than do the male members of the family. Women's work can broadly be classified into two spheres - the domestic sphere and the production sphere. The following chart suggests that the women's contribution in both the spheres is relatively more. Similar observations have also been made by Saradamoni (1982) and Mencher (1987).

It has been revealed from the study that women work for relatively longer hours with shorter breaks. On an average women work for not less than 13 hours a day while for male it is not more than 10 hours a day. Still women's work is not valued in economic terms. In fact, women work at home as well as outside. There is practically little or no free time left with them for rest or relaxation.

The work a woman does at home or outside is often monotonous and of nagging nature. For instance, the work of transplantation is very much time consuming and backbreaking. It has been observed that due to such type of works women often suffer from certain ailments caused by the profession. In such case too, very rarely they go for proper medical treatment. Women's health is very much neglected in village society. It is true that among poor people where bare subsistence is difficult, better health care and medical aids belong to the category of luxury for both men and women. The only luxury the men in such a situation may avail of is by taking rest at

Chart-1
Gender Bias in Subsistence Activities

Activities	Men	Women
A. Domestic Work		
1. Cleaning the House	×	√
2. Collection of fuel and water	×	√
3. Feeding animals	×	√
4. Cooking	×	√
5. Washing Utensils and Clothes	×	√
6. Child care	×	√
7. Marketing	√	√
B. Cultivation Work		
1. Ploughing	√	×
2. Sowing	√	×
3. Transplanting	×	√
4. Weeding	×	√
5. Harvesting	×	√
6. Cleaning and Processing	×	√
7. Storing	×	√

home without doing any manual work. Women in general are denied even such rest. The work load and responsibilities of women of the well-off section is not that hard like that of poor women. But by and large their life style is culturally circumscribed. Women of relatively higher castes and higher income group do not go for manual job. Their life is relatively comfortable but social position remains almost the same. The women of lower castes and lower income groups mostly go for wage labour. This suggests that when there is no other means of subsistence than human labour, cultural impediments or constraints do not seem to be at work. Women put their entire labour for survival of the group.

Women's employment as agricultural or casual labour is almost pan-Indian in nature. Women workers primarily depend on agricultural

Chart 2
Work and Rest in Hours

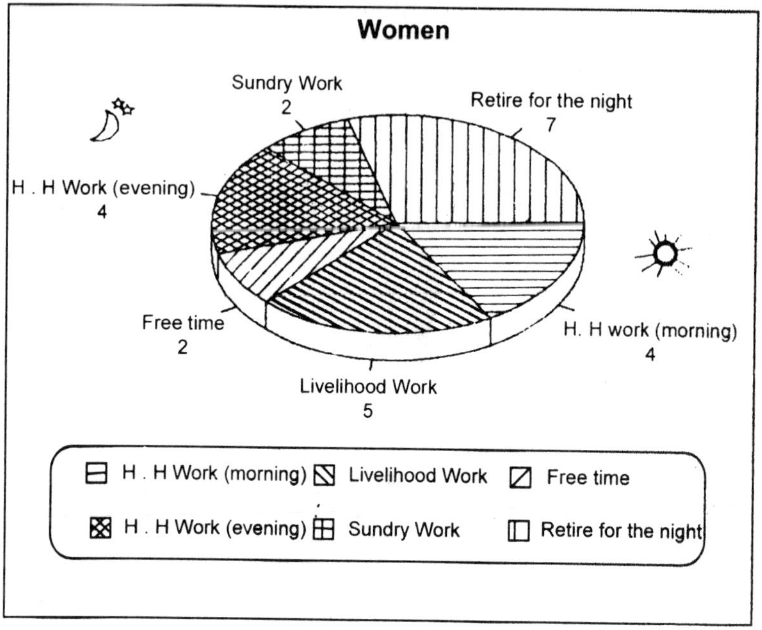

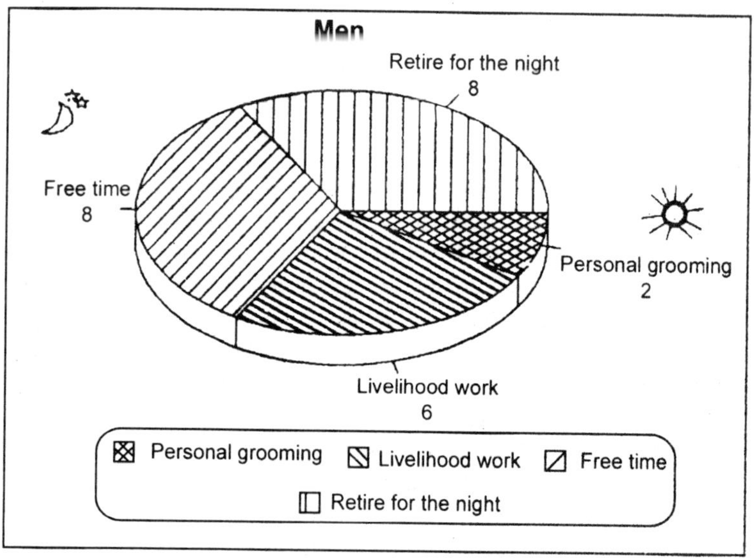

labour. Agarwal in this context commnets "while the dependence on wage work has been increasing for both men and women, the increase has been greater for women : by census figures, in 1961, 25.6 per cent of rural female workers and 16.2 per cent of rural male workers were agricultural labourers; by 1981 the figures for women and men had increased to 49.6 and 24.3 per cent respectively, namely agricultural wage work as their main source of earnings (1992 : 37)". This suggests that women have very little choice or scope for employment beyond their immediate surroundings. Due to higher domestic responsibility, they prefer to work near their home even with less wage.

Another important finding is that women spend their entire earning for the family and for spending money on themselves they are required to ask for permission from their respective husbands or heads of households. Conversely, men particularly from poor households, spend at least one-third of their earning if not more, for their personal amusements, including indulgence in various kinds of addiction. Among the low-income category the family is benefitted where women go out for work. Their children get better nourishment. But it cannot be said that as the women earn they enjoy relatively better treatment. Often women are found malnourished as because priority in terms of food and rest go in favour of the males.

The process of socialization too, helps to perpetuate the system based gender inequality. For the girl child, the entire system is rather apathetic - they have no childhood, they are victims of unequal treatment and many other forms of discrimination. Even the well off families do not encourage expenditure on girls' education. Among the poor from the age of five they are supposed to help their mothers in the work of baby sitting. At the age of 10, they behave like grown up girls, sharing the same load of poverty as their mothers do. On the other hand boys of that age roam freely, can attend school and learn any trade. The sharp gender inequality gets reflected in the high infant mortality for girls and skewed sex ratio of the country.

Women in the rural set up in general are not aware of their rights and privileges. Their attitude is fatalistic and they have accepted their subservient position. The gender based process of socialization creates a sense of inferiority among women. It sets two norms - one is for making a person who is useful to society, the other is merely a mode of genderization which dictates the gender role for women and creates a gender bias in the society. A boy, irrespective of his economic or caste background, grows up as an individual with dignity and respect. He can think for himself, he is for the society and the society is for him. On the other hand women's lives are out and out for others, their survival too depends on the mercy of others. They themselves do not honour their being, as if they are born to be ill treated.

Though development activities have not done any major good to the life of rural women, atleast women have been exposed to the outside world through some general developmental programmes implemented in their respective villages or due to improved communication network or electronic media. They can perceive that there is a world beyond their own village society where women are relatively better placed. They also vaguely aspire for that sort of life for their children. It is almost universally observed that poor women very earnestly plead for employment opportunities through which they can provide some comfort to themselves and their family members. It proves that women in general are more concerned about the well-being of their families. The outside employment gives women some freedom and some sort of self-confidence though does not ensure better status in society. Hence it is expected that if women folk can develop themselves, the overall development of society may be augmented at a faster pace. The development of women does not depend solely on the role that women play in the development process. Nevertheless, gender inequality acts as a great barrier to women's development. A shift is necessasry in the development perspective and women's development as such should be integrated to the overall structure and functioning of the society.

References

Agarwal, B. 1991 : *Land of Ones Own,* Cambridge University Press.

Agarwal, B.1992: "Rural Women, Poverty and Natural Resources : Sustenance, Sustainability and Struggle for Change", in *Poverty in India*, (eds.) Barbara Harris, S. Guha and R.H. Cassen. Bombay Oxford University Press.

Banerjee, N.1989: "Trends in Women's Employment, 1971-1981. Some Macro Level Observations". *Economic and Political Weekly*, April 29,1989.

Boserup, Ester 1970 : *Women's Role in Economic Development*, London : George Allen & Unwin Ltd.

Dandekar, V.M., 1986: "Agricultural Employment and Poverty", *Economic and Political Weekly*, 21,1989.

Desai, N., 1986: "Women Production and Reproduction in Industrial Capitalism : A Comparison of Brazilian and U.S. Factory Workers" in *Visibility and Power* (eds) L. Dube, Eleanor Leacock and Shirley Ardeners, Delhi : Oxford University Press.

Dube, L. Eleanor, Leacock and Shirley Ardener,1988 : *Visibility and Power*, Delhi : Oxford University Press.

Evans Pritchard E.E.1965 : "The Position of Women in Primitive Society and in Our Own," (1955), in the *Position of Women in Primitive Societies and Other Essays in Social Anthropology,* London : Faber and Faber Ltd.

Krishna Raj., M., 1988 : "Women Studies : Case for a new Paradigm". *Economic and Political Weekly* 30.

Lowie R.H. 1920 : *Primitive Society*, New York : Horce Liverright.

Meneher, J.P., and "Muddy Feet and Dirty Hands, Rice K. Saradamoni : Production and Female Agricultural Labourers". *Economic and Political Weekly,* 17(50).

Miller, B.D., 1981 : "The Endangered Sex," : *Neglect of Female Children in Rural North India*, Ithaca, New York, Cornell University Press.

Pandey, R., 1989: *Women from Subjugation to Liberation*. Delhi : Mittal Publications.

Report of the Committee on The Status of Women in India, Towards Equality, Government of India, Ministry of Education and Social Welfare, New Delhi, 1975.

Sen, Amartya, 1997 : "Facility at 50", *The Telegraph,* Calcutta, June 30th, "Beyond the Ballot", *The Telegraph,* Calcutta, July 1st.

Sen, Gita and Chiranjeeb Sen, 1985, "Women's Domestic Work and economic Activity : Results from National Sample Survey", *Economic and Political Weekly,* Vol. 20. 17.

V. Shobha, 1987, *Rural Women and Development*, Delhi : Mittal Publications.

Acknowledgements

The author sincerely thanks Dr. R.K. Bhattacharya, the Director of Anthropological Survey of India for his initiative in her participation in the Women's Day Seminar and for granting permission to utilise the data generated by the project 'Women, Poverty and Rural Development' sponsored by the Anthropological Survey of India of which the author was the coordinator.

9

A Micro-Study of Women and Agency in Chhattisgarh Region in Madhya Pradesh

Kakali Chakrabarty

In every society women play a key role in the maintenance of social conditioning of an individual. Anthropologists call it enculturation. Through this a woman not only gains status in society but also occupies the role to steer the family.

The role and status of women vary with the natue and structure of societies such as matrilineal, patrilineal, tribal, rural and urban. Each and every society is guided and governed by certain norms, traditions, values, ideals and practices, which control an individual's behaviour, actions and interactions, their modification and its acceptance. Each and every activity in society is the expression of a particular social situation, i.e., the social conditioning, which forms the basis of social atmosphere in a domestic set up.

In anthropological studies 'role' and 'status' are two basic concepts used in understanding and analysing social behaviour of a group or an individual in the total social perspective. The term 'role' in general represents the behaviour expected from an occupant of a given position or status. In the definition of role two features are emphasised, one is 'expectations' and the other is 'enactments' or 'conducts'.

The term 'status' is used in the field of social anthropology as a synonym for any position in a social system. Age, sex, birth, genealogy and other biological and constitutional characteristics are very common bases of status. Status connotes evaluation and in this sense status is gratification, its loss a deprivation (*Encyclopaedia of Social Sciences* : 253). In this context it is to be noted that status or social position is always to be viewed in relation to a counter position and therefore the unit of analysis is not the status itself but the relationship of the two statuses.

Therefore, the study of differenciated role of women in various fields of activities in social, familial and economic life is an essential parameter in understanding their social position or status in a group or a family or in a society. With the growing consensus worldwide, in the last few decades, about the predicament of women's lives, their exploitation, deprivation, and social subordination to men, much emphasis is laid on these two concepts, i.e. the role and related status of women in analysing social realities.

This is a fact that women are more visible in anthropology than in any other social sciences. Although it is undeniable that in earlier ethnographic accounts women's activities were not studied as a meaningful category for understanding gender role in society and everything had been analysed from men's perspective. It is only during the last few decades, specifically after the seventies, that there has been a sharp change in the focus of anthropological studies and special attention has been given in analysing women's activities from a totally different perspective and that is the women's perspective. Women's activities have been analysed in view to understand the contribution of women to the society as a social actor independent from their counterpart, i.e., the men. The year 1975, the year declared as The International Women's year, can be regarded as a landmark for the conscious and meaningful attempts to understand women's issues worldwide.

The phenomenon of women's subordination to men has been analysed and interpreted by social scientists from different points of view and a number of theoretical frameworks have come up. They are: biological determinism, economist view, feminist approach and so on. Biological determinism put much stress on women's reproductive functions as governed by biological constraints and argues that such functions in turn shape the social lives of women, make them confined to the arena of child rearing and caring within the domestic front. Economist viewpoint identifies absence of parity in role of women in the production system as the prime cause for women's subordination. Engels (1968 : 569) relates this development of women's subordination with the introduction of private property based on economy of surplus, sometimes at the stage of barbarism, the period in which knowledge of cattle breeding and land cultivation was acquired. He stated that 'The Savage' warrior and hunter had been content to occupy second place in the house and give precedence to the woman. The 'gentler' shepherd, presuming upon his wealth, pushed forward to first place and forced woman into second place. He argued that 'the wife became the first domestic servant, pushed out of participation in social production ... When she fulfills her duties in the private service of her family, she remains excluded from public production and can not earn anything' (Ibid : 501). Feminists look at the phenomenon of women's subordination as being rooted in the hierarchical division of labour anchored in the organisation of housework and child bearing and rearing.

Privatisation of property and women's exclusion from public production resulted in monogamy through which men obtained sexual monopoly over the individual woman on which the basic ideas of patriliny rests. Joan Smith (1983 : 104) proposed that neither economism nor biologism alone can explain women's subordination. According to her 'unpaid domestic labour and child bearing and rearing - the roles assigned to women ... are one form of social labour that shares important features with myriad of other activities. ... Subsistence cropping, informal marketing, informal exchange of services (rides to work and child care exchange) for example and the multiplicity of other activities that are non-waged and subordinated to those more conventionally, defined as part of the economic system.'

The interim conference of United Nation's Decade of Women in Copenhagen in 1980 produced an observation that women represent fifty per cent of the world's adult population, compose one third of the paid labour force and actually perform two thirds of the world's working hours; yet they earn only one tenth of the world's income and own less than one per cent of the world's property (Bjorkman,1987 : 1).

In her famous volume *The Second Sex (Le Deuxieme Sexe)* Simon de Beauvoir (1972 : 736) observes that 'woman is the victim of no mysterious fatality; the peculiarities that identify her so specifically a woman get their significance placed upon them'.

To understand the lives of women in India it would be worth to have a glance at Elisabeth Bumiller's realistic expression documented in her book *May You Be The Mother of Hundred Sons.* The very title of her book rightly touches upon the very basic ethics of Indian Cultural tradition that determines woman's place in a society. She writes (1990 : 11) 'the typical Indian woman representing about 75 per cent of the four hundred million women and female children in India, lives in a village. She comes from a small peasant family that runs less than one acre of land, or from a landless family that depends on the whims of big farmers for sporadic work and wages. She can neither read nor write, although she would like to, and rarely travelled more than twenty miles from her place of birth. ... She does not own land in her own name, or even jointly with her husband. ... Her occupation is field work, chiefly harvesting, planting and weeding, for which she often receives ... half the wage that a man receives for the same amount of work. She has to juggle this labour with her full-time job, the care of the house and the children. Her husband does not help her; indeed, he does not even consider what she does at home as work'.

This is no exaggeration of the situation that prevails in a traditional Indian rural family. It is important to note here that to understand the lives and predicament of women one is to start his or her journey from the level of household where in most Indian societies production and reproduction of social life is carried out. Production in anthropological terms is to mean the subsistence economy of the people through which they make out their livelihood. Reproduction in a simple term is viewed as a regeneration of labour in the domestic front through cooking, washing, childcare, collection of fuel and water and so on.

It is commonly argued that domestic works such as housework and child care are 'unproductive' as in conventional Marxist analysis it is stated 'non-work' or at least not productive. But in recent years there is a growing awareness towards the fact that it involves a huge labour input though unwaged and therefore virtually cannot be ignored as unproductive. It can also have a productive value in the form of saving, budgeting or the provision of unpaid services to the household unit.

In this paper an attempt has been made to analyse women's productive and reproductive role in a micro situation in comparison to that of males. The paper also intends to highlight how social conditioning of women acts as one of the important underlying force to uphold the ideals of patriarchy making women the main actor. The observations made in this paper have basis on empirical findings of anthropological investigation in the rural area of Chhattisgarh in Madhya Pradesh, located in the central part of India. Chhattisgarh is a place which is historically known. It is the abode of tribal peoples and a place which has been the homeland of Rajmohini Devi, the tribal reformist leader and Teajan Bai, a Pandavani performer of great excellence. Historically the region was once ruled over by Haihaivansi Rajputs who are believed to have had thirty six *(chhattis)* fort *(garh)* from which the region derived its name.

The name of the village is Achholi, a multiethnic society consisting of a number of castes, tribes, religious and linguistic groups. There are altogether twenty four ethnic categories of which fifteen are local and rest are immigrants. The present paper deals with the observation made among the local population which comprises twelve castes and three tribal groups. The castes are Sahu, Kurmi, Lodhi, Lohar, Yadav, Mahar, Panka, Kalar, Satnami, Gada, Marar and Mehtar. The three tribal groups are Gond, Pardhi and Kawar. Among the local population Sahus are the traditional peasant caste and they are the main landholding community. About 80.50 per cent of the total Sahu households practise cultivation either as primary or secondary occupation. Lodhis emerged as second major agriculturist caste. Satnamis are also traditionally engaged in agriculture either as owner cultivator or as wage labourer. Among the tribals, Gonds emerge as major agriculturist group and in landholdings they come second in rank. Landlessness is also present in high percentage (42.86 per cent) among the Gonds and this landless section mainly depends on wage labour. The other tribal group, the Pardhi earn their livelihood by their traditional occupation of mat weaving. Yadav, the traditional cowherding caste are now mostly associated with agriculture. One Lohar household is engaged in their traditional vocation of iron smithy. In the village society the Sahus, being the main landholding group, command greatest economic power and status which empower them with a dominant role in the political sphere also.

The village economy is basically an agrarian one. Besides agriculture other occupations are wage labour, mat weaving, small scale trading, carpentry, masonry, cow herding, ironsmithy and salaried jobs in government and private sector. The society is patriarchal and families are patrilineal (i.e. the descent is traced through male line). To understand women's issues in their proper perspective it is very much required to have a close view of women's activities in various spheres of life. Hence, it has been attempted to examine the extent of participation of women in two apparently different but interrelated domains of life. One is that of household-family system and the other is the production system or the economic organisation.

The empirical findings from the micro-situation of Achholi, regarding the participation of women and men in household chores and in sharing of household responsibilities is presented in table 1.

Table 1
Participation of Women and Men in Household Activities

Particulars of Households Chores	Women (N = 78)		Men (N = 72)	
	No. of Participants	%	No. of Participants	%
Cooking	57	73.1	—	—
Cleaning	62	79.5	—	—
Washing	56	71.9	—	—
Fetching Water	56	71.9	1	1.39
Collection of Firewood	37	47.4	2	2.78
Serving Food	39	50	—	—
Looking after Livestock	8	10.25	—	—
Making of Cow-Dung Cakes	3	3.85	—	—

The table gives us a clear idea about the participation of both sexes in household activities. Number mentioned against each category of work is overlapping for each category of work all 78 females and 72 males have been taken into account. Out of a total of 72 males not a single person participate in cooking while out of 78 females 57(73%) participate in cooking. Similarly the jobs like washing of clothes, serving food to the family members, cleaning of used utensils, collecting potable water, looking after the livestock etc. are exclusively done by the womenfolk. In case the only adult woman in a nuclear family falls ill, any of female relatives of the family extends her services for that period. In joint or extended families womenfolk manage the household chores amongst themselves.

Household is perhaps the most important frontier where women play a pivotal role. Division of labour between the sexes and the gender relations is also most clearly visible in a household-family set up. In the rural Indian set up the social boundary of a household, i.e., the unit of residence is often found overlapping with that of a family, an unit of kinship bondage. It often comes out of various studies that though conceptually the two units are identified separately but in practice, the fields of interactions in the two units often coincide with each other.

In a rural Indian set up the household work starts with the set of dawn. Such chores include all kinds of domestic works including child care and rearing. And the jobs come under the purview of domestic work including cooking, washing of clothes, cleaning of utensils, sweeping of household premises, courtyard, cow shed etc., giving fodder to domesticated animals, looking after them, bringing of potable water, collection of firewood or cow dung for fuel resources, maintenance of house and so on. In this village society such jobs are exclusively assigned to the womenfolk of the household. It is obvious in such situations that in household chores participation of males is almost nil. Sometimes stray instances are found where a male person is taking part in collection of firewood or in bringing water.

(A) In understanding the role of women in chores composition and size of a household and/or a family are two important factors to be considered. Number of working hands in a family is an equally important factor to evaluate the workload on an individual female member. Composition of a family or a household is important in analysing one's role and power one enjoys. It is commonly observed that there may be some differential power adhered to women depending on one's kinship relation but in a patriarchal society women in general hold secondary social status to that of men. No less important in this regard is the size of a family and the ratio between the number of female working hands and the number of male members she is to serve. It is a common picture that there always be more than one dependent adult and minor on a single female. It is interesting to note that in addition to the discrimination between the sexes there is discrimination among the females depending on one's age, kinship ties and related authoritarian power. (B) Kinship in an extended family is another important factor to be considered while analysing the work participation of members in a household. Besides, kinship in a society not only shapes the composition of a family but also determines one's right to the economic resources. Care of the young kids till their mother remains busy in work. She enjoys enough leisure while her daughter-in-law hardly gets any free time for herself. But often it is observed that she extends her hands in the economic frontier. An unmarried girl in an extended or joint family is exempted from active household work but she is a potential working hand for the family. A close observation reveals that smaller the family size lesser is the ratio between the dependent and the potential working hand and bigger the family size greater is the ratio, i.e. the workload on a single adult female increases with the increase of the family size. Table 2 gives an analysis of the empirical findings in work, though is not given proper recognition in a patriarchal society and it involves huge labour input which comes from the female members in a family.

Table 2
Size of family and the ratio of potential female working hand and dependents in relation to household chores (average number of dependents per single female)

Size of Family	*No. of Family*	*Distribution of Members in Terms of Sex*					*Potential Female working hand and dependents*		*Average ratio of dependents per single female*
		Adult		*Children*		*Total*	*Adult Female*	*Dependent*	
		M	*F*	*M*	*F*				
Small (2-4 Mebers)	16	10	22	10	10	52	22	30	1 : 1.36
Medium (5-6 Members)	22	40	35	23	21	119	35	84	1 : 2.40
Large (7-10 Members	6	11	13	9	12	45	13	32	1 : 2.46
Very Large (11 and above Members)	2	11	6	6	5	28	6	22	1 : 3.66

Note: Two households consisting of single member have been excluded from this analysis.

Another important activity for a family is the collection of firewood which is the main fuel resource in this village. Collection of firewood in Achholi is a female specific job. For collecting firewood one is to go far off from the village, to the hills and forests which is about 5 to 6 kms one way and for that she is to walk down all the way. It is almost a full day's job.

Marketing and shopping for daily requirements is another routine job done mainly by the womenfolk.

Besides household works women take active role in subsistence economy. Activities related to subsistence economy may not always be income generating like family labour in an agricultural field which always goes unpaid.

India is basically an agrarian society and in traditional agricultural economy womenfolk constitute the major labour force in most parts of the country. In some parts women are tabooed to touch a plough, in some they are not. In the Chhattisgarh region of Madhya Pradesh women even participate in ploughing operation.

For the traditional agricultural economy in this region womenfolk do all the major agricultural operations. Similar to the picture available in

Table 3
Participation of Women in Economic Activities

Economic Activities (Occupational Categories)		*Women's Participation (N = 78)*				
		Primary Occupation		*Secondary Occupation*		*Total*
		No	*Per cent*	*No*	*Per cent*	
Agricultural Sector	1. Cultivation (Own Land)	21	26.92	6	7.69	27
	2. Agricultural Labourer	35	44.87	19	24.35	54
	3. Kitchen Garden	2	2.56	—	—	2
Non-Agricultural Labour	4. Construction Work	3	3.85	—	—	3
	5. Bidi Rolling	1	1.28	—	—	1
	6. House Maid	1	1.28	—	—	1
	7. Cattle Herding	1	1.28	—	—	1
Trade/Business	8. Tea Stall/Betel Leaf Shop	2	2.56	—	—	2
	9. Milk Selling	—	—	2	2.56	2
Traditional Callings	10. Mat Weaving	4	5.13	—	—	4
	11. Bird Catching/ Hunting	—	—	1	1.28	1
Others	12. Peasion	1	1.28	—	—	1
	13. House Wife	4	5.13	—	—	4
	14. Secondary Workers	3	3.85	—	—	3

Note: 1. Housewife here includes those who do not participate in the economic activities directly but bear the responsibilities of household work and indirectly help in economic activities.

Note: 2. Secondary workers are those who because of their old age are not included in the main workforce but contribute their labour to the productive system according to their working capability.

other parts of rural India, a close observation of this village also shows that a majority of the women workforce engaged in the agricultural sector are wage labourers. Table 3 reveals that agriculture forms the mainstay in this village society and a majority of the womenfolk are engaged in agricultural activities either in family land or in other's land.

Role and participation of women in production organisation varies with the nature of the production system, thereby different in agricultural and non-agricultural sectors. In the present field situation participation of women in non-agricultural sectors is mainly on wage basis while in agricultural sector family labour is often an unpaid job. Agriculture is, however, dependent on both family labour and wage labour. Agriculture, being the mainstay of the people in the area, offers largest employment opportunity to the rural women. It offers employment almost round the year and also requires a huge labour input, and thereby can accommodate a large section of the labour force. Ploughing, transplanting, weeding, harvesting, husking, storing are the major operations in agriculture. Ploughing, as has already been stated, is not taboo to women here but is conventionally done by menfolk. Transplanting is the major operation next to ploughing. It is mainly done by the womenfolk. Pulling out of the seedlings from nursery bed and making small bundles of it, is mostly done by the menfolk, preferably by the family labour, while actual job of transplanting the seedlings is exclusively done by the women. The job of transplantation demands patience, efficiency and a habit of hard work which the village women are very much used to. For transplanting seedlings one is to work in kneedeep water and in forward bending posture for about 8 hours a day or more as the seedlings pulled out of the nursery bed require to be transplanted immediately. Weeding is another female specific job. The next major operation is harvesting which involves reaping and gathering in of grains. It is the womenfolk who mainly do the job of reaping while menfolk remain busy in making bundles, locally called *gattha* Husking is another job done by womenfolk in the house. For commercial purpose they sometimes take the help of husking machine available at the nearby town of Dongargarh. Storing is done by menfolk with the help of female members of the family. Distribution part is exclusively taken care of by the menfolk.

Let us have a look into the role of women in other occupational pursuits. Mat weaving is another occupation which involves family labour. Mat weaving requires specialised skills which one learns from one's own family since childhood. Both the sexes take part in mat weaving but participation of women is comparatively more if we take into account the actual working hours.

In wage labour also women actively take part. There are altogether 41 women (52.56 per cent) out of a total of 78 who showed wage labour as their primary occupation while 10 others (24.35 per cent) are engaged in this as secondary occupation. Out of 41 females working primarily as wage labourer, 35 (85.36 per cent) are found engaged in agricultural activities, 3 women are found engaged in construction work and even less, i.e. one female each is engaged in bidi rolling, cattle herding and in the occupation of housemaid.

In many cases seasonal rhythms of various occupations complement each other. Thus, the Pardhi mat weavers supplement their earning though agricultural wage labour; or an agricultural labourer seeks employment in non-agricultural sector in lean season.

The above facts show that women not only have an active role in household chores but also play an important role in subsistence level. In lean seasons when job opportunity is less it is the woman in a family who keeps her labour available even on a meagre wage rate just to maintain her family. During this time men usually move out to towns for construction work or other kind of mannual labour where they can get higher wage rate. But as the job opportunity in towns is not assured the womenfolk can hardly have any choice other than to work on low wage. Therefore, their income is crucial in lean season for maintenance of a family.

Table 4 presents a quick view of the participation of both sexes in agricultural operations as discussed below.

Table 4

Participation of Men and Women in Agricultural Operation

Categories of Activities/Operations	*Participation of*	
	Men	*Women*
1. Ploughing	√	√
2. Transplantation		
(a) Plucking off seedlings	√	
(b) Making Bundles	√	
(c) Transplanting the Seedlings		√
3. Weeding		
4. Harvesting		
(a) Reaping		√
(b) Making Bundles or Reaped Crops	√	

5.	Winnowing		√
6.	Carrying of Harvested Crops from Field on		
	(a) Headload	√	√
	(b) Bullock Cart	√	√
7.	Storing	√	√

* Though women are not tabooed to plough the field but it is conventionally done by the menfolk. Only a solitary instance is found where a widow ploughs her own field herself. She also ploughs the field of an absentee landlord against payment.

It is an empirical fact that women are never allowed in the traditional village council. Neither they are allowed to hold any portfolios nor they are invited for their views to settle down any social issues. Traditional village councils everywhereare strictly men's domain. Through this negation women are totally excluded from the arena of social control in a partriarchate society. Ironically enough women in this part of rural India (Chhattisgarh area of Madhya Pradesh) never feel deprived for this rather they accept it as a natural phenomenon of sexual demarcation.

Decision making is another important parameter to evaluate one's position in a social group or in a family. It is observed in general that in the sphere of decision making women are invisible, although they are not absent altogether. In this rural society women hardly enjoy full freedom in terms of decision making whether it is regarding family matters or regarding her ownself, like her own employment, or visit to her parents place, or spending her own income etc. In decision making a women's position and kinship status in the family is important. In nuclear family consisting of husband, wife and their unmarried children, the husband acts as head of the family and he holds the decision making power although on many occasions he seeks opinion or support from his wife. In families where widow mother lives with her married son, she being the eldest member of the family enjoys previleged position in decision making in comparision to her daughter-in-law. Kinship relation plays an important role in this regard. An adult son seeks opinion from his mother but dominates over his wife's wishes. In a joint family it is the eldest male member (or the father) who takes decision in consultation with other adult males/his sons. In such a family the mother, i.e., the wife of the head of the family enjoys a relatively privileged position in relation to other younger female member, i.e., her daughters-in-law. Her view are duly regarded though the ultimate authority lies with the male head. The daughter-in-law in such a family has no role in decision making and for enjoying the status of a senior woman she is to wait till her turn comes.

In any social system rule of inheritance speaks of gender differentiation and the pattern of power structure. In a patriarchal social system where power lies in the hands of males rule of inheritance certainly speaks of male dominance. In a patriarchal society property inherits in the male line, i.e., from father to sons. In case there is no male issue then only property goes to female children. Unmarried girls are the responsibility of their brothers after the death of their parents/father. The Village Achholi speaks the same story.

In the studies evaluating the role and status of women in a given social system, it is often overlooked to take an account of women's perception about their ownself, their acceptance and annoyance towards the social position of status they are adhered to within family or in society. Traditionally women are denied of entry in many fields of activities for instance in socio-political organisation, in management and controlling of economic resources and its ownership, in decision making, in education, in health care and so on. Situation has changed a lot in modern era, particularly in post-independence period, but the change is relatively slow in rural India in relation to urban societies. It is observed in this part of rural India that women, in general, accept their subalternity as a tradition and they never think otherwise. A few who ideally speak against the present condition, don't show the same spirit practice. They never questioned the tradition prevalent in the society. Moreover, a majority feel that men's superiority and women's subordination is natural in human society. It is to be noted here that much of women's productive labour takes place in the home based economic organisation, in household work, in kitchen garden and in kitchen, in child care and so on which often are overlooked as meaningful economic category. Therefore, women's labour goes unrecognized both at the family level and at the social level. In this regard, it is to be mentioned that no single, simple equation is adequate to analyse the gender inequality and many factors together responsible for the subjugation of women. All these factors are interwoven in a social network.

Women, who play a key rôle in subsistence economy and in maintaining a household surprisingly have hardly any existence in the sphere of decision making. Access to and rights over the economic resources is another factor that ensures empowerment of an individual in family and in society, which the women are often deprived of. Inspite of her major contribution towards economic and occupational activities and towards the maintenance of livelihood, a woman does not enjoy any right over property or the economic resources either in their natal family or in her husband's family. Economic and social dependency on her male counterpart makes her vulnerable to exploitation of male chauvanism and male dominance. The socialisation process acts as an important underlying force in this respect. In a traditional rural Indian family a girl child is considered as a potential working hand in household chores and she is trained up as a helping hand to the mother so that in her turn she can carry on the responsibility of household work. But a male child of the same age is totally exempted from such exercise. Though it is the female, the mother, who plays the key role in socialisation in one's early age but interestingly while transmitting the social ideals she acts as a representative of male dominated philosophy, i.e., patriarchy. Therefore, in a male dominated society it is the women who uphold and ensure the continuity of patriarchal values unknowingly through the process of socialisation and this forms the social conditioning of an individual. A girl is taught to be submissive to males and the values of female subordination is germinated in the social psyche.

Another point is to be mentioned here is the social importance attached to each and every work. In agricultural operation though transplantation is the most difficult and laborious job, yet it is given lesser importance than ploughing which is conventionally done by the men in this society. Like the household chores which are never considered as a productive work by the men.

The reflections of patriarchal values are also remarkably visible in the self-perception of women in regard to their social position or status. The secondary position in relation to men is accepted as normal occurrence in human society and cannot be thought in any other way. Moreover the notion of men's superiority is so deep rooted in the social psyche that neither men nor women can even think of challanging it. Instead women have accepted their subjugation to men as an universal phenomenon based on the natural differences between the sexes. Likewise the arena of decision making is rooted as men's domain in women's psyche. The learning process and the social conditioning in one's early age through socialisation transmits such patriarchal values to the new progeny. And thus the labour power which could be a source of authority for the women became instrumental under the control of men.

Awareness is another important factor to be mentioned while analysing the gender role in this particular social setting. Womenfolk in a rural society live in a very close-knit boundary, both physical and social.

Their world encompasses itself within the small periphery of the village and its neighbourhood. Most of them can hardly name the Prime Minister or the President of the country. The various provisions made for women in the constitution of India had never been reached to their knowledge. They are equally ignorant about the ideas of women's liberation movement that had hit the world's consciousness decades ago. They never made any attempt to compare their own condition to that of men. Rather sacrificing one's own health, energy and interest in favour of husband or son or brother is appreciated with high esteem. Lack of exposure and education make women victims of ignorance which results into lack of confidence over their self, a sense of incapability at intellectual level and acceptance of male dominance as a natural phenomenon. Therefore, first and foremost attention is needed for education because only education can help women to become free from their mental dependency. On an average, the literacy rate in rural India is far less than that of urban areas and the rate is even lower in case of females than that of males. Though a good number of female children in Achholi are sent to schools for formal education but when the family is economically poor then it is the male child whose education is given priority over that of a female child. Female children are often taken out from schools for many reasons. Sometimes it is economic,sometimes it is social or matrimonial. Age at marriage for girls is about 18 years and for a girl child marriage is considered as the ultimate goal. In Achholi there is no higher secondary school and for higher schooling facility one is to go either to Dongargarh town which is 4 Kms away from the village or to the neighbouring village, namely Belgaon, more or less at the same distance. In many cases girls are dropped out from schools only because they are not allowed by the guardians to go out the village for schooling. The traditional value system and lack of government facilities together form such social situation.

Government's planning stresses economic upliftment as the priority requirement and the various economic schemes have been undertaken keeping in mind especially the exploitation on women. Economic independence of course will help them to achieve some voice in the existing family situation but until and unless women's participation in the total productivity of the country is proved indispensible it is quite difficult to achieve a status equal to that of the other half of human race.

The reasons for deprivation of women from equal access to resources with that of men, from power, from the control over their ownself, from education, from freedom of movement, from freedom of expression, from equal social status to that of men and so on, are thus multifaceted. All these factors together and many more, that many come up from various individual studies, may explain the subjugation of women to men. Planned development, keeping in consideration the factors responsible for inequality is needed from the part of the government to change the condition of lives of women in rural India which automatically will have a chain impact on the lives of their urban counterpart. An ideological orientation is also needed while formulating the plannings of development. Women's existing responsibilities for reproductive work is not to be ignored. Moreover, the double burden of women's productive and reproductive role is to be analysed with utmost importance. It needs far greater attention to provide benefit to women. Women's labour, either waged or non-waged, productive or reproductive, in subsistence economy or market economy, is required to be recognized and properly attended. The responsibility thus comes before humanity to identify each and every such factor, to eliminate them from the social conditioning and to establish a total harmony between the sexes for the greater cause of human society.

References

Beauvoir, Simone de 1972 *The Second Sex*, Penguin Books, England.

Bjorkman, James Warner (ed.) 1987 *The Changing Division of Labor in South Asia,* Manohar Publications, New Delhi.

Bumiller, Elisabeth 1990 *May You Be The Mother of Hundred Sons,* Penguin Books.

Engels, Frederick 1968 'The Origin of the Family, Private Property and State in *Selected Works of Karl Marx And Frederick Engels,* Progress Publishers, Moscow (First published,1891).

Sills, David L. (ed.) 1968 *International Encyclopaedia of Social Sciences,* The MacMillan Company and the Free Press, New York.

Smith, Joan 1983 'Feminist Analysis of Gender : A Mystique' in Marian Lowe and Ruth Hubbard (eds) *Woman's Nature,* Pergamon Press.

10

Women in Environmental Management

Sri Mallanath Mukherjee;
Dr. Malay Mukhopadhyay

Introduction

Women have primarily been associated with the home and men with the 'world of work'. The compartmentalisation between home and work led to a gender differentiation of such an order that even in contemporary situation men and women are treated at different footings, particularly in developing countries. It is also observed in India over the last several years that women have been neglected in developmental and environmental issues.

The increasing trend of market economy, urbanisation in India has seen an increase in marginalisation among women. This is partly because of the very nature of 'development path', followed in post independence period in India. This path is based on a model of improved well-being through the universalisation of needs, productivity and growth. It is actually an extension of modern capitalist patriarchy's economic vision based on the exclusion of women from the productive process (Shiva 1991).

The displacement of women from productive activity by the expansion of modern technology and urban growth was rooted largely in the manner in which development projects appropriated or destroyed the natural resource base for sustenance and survival of women.

The growing perception of this sort of neglect tend to make women more ecologically conscious. The problem and crisis of environment and day to day life are closely related more with the women than men. There is also a strong line of thought that endorses women's special consciousness of ecological issues which supposedly makes them better managers of natural resources.

Women's consciousness of the environment and therefore their constructive approach is then not something inherent arising out of their being women, as is often propagated. It is rooted in their roles and work tasks, which lead them to interact extensively with natural resources for survival. The impact of environmental degradation is felt more actively by women who interact with it for survival. It is only in some aspects of environmental deterioration, such as pollution caused by deforestation, mining operation, use of pesticides, chemical fertilizer in agricultural fields, industry, that most women may be affected similarly as a consequence of their gender functions.

Therefore the problem of environmental degradation and resource management is not only perceived by women but they have devoted themselves in policy making and conservation practices. The paper here examines the actual place of women in resource management to achieve sustainable development.

Environmental Perception of Women

Most of the environmental research done so far in India emphasises its physical aspects and changes over time and space. However geographers of late have studied environmental perception and have stressed that the image of the world that each person carries inside his head is as important as the objective environment of the outside world. The mental images are the subjective environment that is environment as perceived by human beings. The explanation of man regarding environment problem is founded upon the premise that environmental cognition and behaviour are intimately related.

Women relate to environment more closely than their male counterparts. Women see, perceive, utilize and interact with their environment in a different way than men. It is because of the fact that women in rural areas engage to collect fuel wood for cooking, bring water from tube wells or rivers and arrange food for the family members. This behavioural approach has taken the view that deeper understanding of human and environment interaction can be achieved by looking at the various processes through which she comes to know environment in which she lives and by examining the ways in which these processes influence the nature of her resultant behaviour.

It should be clear that women, as the world's most important food producers are directly dependent on a healthy environment. It is also becoming more and more obvious how much rural women themselves are conscious of this dependence and how much they know about this natural environment, soil, crops and forests. As a rural woman from Zimbabwe said 'My environment is the basis of my economy and my total survival. It is from the land that I get my food' (Nyoni : 1985).

In Raniganj coal belt of West Bengal for example we found women are greatly concerned about the health of their family members particularly those who work in the mines. Deterioration of agriculture and deforestation are pointed whereever changes are perceived by women. The women belong to different ethnic and religious groups, various economic classes and have different social status. Accordingly their perception of environmental changes varies and adjust itself to the new environment immediately.

Women and Community Life

Seventy five per cent of the world's population lives in the developing nations of the world and 75 per cent of third world population is in rural areas. So in broader sense term 'rural women' refers to the women of this world. The women of third world countries play major role in managing natural resources. Their tasks in farming, animal husbandry as well as in the household make them the daily manager of this living environment. An Indian agricultural labour's day is typical, she cleans the house, washes clothes, prepares food for her husband and children. She works in agricultural field. On her way back home she collects fuel wood and if necessary, drinking water. Therefore women are directly related with their immediate environment.

Women of developing world feel any crisis more quickly than men. The burden of fuel wood crisis is borne by women because they take the responsibility for meeting household energy needs through its collection, preparation and use. To tackle the problems regarding the shortage of fuel either as wood or charcoal they prepare one meal a day instead of two. In other cases where formerly nutritious food such as pulses were eaten, these are now being replaced with less nutritious alternatives which do not take so long to cook. They experiment to find ways of reducing fuel consumption. Water is needed for many purposes in a household which is mainly collected by the women in a family. Women have to decide where to collect water from, how to draw, how many water sources can be used and depending on their quality distinction is made in purpose—drinking, washing and in the kitchen. The provision of safe and pure drinking water is a pre-requisite for environment management.

The women of tribal community used to collect medicinal plants seen around the forest. They know the use of individual herbal plants in their proper quantities and keep up its use among the community which is also a conservation of the indigenous species in our ecology. Women have extensive knowledge of plants, animals and ecological processes around them.

Women—Natural Resources and Environment

Since the beginning of the nineteenth century the explosive growth and expansion of the world's population accompanied by new technological advances have dramatically modified the earth's landscape. In America and Australia most of the vast forests and grasslands of the midlatitudes and subtropics were converted to crop and grazing land in little more than a Century. In the tropical regions vast areas of rainforest are being cleared, resulting in the eradication of countless species, many with potential values as sources of food and medicine. If the present rate of degradation continues, almost one-fifth of the world's arable land will disappear by the year 2000. The World Commission on Environment and Development (1987) expressed the view that the scale of environmental destruction is alarming. But it is indeed something that both men and women are deeply concerned about the rapid scale of deterioration and have involved themselves to regenerate the natural environment.

However women are more closely related with natural resources and environment. For centuries women have been used to gather forest products in meeting their basic needs. But they rarely collect entire trees, they collect only twigs, small branches and often dead wood, so destruction is limited. Experiences from all over the world prove that women have organised many movements against forest loss. India's Chipko Andolon is prominent among such . In the Reni forests of the Chamoli district U.P. women were confronted with the prospect of 2500 trees been destroyed by commercial enterprise. When the contractor arrived, they went into the forest, joined hands and encircled the trees. The women told the contractors that before cutting the trees, they would first have to cut off their heads. Through this protest the forest was saved. Kenya's Green Belt Movement by the National Council of Women is another example of natural resource development. Women's groups are actively involved in the Kenya Energy Non-Government Organisation (KENGO), a platform with the objective to safeguard energy supplies and a programme of reforestation using indigenous trees.

The rural women of Bangladesh come out from the home by rejecting the tradition of seclusion only for work and socio-economic change. Now the rural poor women are working on road side afforestation.

In 1974, a pilot project on rural development was started in the mountainous region of Larestan in the east of Iran. The main objective was to promote sustainable development of natural resources through the use of appropriate technologies. It was hoped that external dependence, a dominant characteristic of undevelopment, would gradually be eliminated. Under that scheme the rural industries and domestic economic units were formed exclusively by women. They decided to improve family living standards by promoting the weaving of handicrafts using traditional motifs. The agricultural unit aimed to promote sustainable development through the use of scientifically and environmentally appropriate cultivation and animal husbandry method. The unit also tackled the reduction of malaria mosquitoes by relocating the habitat of the larva, by improving human and animal hygiene. The agricultural unit installed a biogas plant having the objective of energy supply, environmental care and recycling of organic wastes back to the land.

In Malayasia, the Consumers Association of Penang (womens wing) is fighting industrial pollution of their rivers. There has been an alarming decrease in fish production, the serious effects of which have been felt in the local community particularly by women. Women along the coastal area of Papua New Guinea are starting to look after environment besides the sea where people collect salt for cooking.

In case of mining operation, local people along with their families were employed in the Raniganj Coal Belt area of West Bengal at the initial stage. The Bauris (local tribe) were the first to bring their women folk into the collieries and their contribution in the early development of Indian Coal Mining Industry was quite significant. Women in collieries were initially employed as 'gin girls' but switched to various other kinds of surface and underground work when the mechanical system of lifting coal from shallow shafts was phased out. The main role performed by women in the early decades to the present century was however that of a loader of coal broken by their male partners (Roychowdhury 1966). That the women working in the mining activities were aware about their health and surrounding environment was observed from the survey report.

Women-Policy Making and Environment

The role of women in administration and policy making from grass root level to international level has opened a new dimension in environmental management practices. Women with special perceptions, experiences and needs have brought about a change of behavioural approach in utilising resources. Women have a strong ability to work together. They can share their experiences and skills to take effective action. Some of the most successful evidences of women's organised initiatives are the Chipko movement of northern India, Narmada Banchao Andolon of M.P. and Maharashtra and Baldia Sanitation project in Pakistan. Now women have organised themselves in form that explicitly articulate their concerns. Many development Projects designed by planners in co-operation with local women have been installed in different parts of the country. Active participation of the women is more satisfactory than that of male participants. These women have organised themselves into cooperative work groups and all decisions are governed by the working women. Such foras organised by the women and for the women are listed here. Worldwide - world women working for women dedicated to the Environment was founded in 1982 with a view to - (a) educate the public and policy makers about the effects specifically on women of the destruction of natural resources and ecological system and to present women's perspectives on these issues, (b) increase women's involvement in the design and implementation of development policies, (c) support and expand the influences of women in organisation engaged in environmental and natural resources activities, (d) encourage women individually and collectively to take up environmental and natural resources management goals (J. Martin-Brown, Worldwide News 1986).

The Young Women's Christian Association (YWCA) is a worldwide network of thousands of women. They are working on a number of environmental issues like energy related issue, pollution, the need to restore damaged trees, pressure of population on ecology etc.

Conclusion

So, in conclusion it can be said that the perception of women in environment is one of the important tools for the preservation of our environment. Women are the ones who could make a major contribution to rehabilitation. They have the knowledge and capacity for resource management. Thus with this changing and degraded environment participation of women should be increased significantly. Till today it is also observed in such societies that rural women cannot participate actively due to social and religious orthodoxy. Thus, mass awareness campaign and social education programme by involving women should be carried out. The study of women in environment is not only desirable but also necessary for future planning and development.

References

1. Brydon, Lynne & Chant, Sylvia; (1989) *Women in the Third World,* Edward Elgar Publishing Limited, Aldershot, pp. 91-120, 213-240.
2. Dankelman, Irene and Davidson, Joan; (1987) *Women, Environment and Natural Resources,* Earthseon Publications Limited, London, pg.42-63.
3. Kondiyoti, Deniz; (1985) *Women in Rural Production Systems* : Problems and Policies, UNESCO Publication, Paris, pp. 91-108.
4. Miss Maria (1986) *Indian Women in Subsistence and Agricultural Labour,* Geneva, International Labour Office, (also published by New Delhi : Vistar,1987).
5. Ray Chowdhury, Rakhi (1996) *Gender and Labour in India,* Calcutta, Minerva Associates Pvt. Ltd., pp. 45-70.
6. Shiva, M. (1994) 'Environmental Degradation and Subversion of Health,' ed. by Vandana Shiva—*Class to Home-Women Reconnect Ecology, Health and Development*, London, pp. 43-60.
7. Venkateswarn, S. (1995) *Environment Development and the Gender Gap*, Sage Publications, New Delhi, pp. 118-130.

11

Women Empowerment and Status in Joint Forest Management

Ishita Naha

Dr. (Mrs.) Sutapa Mukhopadhyay

Introduction: The Plight

Not long ago, Madhabi Matey can still recollect the pain that tormented her everyday when the time to go for her daily gathering would come. The long walk into the forest was neither pleasant nor fruitful. With no trees to give shade or relieve her from the scorching laterite heat, the search for fuel made her life more wretched day by day. After this hard and torturous ritual, her body felt numb and exhausted like the forest itself, but she knew that rest was far away for her chores at home were yet to be done. The worst part of all these she felt was the thought that time and again she would have to come to this forest for the daily needs of her family, if caught by the forest guards, she knew what harassment awaited her. They tell her that she is a thief as she has no right over this forest that surrounds her village. Strange world she wondered, the stigma of being called a thief troubled her wretched mind in her wretched body from time to time.

Looking Back: The Good Old Days

Madhabi thought her misery to be an age old story and that every other rural women bound to face, knew only half of the story. In ancient India, forests were managed in small patches by local rural communities. Most of the people depended on the forest resource for their survival, ranging from food to medicine. The connection of the people with forests in Indian culture is stamped as 'Aaranya Sanskriti' and the forest as 'Aranyani'. Both tribal and non-tribal people of this country depended on the forest for economic, social as well as religious needs. Economic and social needs are relatively easy to understand as the role of forest in these two fields is still the driving force behind many action programmes. What surprises us initially is the religious role of the forest.

The religious aspect sprang from the use of different leaves during different festivals and rituals. In many parts, tree worship is still not an uncommon sight. Among tribals this association is more deep rooted. For example, some tribes have their *gotra* named after a tree which according to their legend helped that family at their time of crisis. As a result, their forefather had promised to protect that tree and worship it. The promise runs down to the descendants, and the different *gotra* protect and nurture different trees. Again, tribes in Chota Nagpur have 'Ambiha' where the bride and groom are first married to a particular tree so that the good qualities of the tree pass down to them as a blessing from the tree, the mother of all forest resources. In all these customs and rituals the women played a pivotal role for in India women play a centre role in 'informal management system'.

Colonial Privatisation: Paradise Lost

During British rule and particularly in the mid-nineteenth century things took a wrong turn. The British, realising the scarcity of forest resources and need for judicious use of forest resources drew up a plan of restriction, a common feature of colonial powers. Memorandum drawn in August 1855 by the fledgling Forest Department under the British India Government brought along a trail of bloodshed and conflicts. The most gruesome effect of the restriction was felt by the forest dwellers whose very existence depended upon the forest. This 'Privatisation of Common Property' (Singh, 1987) also started the saga of deprivation and mishandling of forest resources. The transfer of control from communities to the Government crushed much of the essence of traditional management.

The glory of the by gone days were soon forgotten. Scarcity of resources resulting from undue restrictions eroded the traditional ties and the people who were the protectors turned destructors. Necessity became an eye-opener for the forest dwellers and made them see the fruitlessness of clinging to a tradition which in return gave nothing but only robbed them of their basic needs.

Gender Play: Carrying the Cross

In this degrading senario, women became the worst victims and the fate of Madhabi Matey became the rule of the day for every rural poor woman who depended on her environment. Women were the butt of environmental deploration. The assessment of the impact of the process of 'privatisation of common property' on women unearthed gender issues. The main alternative available and to some extent accessible, to the traditional economy is the settled agricultural system which, as it is generally practised is based on male ownership of land. The impact of this system has been so great that today in many slash-and-burn areas of eastern India, even slash-and-burn land is individually owned, distributed and passed along the male line.

Women from lower-income groups face gender specific causes of disempowerment which occurs as a result of kinship system prevailing in most of the regious. These norms in their course give out a strong sense of female seclusion and also a gender based division of labour. What is significant at this point is that women are deprived of the right over food production resources but are depended on as food suppliers of the family.

Thousands and thousands of rural women, in their daily chores of gathering, sowing, cooking, washing are in direct contact with their immediate environment. Environment problem to them is a living fact with deforestation, lowering of water table for irrigation, drying out of safe water sources etc. These deteriorations in the natural environment have a direct effect on the direct receptors, that is the rural poor women. Deforestation means walking further to collect daily fuel, water table fall leads to harder and longer search for water. The more time taken by such work, the less time she can give to her children and family life suffers. Children are left unkempt, picking up diseases is rampant. She now does not even find enough time to contribute to the family income. As a result the family standard is also lowered. With loss of faith, loss of custom and ritual, loss of tradition, loss of health and income they become thieves of the groves that they had once pledged to nurture.

Joint Forest Management: A Positive Stance

The progressive deterioration of forest over time became a cause of great concern not only to the forest dwellers, but also for the people living away from the forest. Therefore an urgent need to explore alternative organisational arrangement for the protection and construction of forest became a priority. Experiements started and there emerged the concept of 'Joint Forest Management' (FPC) which is also known as 'Co-Management of Forest' or 'Participatory Forest Management'.

The Management Scheme had its origin in Arabari. Arabari is a small village some 20 kilometres from Midnapore town. In 1971-1972, A.K. Banerjee, the then Divisional Forest Officer after many failed attempts to regenerate and protect the forests, realised the cause of the failure as due to the heavy dependence of the forest dwellers on the forest. With this realisation the concept of Joint Forest Management emerged. Whereas, earlier in line with the memorandum of August 1855, the Forest Department (FD) took for granted that the management of forest and its resources was exclusively their duty, this changed concept opened windows of thinking. People's right was now recognised and given importance. A decentralisation of power was planned.

A radical change was planned and the people too readily accepted the idea as they now could also gain from forests produce and small timber. The gains were apparent:

(1) It ensured a profit, that is one-fourth of the income from rotation felling of ten per cent of the area.
(2) It was in support of and in consonance with the at tempts of villagers to prevent encroachors, who depleted their natural resource base.
(3) It gave them self-confidence and also promised them their lost glory.

Though it was started in 1971-1972 the idea gradually took flight in July 1988. In the meantime however, the idea of Forest Protection Committee had gained popularity to the neighbouring districts. Forest Protection Committee became the vital link in regeneration of the forest and the successful implementation of the programme.

Forest Protection Committee: Women Empowerment.

The introduction of the decentralisation in forest management had as already pointed out, a positive effect on the people. It was reminiscent of the old 'aranya sanskriti' of the country. Therefore in forming the FPCs, the vision of ancient managerial system of bringing the forest and the people together was evoked. It refers to the collaborative attempt that with preciseness shifted the power of control from the Government office to local populatrion, participatory management, as it may be called. Protection of forest has now become important more for the need of the village than for the mare regeneration of the forest. Efforts were made to revive the tradition, the murder of which had led to such immense suffering which spread from economic, social, religious to climate, soil and the overall environment.

The most important part of the bargain was the boost it gave to women's empowerment in the formal structure and in the process of decision making. A novelty occurred and women were invited to come out from their informal management structure. Women were given their due reverence and the powerful economic, social and religious role played by them for environment was recognised. Her pivotal role in rural environmental management was now after centuries acknowledged and ways to release their potentialities was given importance.

With women's empowerment in FPC efforts were made to break loose from the on-going of dis-empowerment suffered by women in India. The first reaction observed in villages where women's active participation was sought was that of surprise. It was hard to reconcile with the idea that women too could officially represent a household as the member of the FPC. However women's involvement became a significant contribution to the efficient functioning of the FPC as in practice, the main offenders of the forest resources were identified as female members instigated by her socio-economic conditions.

The empowerment, in its turn opens new horizons in some areas. The success of women's empowerment was stamped by Chipko Movement. The Movement not only threw a gender challenge but also gave a strong impetus to women for their participation and involvement in Joint Forest Management. The movement typically exemplifies women's managerial technique in contrast to their male counterparts. It highlights the world and thought of women which extends from small family structure to larger family units encompassing the whole environment under her affectionate control seeing her environment as an extended family which needs similar nurture and protection.

Status of Women in FPC : Myth and Reality

There are some well accepted parameters adopted by sociologists and social scientists all over the world to assess the status of women in society. For example:

(a) Value given to the opinion of women.
(b) Equal formal status for women in social and official gathering.
(c) Equal opportunity for food, health, treatment, clothing and also to earn her living.
(d) Autonomy for expenditure, selection of nominee.
(e) Self recognition and self-esteem to stay away from home as man remains.

Among several other indicators the above mentioned are directly relevant to assess the status of women in FPC's.

In India, female membership in FPC ranges from 2 per cent to as much as 60 per cent. This is owing to two reasons, firstly, the traditions that confer on men the responsibility of protection; secondly, the poor participation may also be tied to the internalisation of the dominant values which idealise women as submissive and non-aggressive.

The rationale for promoting greater participation of women in the FPC's reflects more a pragmatic attitude than a desire to raise the social status of women. Women are seen as the prime forest offenders and FPC empowerment of women revolves around this fact. Clearly, daily reality of women living in forest areas or in rural India is often quite different from the way in which that reality is interpreted. For example, status of women was said to have been given a boost by their enrolment in FPCs. In reality, the very process of empowerment through FPCs is externally induced. Women in reality live in constant fear of losing their livelihoods, of starvation, of losing their children to illness and being thrown out of their homes. Traditional attitude towards women, which result in a lack of mobility, a lack of value of women's worth and a position of deference to male opinions, compound their problem. All these had led to the sense of helplessness suffered by women. As a result they are not able to hold their own within their family and community structures.

The status of women in EPC is reflective of her status in the community. Survey revealed that women decision are not vocal due to the presence of men. In sitting arrangements, women are given rows behind men, a thing naturally accepted by the women too. However, examples are not rare where women were vocal and direct. At these areas where the participation of men and women were found equal, the sitting arrangements were altered, women were giving patrolling duties and power similar to men FPC members and cross-check of women statements with males were avoided.

In the contemporary period the status of women as viewed by the majority of the society is directed by the literature, religious texts, historical process of evaluation of society, etc., this is exclusively an urban phenomena. In larger India the covert norms, the value system which is deeply rooted provokes the superiority of men over women. The activities of women are judged through their parameters which can be strongly felt in the rural areas where FPC are at work. Thus, acceptance of women as equal to men or acceptance of their activities as envisaged by FPC are going against the mass code of ideal women in the country structure.

Conclusion: All well that ends well

In the early Vedic period women engaged more or less equal socio-cultural rights with men. The reason behind that as mentioned by Atlekar is that the Aryan men busy in war and conquests. The women have do not a lot of productive work and so they were taking major decisions also. Then with social evaluation came the conflict between two types of

"Production fucntions". As the society is undergoing a transitional period this conflict becomes inevitable.

In such situation, women are cornered and experienced a lack of power, subordination in multiple roles or identities: as workers, as members of low income groups in meeting their basic needs and as women negotiating gender relations. The role of Joint Forest Management at such crucial juncture is a notable experiment in the institutional change for ecological development. The formation of FPC and its drive towards women participation can be interpreted as a door-way to women empowerment and status-identification in rural structures.

Intially the Forest Department encouraged female participation due to rise in female offenders. More than humanitarian considerations of equality and social status, it was the gender—specific role based on sheer necessity emerging from the inability of the men to handle the situation that led to the promotion of women representation in the FPCs. But their active involvement is impared by the domination of male to keep the women in their 'culture of silence' or pressure creating diffident to express themselves freely and spontaneously. Women are discouraged to share and raise issues in open meeting and it is left to their husbands who assures them woudl represent their wives views at open meeting. But there are old tricks and women are beginning to seek through them as involuntarily the FPC's initiative and the other organisations working at the grass-root level have succeeded in organising women showing them their own strength.

However the full achievement of the objectives of women's complete involvement and representation is yet to be achieved by the Forest Department and the Forest Protection Committees. The contradictions inherent in the forest policies, forest act, social status, gender bias etc. are yet to be resolved. The contradictions may be given a picturesque portrayal as a "goddess whose one hand blessed the people with prosperity while the other restricted their rights."

References

1. Adhikari, N., Yadav, G., Kumar, S. & Ray, S.B. Process documentation of Women involvement in Forest Management at Mahespur, Ranchi District. Working Paper No. 8, IBRAD.
2. Ali, A., Saha, M. & Bhadra, R.K. Profile of Bamunmara Forest Protection Committee, Midnapore. Working Paper No.19, IBRAD.
3. Carr, M. & Chen. M. & Jhalvala, R. (1996). Speaking out - Women's Economic Empowerment in South Asia.

4. Naha, I. (1998). 'Parivesh Anubhutite Mahilara : Ekti Ruprekha' Parivesh O Unnayan, ABBOPS.
5. Mukherjee, R. and Ray, S.B. (1994). Influence of Social Institution on Women's Participation in PFM : A Case Study from Sarugarh, North Bengal. Working Paper No.17, IBRAD. Calcutta.
6. Ray, S.B., Yadav, G. and Mishra, C.G. (1996). Facilitating Institutional Change for Joint Forest Management. Working Paper No.35, IBRAD.
7. Vegas, P. and Menon, (1995). Bringing Government and people together : Forest Protection Committees of West Bengal - Role and Participation of Women. Women and wasteland Development in India, Edited by A.M. Singh and Neera Burra.

12

Empowerment of Women Through Panchayati Raj Institution

Maitreyi Chaudhuri

Introduction

In Indian constitution there are provisions for equal rights for all citizens irrespective of their social and economic status. However such provisions exist only in pen and paper for millions of economically and socially disadvantaged groups of people of India. The Scheduled Caste (SC), Scheduled Tribe (ST) people and the women are included in these groups. These people are unempowered economically, socially and politically.

According to Beteille (1999), "Empowerment is a way of addressing the problem of rights that remain uninforced". Empowerment is a way of making the disadvantaged group of people aware of their rights and creating a situation where they can freely enjoy their rights and play a vital role in social, economic and political decision making process. The present paper deals with the problem of political empowerment of a particular section of Indian population viz. women.

In India women are in a much worse position than men not only in terms of sex ratio, life expectancy, literacy rate (Census of India,1991), nutrition (Batliwala,1985; Sen and Sengupta,1983), work force participation, wage earnings (Mukherjee,1996) and work time disposition (Jain,1996), but also in terms of their acess to power structure (Mukherjee,1996) which controls and guides the development programmes of a society. Since access to political opportunities and particpation in political decision making process are important components of capability and autonomy, discrimination in this respect leads to wastage of women's talent and efficiency which are necessary for an all-round development of a country. One of the three variables used in the construction of Gender Empowerment Index (GEM) is the relative share of women in administrative and managerial positions (UNDP 1995). Women need to be involved in the decision making process in order to bring their demands in the national agenda. The entry of the women in the decision making bodies will ensure restructuring of the institutions and lead to a solution of issues related to women's rights.

In order to ensure empowerment of women in political arena, the issue of reservation of one-third of the seats for women in grass-root level organisations was taken up by different women's organisations and social thinkers. Accordingly, the Government of India passed the 73rd constituional amendment which was followed by the 74th amendment mandating reservation of one-third of the seats for women in all village, block and district level elected bodies. There is also the same reserved quota for women in the positions of chairpersons and deputy chairpersons in these institutions. Since the Panchayati Raj Institution (PRI) plays a vital role in ensuring people's participation in the development process, it is felt that political empowerment of women through reservation of seats in PRI will train them up in exercising their power in decision making and remove social and economic discriminations against them.

How far the above goals of reservation have been achieved in reality needs to be examined on the basis of empirical findings. This has been done in the present paper. The role of the female Panchayat members in the political decision making process has been examined critically on the basis of data collected by interviewing the women Panchayat members of Bolpur Sriniketan block in the district of Birbhum, West Bengal.

The Study Area and the Sample

Bolpur —Sriniketan block consists of nine Panchayats. Out of these, three Panchayats were selected on the basis of random sampling. The selected Panchayats were Kankali, Sarpalehana and Ruppur. These three panchayats had 21 elected women members at the time of our survey during 1997-1998. Of these women members, 5 belonged to the Scheduled Tribe (ST) group, 9 to the Scheduled Caste (SC) group and 6 to the General Caste (GC) group. There was one Muslim woman in the sample. The level of education of these women was low on the average. Out of 21 women 9 were just literate and 5 completed the primary level, three discontinued their education after class IX and 2 passed the School Final Examination. Among the GC group, there were one B.A. and one M.A. degree holders. A majority of the members belonged to the low income group and worked either as agricultural labourers or share croppers.

Performance of the Women Members

In order to study the role of women as Panchayat members, data were collected on (a) attendance in Panchayat meetings, (b) participation in developmental activities and (c) motivation behind contesting the Panchayat election.

(a) *Attendance in Panchayat meetings:* Panchayat meetings are held once a month. These are generally held after 1 pm. At the time of our survey each member used to get Rs. 20 for attending a meeting[1]. The Panchayat records showed that eleven out of twenty one members attended more than 50 per cent of the meetings held between April, 1997 and January, 1998. Two ST members and one GC member did not attend any meeting. The tribal members were found to be very reluctant to attend the meetings. One SC member and two GC members attended all the meetings.

The major reasons for irregular attendance of the women members in Panchayat meetrings are summarised below:

(i) *Shortage of time :* Household chores and caring and rearing of children took so much time that it was not possible for most of the women to attend the meetings regularly. This was true even for some educated and employed women from the tribal and the Muslim community. One tribal school teacher could not attend any meeting due to lack of time.

(ii) *Loss of a day's wage :* Since a large number of women members worked as agricultural labourers or daily labourers, they had to sacrifice their day's wage (which was much higher than Rs. 20) for attending the Panchayat meetings. Moreover, in most of the case, their husbands or adult sons had to escort them to the Panchayat office even sacrificing their day's work. The tribal women used to be employed for a major part of the year either in agricultural or in off farm activities. To them attending Panchayat meeting was a sheer loss.

(iii) *Poor transport facility :* Some of the villages were not properly connected with the Panchayat offices by bus routes. The women members from these villages had to walk a long distance either to reach the nearest bus stops or the Panchayat offices. Out of the 21 women members 6 had to walk or cycle more than 3 kms to reach the Panchayat office.

(iv) *Superstition :* Two tribal women reported that they considered women's involvement in politics as ominous. They believed that they had lost their husbands only because of their involvement in political activities. After their husbands' death they stopped attending the Panchayat meetings.

However, the picture was not too gloomy. A detailed analysis revealed that out of the eleven members,who had attended more than 50 per cent of the meetings, three had attended 70 per cent to 80 per cent of the meetings and another three had attended all the meetings. For the first group of the elected Panchayat members this attendance rate was not at all insignificant. That the women members were becoming gradually aware of their responsibilities was quite evident.

(b) *Participation in developmental activities :* The women members, whether they work in agriculture or in service sector or remain simply as housewives, have to perform all the domestic chores. So it is quite natural that they take up political careers as an extension of their domestic roles and thus their activities are limited. It was found that twelve out of twenty one members could not devote any time in developmental activities of the village. The developmental work was done by their husbands, sons or party leaders. A majority of them were unaware about their political responsibilities, nor had they any knowledge about the development programmes of the Government. They had only to put their signatures on the loan applications made by the villagers.

There were active members also. Nine members were found to devote some time to the developmental activities. Out of these nine women, three GC, three SC and one ST member were fully aware the responsibilities entrusted to them by the Panchayats. Four of these women members were associated with women's organisations. However, they failed to involve other women of their villages in the activities of the organisations. They had formed the village committees to discuss and fix agenda for development. Unfortunately, very few women from the villages attended the meetings. So it was very difficult to finalise any programme for the development of women. In spite of all such problems, these members were able to do some developmental work for their villages. The work done by them may be classified as follows:

(i) monitoring the activities of the Anganwadi workers,
(ii) running the training centres under the programme of Development of Women and Children in Rural Areas (DWCRA),
(iii) arranging the installation of tubewells for drinking water,
(iv) development of village roads,
(v) identifying the IRDP beneficiaries and signing their loan forms,
(vi) working as instructors in Audit Literacy Programme,
(vii) formation of women's organisations in the villages,
(viii) settling family disputes,
(ix) counselling the married couples about small family norms.

Some of the women members, though aware of their responsibilities, could not do any developmental work in their villages mainly because of the following reasons:

(i) shortage of time,
(ii) lack of proper education and training,
(iii) lack of support from the villagers,
(iv) lack of cooperation from the party leaders,
(v) prevalence of tensions and violence in the politics,
(vi) superstition.

(c) *Motivation behind contesting in the Panchayet election:* Fourteen out of twenty one women contested for Panchayat membership only on request of their husbands, relatives and party leaders. Five of these members reported that earlier the seats were held by their brothers, cousins or husbands. When the seats were converted to women's seats, they were pressurised to cotest in the election. In one case, the member was even allured by the false hope of monetary gains. In most of the other cases, the husbands or some relatives of these members were either active party workers or had a close contact with the Panchayat officials. These fourteen women neither had any political awareness nor any intention to do any developmental work. They even expressed their desire to be out of politics after the expiry of their term. Seven women members (three SC, one ST and three GC members) contested in the election quite willingly. It may be mentioned that two GC members, who were also highly educated, had been involved in political activities prior to 1993. These seven women were found to be very proud of their new political power and responsibilities. They were very eager to remain in politics in future also.

In spite of all these shortfalls, the policy of reservation has not proved to be totally futile. Even some of the unwilling members were becoming gradually aware of their duties and gaining knowledge about the social and political situation of the country. Since they had to sign the loan application forms of the target group of beneficiaries under IRDP and ITDP programmes, they, at least, came to know about the existence of these programmes and their objectives. They also were able to realise the importance of education. Three just literate members reported during the survey that mere literacy was not enough to discharge properly their duties as Panchayat members. They also felt the need of knowing a little bit of English. They suggested that appropriate training programmes must be organised for the women Panchayet members. It appears that the members have been able to identify some of their deficiencies and it is hoped that they will be able to overcome these in future.

Concluding Observations

Reservation for women in different political bodies aims at giving women a proper position not only in the political decision making process but also in the domestic sphere. The present survey, however, reveals that within the households the situation has not changed. A majority of the women members did not have the freedom to respond to the interviewers. Most of the questions were answered by the male members of the households and in a few cases, the women Panchayat members even did not appear in front of the interviewers.

As discussed earlier, a vast majority of women members were not at all willing to contest for the Panchayat seats. They had to do so only on the requests from their husbands relatives or party members without any prior knowledge of their political responsibilities. Many members confessed that in the beginning their husbands used to attend the meetings on behalf of them. However, this was not allowed later. In order to reap the benefit of reservation the participation of women in Panchayats should be spontaneous. If only the wives, daughters, sisters and other female relatives (*"bahu beti* brigade" as mentioned by Krishnaraj,1998) of Panchayat members and party leaders are inducted in the Panchayati Raj system, the purpose of reservation is lost. There should be a constant search for leadership among the women. Women with leadership quality should be identified and properly trained to perform their political responsibilities. Special care should be taken to train up the tribal women as successful political leaders. This requires identification of their problems, customs and traditions and designing the training programmes accordingly.

Last but not the least, the factor is the cooperation from the male members of the households. Instead of retaining political control with them by making their wives, daughters or sisters, Panchayat members, they should share household chores with the women so that they get enough time to perform political activities themselves. The women members should be allowed to identify the problems of their villages and chalk out plans for development. Attempt should be made to inculcate a sense of confidence among the women and this can be done only through the continuous help and support from the family members.

It should be remembered that reservation for women is not an end but only a means of enabling them to emerge as independent individuals in the outer world. The present survey shows that, as the first group of elected members in the reserved seats, the performance of the women was not very poor. They are gradually becoming aware of their responsibilities as well as of the development programmes. They can assess their progress and identify the reasons for failure. But still there are miles to go. It is expected that in future, proper education, training and cooperation from family members will help the rural women to emerge as successful political leaders.

References

Batliwala, S. (1985): "Women in Poverty : The Energy, Health and Nutrition Syndrome," in Devaki Jain and Nirmala Banerjee (Eds), *Tyranny of the Household : Investigative Essays on Women's Work.* Vikas, New Delhi.

Beteille, Andre (1999) : "Empowerment : the Indian Way", EPW, Vol. 34, nos. 10-11. Census of India, 1991.

United Nations Development Programme (1995) : Human Development Report, Oxford University Press, New York.

Jain, Devaki (1996) : "Valuing Work : Time as a Measure", EPW, Vol. 31, no. 43, October, 26.

Krishnaraj, Maithreyi (1998) : "Women and Public Domain: Critical Issues for Women Studies," EPW, Vol. 33, February, 21-27.

Mukherjee, Mukul (1996) : "Towards Gender Aware Data Systems : Indian Experience", EPW Vol. 31, no. 43, October, 26.

Sen, Amartya and Sengupta, Sunil (1983) : "Malnutrition of Rural Children and the Sex Bias, EPW, Annual Number, Vol. 18, Nos. 19-21.

Acknowledgements

The author is thankful to Sri Anshumoy Chatterjee, Sri Kalidas Hazra and Sri Manab Roy of Palli Charcha Kendra, Visva-Bharati, for their assistance at the stage of data collection.

13

I Find My Voice—A Personal Narrative

Ayesha Khatun

I would like to tell the story of how I found my voice growing up in a tradition bound Muslim family inhabiting a Muslim village geographically remote and socially "narrow-minded". Travelling to and from the village is a long hike through mud paths during rains and otherwise over miles of fields. No public transport goes till our village and the nearest railway station is about 15 kms away. As an instance of the narrow-mindedness that prevailed in my village during my childhood I would like to tell about the upheaval that was caused when my father admitted my elder sister to the course leading to a bachelor degree in homeopathy in the nearest town. The battle lines extended from inside the home to the outside, family, kin, extended kin and neighbours. There were not many people who supported my father except the person whose support mattered to my father, his Pir or guru. Everybody tried their best to put a spanner in the works from all directions for quite some time. They quoted religion, social ethics and codes from the Koran and from other learned authorities and their writings. The Koran too must have felt the strain of too many interpretations ! Of course, it yielded the clinching argument that even distant China is not too far to travel for education and my sister was going a few miles ! My father also pointed out that no injuction had been laid against a particular sex. Certainly my father's profession as a primary school teacher (holding the designation of Headmaster/Principal), his scholastic background in Philosophy, religious belief and his commitment to duty are the qualities that stood him in good stead. How boldly he

1. Translator's note: It has not been possible to reproduce the poetry, passion and intensity of Ayesha's words, the words finding voice in the hard earned confidence in self and abilities. Very much like the winged wonder that emerges from its chrysalis, Ayesha rises from her shell to sail forth. Ayesha's words, the words finding voice in the hard earned confidence in self and her abilities. Very much like the winged wonder that emerges from its chrysalis, Ayesha's voice rises above her condition to shine forth in celebration of self.

opened the doors of higher education for his daughter with only doggedness of purpose as his principally.

I am the youngest of the three sisters, the elder two engaged in professions, fair and pretty to look at. I am the dark one, neglected in my childhood and denied the attention due to a growing girl. I certainly consider to have been less fortunate than my elder sisters. I must have been quite a tomboy for which I received more than my share of thrashings. Nevertheless my sisters' achievements filled my eyes with dreams, dreams that would reach out to touch the horizons, everything was possible for me to strive for. What did I dream of - was it becoming a doctor or lawyer . . . no, for me the dream was that I would become a great sportswoman hardly knowing what it entailed. The village is hardly the place for training in sports though there are opportunities to be an expert swimmer or runner, but little else. Also, the village does not take kindly to a girl wanting to go in for sports; my father and brothers too did not bother with the niceties of gently diverting my attention or energies in other directions, instead they imposed their collective will on mine. The next activity that seemed attractive to me was music. I put my heart into learning to sing songs of Nazrul, my father's favourite composer. A traditional Muslim household is hardly a place for the practice of the octet and trying to find a conducive atmosphere became fraught with difficulty. Practising at home was a strict no-no and the only time that I could escape from home was in the blazing heat of the afternoons, climbing over the wall to go to my teacher's house in the next village. The time of the day hardly mattered, there I would practise all the ragas without any heed to the time of the day for which the raga was composed ! However even this pursuit was not encouraged for long and my singing was summarily stopped.

Education remained the only alternative and at that moment not a very attractive option to me. I passed the Madhyamik or Class X examination and I found my father showing no special interest in furthering my course in life. He was spent fighting the many battles for my sisters. I have never been the kind to give up and when my father told me that his Pir was not forthcoming with his permission regarding my education, I decided to put up my own case to his eminence. I did have my share of dejection at my lot that seemed to have more than its share of unfairness, I wondered why this discrepancy between the opportunities of my sisters and me. I managed to convince the Pir my side of the argument, however he and the others in my family drove a very hard bargain, no arguments, no protest and no fighting. This narrow path to the higher portals of learning exacted its pound of flesh, my father was no longer the pillar supporting women's education, he however, never set himself as an obstacle. After my higher secondary or Class XII, I joined college for my undegraduate and a bicycle was my means of transport over 20 kms of to and fro. This time the objections came from right within home my paternal grandmother bustled in with a earful of complaints, it seems that I make noise in class, laugh loudly, ride too fast and so on and on, enough reasons to put an end to my education. My father showing Vidyasagar like maternal devotion however stood by me and explained my rebellious nature and loudness as being the consequence of neglect during my childhood, and he clinched the argument by citing the examples of Ayesha, the Prophet's wife as being a fearless and spirited woman going to battle resplendent on a horse. He also gave the example of the Prophet's wife, Hanufa beautiful and a warrior. My poor grandmother looked through my father's intentions but had no valid argument to put forth. She departed but castigated me in severe terms about the dangerous consequences of my headstrong conduct. Age had very little to do with the objections raised against me, girls of my age, women with whom I shared bonds of affection, everybody and anybody jumped on the bandwagon. My lips were sealed and my protest unworded, it was more than a pound of flesh. I applied to my father for permission to retrench on my hard promise of silence that I was made to vow only to be told that I could have revenge by proving them wrong and making something of myself. But revenge tastes sweeter when it is exacted then and there. I must admit that I got some of my own back when my bicycle bumped into that very officious lady quite by accident, but the storm that erupted put a temporary stop to my education.

It was during this time that a *milad* or religious gathering was organized in the village and the organisers belonged to the faction that was opposed to my father and his rather liberal ways and views. Was it only chance that the topic for discussion was "Muslim woman and the system of purdah" and implicit in which discussion was the spectre of hell in the fires of which a defiant woman would burn ? It was so blatantly directed against my family! The discussion took recourse to partial representation and interpretation of the Koran and it was contrary to every tenet of egalitarianism preached in the Koran and by my father, as if the world canvas of the Koran was being forced to fill the narrow confines of our village pathways and high walls had to be built in order keep out those parts of the holy book which was not in keeping with their mindset. They managed to keep out progress altogether. What a narrow sectarian viewpoint, what exercise of force to pull us back, indeed, the leaders of our religion cut a very sorry picture. Their religious titles entitle them to preach for education in madrashas following an education system in which modern science has no place. Small wonder that Islam has such a downward trend, in spite of the grandness of vision of the founder.

I completed my bachelor with History and my teachers wanted me to pursue my masters at Aligharh Muslim University. This time my father put his foot down. I have always dreamt big and going to AMU was one of my cherished dreams and it was this that gave me the courage to overthrow my father's edict. I went to AMU but did not secure admission. I came back and tried to secure a seat in the MSW (Master in Social Work) offered in Visva-Bharati, the university founded by Tagore. The magnificent and larger than life statue of the Baul at the entrance did not let me enter the portals of that hallowed university and finally after much water under the bridge, I enrolled in the University of Bardhaman for my master degree.

Today after many currents and cross currents, I no longer see myself as unfortunate or in any way less than others. I have a job, not a Government one, but in a multinational NGO, involved in the work of development of villages. What a full circle I have come, I have had to return to villages even more "dark" and underdeveloped, more remote than the remotest with waterways instead of roads as a means of access. I have been more than fortunate to have been able to work with them and receive their love and trust. At present, I am situated in tribal areas in the district of Bankura. The immense human qualities that these people possess, has left an indelible mark on my perceptions.

I come back to the context of my discussion. Somehow my father and I, with hard work and exacting sacrifices have managed to rock the walls of narrow mindedness and open the doors of education to Muslim girls. Those very families, who left no stone unturned and no effort wasted in obstructing our path to education seem to have realized the errors of their ways and are trying to ensure that their daughters are not subject to the same harassment. It is indeed heartening to see girls between 16/17 years engaged in learning, attending schools, colleges, cycling to and fro with no pointing fingers or loud curses - a matter of some pride !

This brings me to another story to highlight some of the realities of our society as it operates in our villages. This concerns a young girl who paid the consequences of love by becoming an unwed mother, as the boy refused to have to do anything with her or her condition as is usually the case. It was as if society had telescoped back to a thousand years and the same story of Jabala and Satyakam was being enacted. The child when born bore such close resemblance to the father that there was no doubt in anybody's mind about the paternity of the child. The mother brought her son to my father with a request that he admit him to his school. He did so and what a storm of controversy broke out. The villagers raised a hue and cry about how wrong it was to admit a child whose paternity was in doubt. My father generous as ever, showed his progressiveness, refused to be scared or cowed down by this babble of protest. He answered that in this world only one child did not have an earthly father and that was Jesus Christ. He also added that only the mother could vouch for the father so whoever's name this woman would take would satisfy him. However he said that for him the mother's name was enough because of the courage, determination and fortitude that she displayed in bearing with her lot was claim enough on the child's identity. With these reasons he admitted her son in his school. The consequence was that we were isolated and ostracized in the village, as if contact with us would pollute others. Let us remember her story too.

What is that I want to find my voice for ? Is it for the losing battle that Muslim women face, having to give up almost without a fight, especially when there are so many safeguards in Islam for women ? It is as if fear is the only instrument that is used to control women, as if women like children need to be controlled, that too by men. The only role that is accepted for women is to look after their husbands, bear a lot of children and mourn their fate. Muslim women are losing their share of father's property, the system of bride price or it has been shamelessly replaced by dowry.Though for legal purposes, a Muslim woman could bang on the doors of justice for her share of the bride price, agreed upon in principle, at the time of marriage, in the presence of witnesses. One can easily imagine the sorry sight of a woman after having been divorced by the utterances of a word only thrice, having to do a sit-in at the court surrounded by her numerous offsprings so that she can claim some financial help. The wheels of justice are indeed slow, help remains far but only the dates of the next hearing are forthcoming ! There are many things that I want to say about the lot of women who seem to be characterised by rejection, dejection, frustration, deprivation, and all other 'tion' words that one can think of in the negative sense of the word. At best their plight evokes our sympathy or expressions of horror and disbelief; it also triggers debates, seminars and discussions but there is need to go beyond. So much has changed, systems of Government have changed, what seems to have remained unchanged is the domination of women by men.

(Translated from the original article in Bengali by Kumkum Bhattacharya)

Index